Masters of Budo

THE INTERVIEWS

JON BRAELEY

Masters of Budo: The Interviews

© 2022 by Jon Braeley

ISBN: 979-8-9867880-1-2
First edition. Print
Published & copyrighted in the United States
Empty Mind Books

Author	Jon Braeley
Photographs	Jon Braeley
Translations	Juan Diego Fonseca
	Baptiste Tavernier
	Hiroshi Onaka

In memory of Hirokazu Kanazawa

TABLE OF CONTENTS

Jon Braeley, Baptiste Tavernier and Alexander Bennett at the
2014 All Japan Kendo Championships, Nippon Budōkan

ACKNOWLEDGEMENTS

I was Sixteen years old when I took my first karate class at the YMCA in Sheffield, England. Coincidentally a year later, this was the same venue for the Sheffield Photographic Society, which I joined when I got my first professional camera. Five decades later I am still training in *karate* and still taking photographs, my passion for both undiminished. I also became a film director. In this time I have met some remarkable teachers and mentors that gave me the reasons to keep doing what I love.

At the age of 22, shortly after receiving my black belt in *Shōtōkan karate*, I started *tai chi chuan* practice after meeting David Barrow, one of the U.K.'s foremost masters. I was always drawn to the teacher, rather than the martial art itself. The same is true today. I have a passion and curiosity for the martial arts that extends far beyond my own practice. As a film director I am fortunate to have been exposed to all the major styles of martial arts from Japan and China to South-East Asia and India. This has reinforced my view that martial arts are connected not by the many varied styles, but by the masters who share their knowledge. I wish to thank the following people who do just that.

First I would like to thank Alexander Bennett, 7th *dan kendō*, author and professor at Kansai University with two PhD's in *budō* studies. Thank you Alex for opening so many doors that would have remained closed. Your book, *Kendo: Culture of the Sword* is always close by. I would also like to thank the artist and musician, Baptiste Tavernier, for being an important part of our team and assisting in our visit to Okinawa, the International Budo University and *jukendo* and *tankendo* taikai.

A special thank you must go to a very talented person, Juan Diego Fonseca who lived in Japan for the last decade and was by my side in the filming of many interviews. Juan Diego proofed the interviews for this book. He is currently a university teacher and director of the Ecuadorian Kyudo Association. Without Juan Diego's hard work, I doubt the *kyūdō* movie, *One Shot. One Life* would have been possible.

I wish to acknowledge my gratitude to Tyler Rothmar and Jeff Broderick for their assistance in Tokyo during the recording of a number of *kendō* interviews.

One movie that could not have been made without the assistance and expertise of Paul Martin, is *Art of the Japanese Sword.* Paul is a leading expert in the Japanese sword, and works with museums and collectors worldwide. He was indispensable in our visit to *Tenshinshō-den Katori Shintō-ryū*, along with Daniel Lee, assistant to Risuke Ōtake. My visit to this revered institution of classical martial arts was only made possible by the faith shown to me from Phil Relnick Sensei. Thank you.

I am also in the debt of professor Uozumi Takashi, now with the Open University of Japan, for sharing his vast knowledge of *budō* history and for his patience and time. Another expert of Japanese studies I wish to thank is my friend, the celebrated author and translator William Scott Wilson, whose work includes the *Book of Five Rings.* I look back with great fondness when I joined William on the road trip for his book, *Walking the Kiso Road* in ancient Japan.

In 2017 I was contacted by Hiroshi Onaka of the World Shorinji Kempo Organization to join them in their 70th year anniversary in Japan and California. Thank you for being my guide at WSKO. I also wish to thank my friend Jaime Rojas, who assisted me in California.

I cannot finish without including my friends Marc Ekasala and Genie Asessor who started with me on this incredible journey as my film crew in 2002. The first steps are always the most difficult and I was fortunate to have both of them by my side. Sadly, in 2006, Marc surrendered to acute depression and bi-polar illness and passed away. Marc, you are always in my heart.

Hirokazu Kanazawa with Jon Braeley and his students,
Marc Ekasala and Genie Asessor. 2002

PROLOGUE

The year was 2001 when I made the conscious decision to interview martial arts masters on camera. Although I had visited Japan and China many times in the past, martial arts was not always the main objective. This time it was different.

When I moved from England to the United States in 1990, I watched cable television for the first time and the reality of martial arts is very different to what these television shows would have you believe. Martial arts masters rarely talk about themselves and do not promote their style over another or sensationalize their practice. In Japan, most martial arts classes focus on repeating a single technique until it is mastered. Not exactly the sound of a commercial blockbuster!

But this was exactly the documentary I wanted to make. As an independent film studio I could tell the story of martial arts without being accountable to sponsors or investors with misleading opinion. More importantly, I could let the masters tell their story in their own words and ignore those with self promotion as their main goal.

My first interview in 2002 was with the legendary *karate* master, Teruyuki Okazaki, who was a student of Gichin Funakoshi, the founder of *Shōtōkan Karate*. I asked Okazaki Sensei why he still practices every day at his age, and his reply is worth putting down here. He said, "*Karate training* is a lifetime to develop yourself as a good human being. I'm training now more than fifty five years but I'm still not good enough and that's why I still challenge myself to be a good human being and I have to show my students a good example. This means practicing every day and this means some day you will be really happy! That's the aim. To be a good human being every day through training."

That year I put a similar question to another Funakoshi student, Hirokazu Kanazawa - one of my own instructors. He replied, "Throughout our life we humans have many objectives. As you move closer to your goals you must try and not have too many disagreements on the way. You must try to be humble in your attitude and in the spirit of *zen* or *budō* we call this '*mushin.*' This means an empty mind in a state of total control so that you can arrive at your objective with the mental attitude to find success in your life." You will notice that not one of these world renowned martial arts masters said their goal was the ability to kill with their bare hands or feet!

Nevertheless, if your goal in training in martial arts is to be able to defend yourself, I say go ahead, find a good teacher and do not give up. That's what I did. I started practicing *Shōtōkan karate* out of necessity. I grew up in a working class neighborhood in the North of England, and a week never went by without feeling threatened. Through hard work and education grants, I became an architect and moved to the other side of the city. Nevertheless, I continued my *karate* practice, and as my environment changed for the better, my reasons for practicing martial arts also changed.

Looking back to the time I received my black belt just before my 22nd birthday, I had mastered the basic techniques of punches, kicks, blocks and throws, and in the four decades since, I have not added too much more. My passion for the martial arts drove me to study other styles and pick up many more skills along the way, but those basic technique remain with me. When I practice they are in my unconscious, occupying no space. This is what Kanazawa Sensei was alluding to with his words, "An empty mind in a state of total control." It is the daily practice itself which brings you to find success in your life and not the winning or the losing. I named my first film *The Empty Mind*. In the following interviews with martial arts masters, I hope you also find their words inspirational enough to help you, not only in your martial arts, but in your every day life.

> **"** *The budō we call aikidō, is one in which you become one with your opponent, and one with the universe*

01.
Moriteru Ueshiba

DŌSHU, HEAD OF AIKIKAI

Chapter 1
INTRODUCTION

Born in 1883, Morihei Ueshiba, the founder of *aikidō* known as *Ō Sensei* is considered one of the most important figures in the history of Japanese *budō*. *Ō Sensei* likened *aikidō* to the sword saying it "Empowers one to cut through and destroy all evil."

Moriteru Ueshiba, the grandson of the founder was born in 1951 and received the hereditary title of *Dōshu* in 1999 when he became the head of the Aikikai Foundation after the passing of his father, Kisshomaru Ueshiba. Like his father and grandfather before him, Moriteru Ueshiba works each day to preserve the legacy of *aikidō* for the future, teaching at the *Aikikai Honbu* Dōjō and spreading the art globally through the International Aikidō Federation.

I have interviewed Moriteru Ueshiba three times. My first interview with Moriteru Ueshiba, took place in 2003, at the Aikikai Honbu Dōjō in Tokyo. I had arranged with the *dōjō* secretary, Masaki Tani, to film the class practice and the interview with *Dōshu* would follow. I decided not to take any chances and arrive early. Being British, arriving anywhere late is unforgivable, but to be late in Japan, for one of the World's most respected Masters of *Budō*, would surely mean I had to commit *seppuku!*

The *aikidō* class *Dōshu* teaches begins at 6.30 am. Unfortunately this meant telling my film crew, Mark and Genie, who do not share my fondness for promptness, they needed to wake up at an ungodly hour. To annoy them further, I misjudged how close our hotel, the Keio Plaza, is to the *aikidō honbu-dōjō*, both being in the Tokyo suburb of Shinjuku. This meant we arrived by taxi outside the *honbu-dōjō* more than an hour before *Dōshu's* class starts. Perhaps a little too early! The streets were empty and the five story *honbu-dōjō* was in darkness. As we waited on the narrow residential street, I felt unease creep over me and I began to question why I chose such an important person for this maiden interview?"

Rather than do nothing I started to set up the camera equipment and the tripod. At six o'clock, the morning light started to peek through dark clouds and I saw a small group of people walking up the street toward us. They wore black hakama pants under their top coats and I felt a feeling of relief. More students arrived and I seized the chance to interview a Canadian, Ben Peacock, just before he entered the *dōjō*. He was half my age and I felt a pang of envy as he talked about his martial arts journey to live in Japan and attend the *aikidō* classes under *Dōshu*.

As we entered the *honbu-dōjō* I was met by an elderly gentleman in the lobby, who introduced himself as my interpreter. The *honbu-dōjō's* Secretary, Masaki Tani had made this a condition for my meeting interview, so I agreed to hire an interpreter, at an hourly rate. Considering the interview was scheduled at 8.30am., it was a surprise to see the interpreter but he explained that he wanted to watch *Dōshu's* class.

There are two main *dōjō* or training rooms and we made our way up to the third floor *dōjō*. It was impressive, spanning the full length of the building with a white cloth padded tatami floor and at the front, the *kamiza*, with pictures of Morihei Ueshiba and his son Kisshōmaru Ueshiba. The *dōjō* was already crowded with students, most wearing black *hakama*, the rank of *yūdansha* (degree holder) or black belt. On the mat at the back were a few older gentleman, some looked to be in their eighties! Our small group walked carefully on a narrow perimeter wood floor to the back. Three minutes before the start of class, the room suddenly quietened and the students, sat motionless in *seiza* (formal sitting posture). The door closest to the *kamiza* opened and *Dōshu* entered, knelt and bowed in *seiza*. He walked to the front, knelt and bowed in *seiza* a second time, before the photos of his father and the founder. He then turned

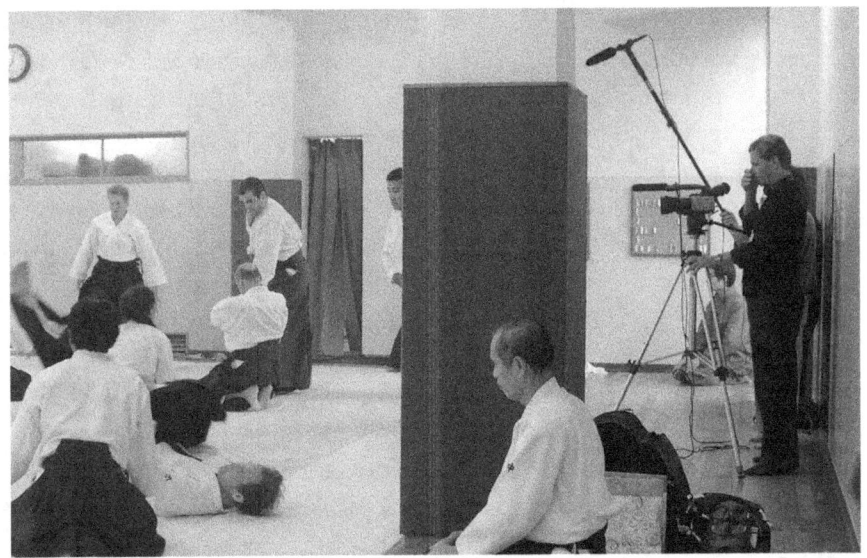
Jon Braeley filming at the Aikikai Honbu Dōjō in 2003

and bowed to the students. Class began immediately, with *Dōshu* and the students going through warming up exercises and stretching.

I will say little of the class teaching here, except to say *Dōshu* appeared to be enjoying himself, at one point coming close the camera and asking if I was enjoying the class! When *Dōshu* demonstrated a technique, with a partner (*sempai*) the students quickly retreat to the back to sit in *seiza* and watch. Sometimes this happens so fast that students just part to make a space for *Dōshu*, making sure not to sit directly between *Dōshu* and the *kamiza*. Throughout the entire duration of the class, none of the students spoke, except to whisper a thank you to their training partner. It was certainly more formal than what I had experienced in most of the *dōjōs* in the United States or United Kingdom.

After class we were taken to the private office of *Dōshu* on the floor below the main *dōjō*. After formal introductions were made, I presented *Dōshu* with a gift. It just so happened that the Florida Marlins baseball team, my local team in the U.S., had just won the World Series. And even though I have never seen a baseball game and have no love for the sport, I bought four signed commemorative baseballs that were in transparent presentation boxes. Knowing how popular baseball was in Japan, I thought they would make good gifts for the *sensei* I would meet. As I handed the gift to *Dōshu* I said that perhaps his son would like it. He held up the ball with a huge smile across his face and agreed it was a perfect gift for his son.

There was only one thing left to do before I left the *honbu-dōjō* and that was to pay the interpreter. In the lobby he handed me a small envelope with the invoice neatly written out. I felt a lump rise in my throat. I had naively expected to pay an hourly rate for two hours. Instead I was billed from the moment he left his home to when he would return, a total of five hours, along with taxi fares for a grand total of 43,000 yen (Japanese currency) or about US$450. Keeping a smile on my face I took out my wallet. I had 30,000 yen, so he accepted the remainder in U.S. dollars, after I offered him an exchange rate far above the banks. I thanked him and tried to hide my embarrassment as I left with Mark and Genie. As we walked to the train station I told them what happened and we all had the same response, "That guy really knew what he was doing!"

My second and third interviews took place ten years later during the filming of the *Warriors of Budo* series. While this second interview at the *honbu-dōjō* was extensive, it did not present any difficulties. However, the next interview was a very different situation. I had arranged permission from the Aikikai Foundation to film at the Iwama Dōjō in the countryside about fifty miles from Tokyo. This was built by Ō Sensei at the beginning of the Second World War and includes the Aiki Jinja (Shrine). Today this is known as the Ibaraki Branch Dōjō to avoid confusion with the Iwama style founded by Morihiro Saito, an early student of Ō Sensei. The *dōjō* is referred to as the 'outdoor *dōjō*' with one wall often left open to the outside garden.

So on a cold November day in 2014, I was on the train to Iwama Station in Ibaraki prefecture with my assistant, Juan Diego Fonseca. The objective was to film the Saturday evening class at the *dōjō* and film the Aiki Shrine close by. Arriving an hour early, we filmed the Aiki Shrine which has a full size statue of Morihei Ueshiba in the grounds, then walked across the country lane to the *dōjō*. I could see why this is called the 'outdoor *dōjō*'... the outside sliding doors remain open during class. At the *dōjō* we met a fascinating lady called Erica Rose from California who had been practicing *aikidō* for nine years. She was an *uchideshi* or a live-in student, who lives on the premises, cleaning the *dōjō* and assisting the instructor, which on our visit, was Hiroshi Isoyama, 8th *dan*. All went well filming the class, which was relaxed and enjoyable. Afterward we were invited to have supper in a large dining hall in the grounds before catching the last train back to Tokyo.

Moriteru Ueshiba

The author enjoying 'Aikidō sake' and sushi at Ibaraki Branch Dōjō

This meal turned out to be a boisterous affair with the local instructors and students serving their own brand of '*Aikidō* Sake.' After an hour of serious partying, we arrived at the Iwama Station in a stupor seconds before the last train left for Tokyo. I am not sure if any or all of this visit rankled *Dōshu*, but a week later I received a message that he would like me to schedule another visit to film at Ibaraki Branch Dōjō, when he would be the instructor. Unfortunately due to scheduling conflicts this visit could not take place for another two months, so I returned home to Miami Beach so I could rent out my home to a new tenant and spend Christmas with friends. The weather was a balmy 25°c when I left Miami in late January, and I arrived in Tokyo to one of the coldest winters in Japan. A large snowman greeted me outside the apartment I had rented, a train stop from Shibuya. I was filming *karate* the next day so I decided to keep as warm as possible under the futon and sleep!

A few days later I was on the train to Iwama Station with Juan Diego. I was worried that my down jacket was not enough to keep out the cold of the Ibaraki countryside in the winter. I was right. By the time we walked to the *dōjō* from Iwama Station the sun had gone down and I was shivering. I was wearing two pairs of socks but my feet were blocks of ice. Before boarding the train in Tokyo, we bought chemical hand warmers at a convenience store, and I had one warming my pocket so I could use my hands to set up the camera. *Dōshu* had arrived and as we waited for class to begin I had the realization that maybe he was here not only to be filmed teaching, but to be interviewed again. "But we interviewed him just a few weeks ago?" said Juan Diego. I replied, "I know but now we are at Iwama, a very special place. I think he wants to talk about this *dōjō*!"

As class practice started I could feel the air get colder and a light dusting of snow had appeared on the ground. My bones were stiff and I tried filming with a chemical warmer in each hand but gave up when I could not operate the camera. Class finished and *Dōshu* stepped out of the *dōjō*. I powered down the camera and began to remove the tripod. Then I noticed the students remaining in *seiza* at the back of the *dōjō*. This was unusual, especially considering how cold it was. Normally the students would keep moving by cleaning the *dōjō* and sweeping the mats. But they sat motionless and I became anxious.

As I began to fix the camera back on the tripod I whispered to Juan Diego, "I think this may be an interview." I had read all I could about the Iwama Dōjō and the Aiki Shrine but I was struggling to think of good questions. I knew we were in trouble. The screen doors opened and *Dōshu* stepped back into the *dōjō*, sat in *seiza* and motioned for us to enter from the rear. We quickly slipped off our shoes and seated ourselves before him with the students lined up behind us in eager anticipation of watching an interview. I had forgotten the frigid temperature and was now sweating!

I began recording the interview. We made sure to use the title of Ibaraki Branch Dōjō and not the former Iwama Dōjō which I knew would annoy *Dōshu*. However by the third question I could see he was irritated and his usual warm smile had gone. Before we asked another question, *Dōshu* interrupted us, "You cannot understand the importance of this *dōjō* and the Aiki Shrine, unless you understand the founders love of farming the land. Please ask me one last question?" So there it was... the reason for this second interview in the Iwama countryside. I recalled the last interview and the words 'bunō ichinyo' (oneness of martiality and agriculture). We asked "*Dōshu*, can you talk about the founders philosophy that *budō* and the growing of crops are as one?" *Dōshu*'s smile returned as he spoke about the farming of one's food as a spiritual part of *aikidō* and why the founder considered this a necessary aspect of *budō*. With this I felt I had redemption at the end an interview that had taken me by surprise. Let that be a lesson I thought as we walked back to Iwama Station to get the train to Tokyo.

Aikikai Honbu Dōjō 2003

INTERVIEW ONE

You are the grandson of Ō Sensei, a legendary budō master and
the current Dōshu. Do you feel pressure for this responsibility?
I cannot say that I have never felt any stress or pressure as you say, in my
life studying *aikidō*. However, since I have been growing up in this environment all my life, I do not have as much stress as people might think I
do. This position that I occupy is something I am used to. (*Laughs*).

What advice can you give a student trying to get to the
next level in their training?
As you have seen, the practice of *aikidō* is the repetition of exchanging
one's technique with one's opponent. The defense of the attack can happen in a split second. Through this fast and strenuous practice, you polish
your technique and your spirit. Nothing is perfect without effort but you
seek perfection from multiple practice. So the *aikidō* that you seek is
attainable only by repeating the practice many times with training each
day. There are no matches or tournament competitions in *aikidō*. Every
day effort is to practice. This is the most important.

Can you talk about 'ki', the internal energy that we hear about in martial arts. This is a difficult subject to understand in the West?

The word *'ki'* is difficult for Japanese people to understand too! *(Laughs).* In Japan, people learn energy or *'ki'* naturally from their daily practice and effort. We all have energy in ourselves, and therefore, we all have *'ki'* within ourselves. By practicing *aikidō*, we learn how to concentrate and use *'ki'* naturally. The natural energy coming out from you without intention is called *kokyūryoku* (breath-power). You learn to breathe correctly through the method of respiration.

In other words, *kokyūryoku* is to concentrate your respiration while in the state of *mushin* (lit. no-mind; emptiness, free from thoughts), and use your full energy in the most natural way. Not against the enemy. For example, when you are caught by the opponent very hard, you don't release the opponent's hand by fighting against the opponent. Watch and find out where the opponent's weakness lies. Where the body is falling, and you use your energy toward the opponent's falling direction. This is called using a technique of "*ki*" or respiration.

We just heard the word 'mushin', can you explain more about this term?

This is a difficult question. If you have various troubles and your thoughts are filled with daily matters during your practice, you are not concentrating during training. As Mr. Braeley mentioned before, *'mushin'* is to empty your mind. This is as if you are a part of the universe.

The technique of *sumikiri* (perfect clarity) is that when you are practicing with the mind of *mushin*, you are fast and spontaneous and your movement becomes to "premeditated silence". This premeditated state is called *sumikiri*. You reach this state of *sumikiri* through the technique of *mushin* and concentration. This technique does not come without great effort. You learn and reach *sumikiri* by everyday practice and effort.

How important is technique? Does aikidō have to be perfect to be effective?

Aikidō is not only about self defense or fighting. The *aikidō* we practice in our daily life also gives you better health of the body and better health of the spirit. But when it comes to practice in class, you practice *aikidō* with various people. You could see in our class this morning that we change partners all the time. Sometimes you win and other times you lose these encounters. From this kind of practice, you learn to use or adapt your technique differently for each opponent. It is not possible that you would use the exact same technique against every opponent.

In *aikidō* we call this *maai*. Through *aikidō* you learn to use this *maai* technique. To use the different techniques with the different opponents. A basic concept of *aikidō* is that you will come to understand the opponent you practice with. My hope is for students to practice more and more *aikidō* and through this will they will learn to understand other people. And to use what we learn in practice in our daily life. This is the spirit of *aikidō*.

Moriteru Ueshiba teaching at the Aikikai Honbu Dōjō 2014
Photo: Jon Braeley

Aikikai Honbu Dōjō 2014
INTERVIEW TWO

How would you define "aikidō"
You are asking me what is *aikidō*? The founder Morihei Ueshiba defined it that through the spiritual pursuit of practicing *bujutsu* or *budō*, from this spiritual training one can become 'one' with the universe. This becoming 'one' is *aikidō*. The *budō* called *aikidō*, is one in which one becomes one with the opponent, and one with the universe. That state of mind is what is called Aiki. It very difficult and hard to understand, but it is based on this, and it is this reason the founder created the *budō* called *aikidō*.

In what way does aikidō practice build 'nigen-keisei' or one's character?

Our founder Morihei Ueshiba taught us that *aikidō* is not a battle of strength with one's opponent or partner, but a feeling of mutual respect. To raise people with correct attitude, a balanced and sincere people. This is what he said is *aikidō*.

How close is today's aikidō to the one created by the founder?

The *aikidō* itself has not changed. What has changed from when the founder Morihei Ueshiba taught *aikidō* and what is taught today is the environment, of life and society. Of course, the people who were around at the time of the founder have passed away, so those teaching are now from different people.

But *aikidō* itself, the *aikidō* spirit, the techniques, the aspect of mutual growth through practice, these things have not changed at all and remain the same when the founder taught.

Can you talk about the Ibaraki Branch Dōjō and its significance?

I will tell you about its history. This *dōjō* we are in now, the actual *honbu-dōjō* in Wakamatsu in Shinjuku, was established around the year Shōwa 17 or 18 (1942-1947). About seventy years ago. During World War Two, Tokyo went through very difficult times with many fires raging in the city.

During this time, the founder Ueshiba Morihei, moved to Ibaraki prefecture's Iwama, nowadays called Kasama City, were he acquired a plot of land. This is where he began to live. The reason was to continue his practice of *budō* and to pursue agriculture as one. He called this the spirit of *bunō icchi no seishin'* (the spirit of the martial and the agricultural as one).

At that time, he created the Aiki Shrine and the outdoor *dōjō*, and from that time to the present day these still stand. However, once the Second World War finished and things settled down, and because this main *dōjō* in Shinjuku withstood the destruction of the war, the second *Dōshu* Kisshōmaru (founder's son) opened its doors for the re-installation of *aikidō* practice.

Also the founder, once things settled down after the war, returned to Tokyo to live. He also continued to live in Iwama. That is the context in which the Ibaraki Branch Dōjō came into being. In the year Shōwa 44 (1969) the founder passed away, but the outdoor *dōjō* practice and Aiki Shrine remain to this day.

Moriteru Ueshiba teaching, Aikikai Ibaraki Branch Dōjō 2015

Nowadays, both myself and my son Mitsuteru, attend practice twice a week at the Ibaraki Branch Dōjō, and do practice with the local people. Also the Aiki Shrine, together with the *dōjō*, are still active today. Both the *dōjō* that the founder created, this Hombu Dōjō in Tokyo, and the Ibaraki Dōjō are still running. Today, the Ibaraki Dōjō stands as the Ibaraki Branch Dōjō. I serve as the *dōjōchō* (head of the *dōjō*) for both of these *dōjō*.

What about the development of aikidō outside Japan?

Many more people now practice *aikidō*, and each person has a different way of thinking. Their bodies are also different to one and other, so the appearance of *aikidō* might seem a little different. But we have continued to strictly pass on the *aikidō* that the founder taught through practice that adheres to the principles. I believe that this is the correct path to follow.

Is there one technique that you feel is the essence of aikidō?

In the method of training, there is always the left and right, both practitioners repeatedly act as both attacker and recipient. They are both there for each other. In this context, they practice with this feeling of mutual respect, nurturing this feeling. *Aikidō* is a time-honored Japanese *budō* and as one it fortifies the body as well as it elevates the spirit. This is the essence of *aikidō*.

What should one consider when facing more than one opponent?

During practice, one does not look only at the opponent, but observes the whole surrounding. When only one point is seen then all the rest cannot be seen, one has to observe everything in its entirety. This is good when facing several opponents. Similarly, in life in society, if one focuses solely in one thing, one becomes unable to see the rest. Advance towards a single thing while observing all the surroundings. I think that this is the *aikidō* way to manage things.

In aikidō what is meant by the term 'shūchūryoku' (power of concentration)?

In *aikidō* we use the term "*ki*", but it is not a thing which you could segregate and point in itself. Through practice we focus the *ki*, that *ki* which all living humans poses, and use it efficiently. It is more fitting then to say we use is to revitalize us, and doing this, live a better daily life. During practice also, revitalize what we posess within. The way to revitalize is through a practice where we can use our strength, focus power and our abilities in a skillful way. Through practice, this revitalization can be cultivated. This is the *ki* in *aikidō*. It is not that this *ki* is a thing in its own, but rather it is the manifestation of the revitalization of the things within us as a whole. This is the *ki* in *aikidō*, you got me?

What does "Aikidō is the Way of Harmony" mean to you?

Aikidō is not about struggling against an opponent, but to build mutual respect, nurture people with correct attitude and sincerity, balanced. This is built through practice. From here comes the 'harmony' of *aikidō*, the becoming one with the opponent, with the universe. This is cultivated by practice that aims towards this state of mind. It is for this reason that *aikidō* is often called "The Way of Harmony."

I might be repeating myself, but during practice we must be balanced, taking care not to become one-sided, so we practice with people who have just began and with those who are experience alike. In those cases we practice at the same time as we guide. This is just like you said, what was it? The Way of Harmony. That is the connection.

You teach early morning each day, can you talk about this?

The early morning practice has been done from the days before the war, how do you say it in English, the Second World War? During the war it was halted. Ever since the year Shōwa 24, that is, the year 1949, it was restored by my father, Kisshōmaru the second *Dōshu*, and it takes place every morning from 6:30 am, like I was doing just before.

In daily life humans awaken when the sun rises, and when it settles we rest. Within this cycle, first thing in the morning is to wake up and purify the body and the heart, to cleanse the self. For this purpose is the morning practice started. It would not be possible to do it as early as 4am or 5am, so it is done at 6:30am which is a time when many people are able to attend. It is before going to school or work, so the time is determined from 6:30am to 7:30am.

Having cleansed both the body and the heart one can begin the day with a positive attitude towards what awaits ahead. This has continued as a tradition for over 70 years now. As you saw before, about 80 people attend the morning practice. Young people, women, elderly people and people from abroad. Many people gather and practice every day. Within the strictness of practices, the *dōjō* is also filled with an atmosphere of mutual respect. I think that everyone together created this magnificent practice environment. You could feel it, couldn't you?

Aikikai Ibaraki Branch Dōjō (formerly Iwama Dōjō)

Ibaraki Branch Dōjō 2015
INTERVIEW THREE

Can you talk about where we are, in Ibaraki?
This Ibaraki Branch Dōjō has been around for about 70 years, since the founder Ueshiba Morihei acquired a plot of land here. Two years afterwards, that is the year Shōwa 20 or 1945, he constructed this 'outdoor dōjō' here. This *dōjō* which was built for the purpose of *'bunō ichinyo'*, that is, to advance the way of *budō*, of *aikidō*, at the same time as farming, and has

remained unchanged. Also, there is the Aiki Shrine that was built before for the sake of faith. It is a world where *budō* and agriculture are as one.

What memories do you have of the founder, O' Sensei?
My oldest memory is from about... 65 or 66 years ago. When my grandfather the founder and my grandmother lived here I used to come here to Ibaraki, to play from time to time. I have memories of playing around the *dōjō* and the grounds of the shrine. That is some 60 some years ago. The first time I did practice here how old was I? I think that I did practice here only after becoming an adult. I did not practice here when I was a kid.

Can you talk about this dōjō in Iwama, the Ibaraki Branch Dōjō?
First, in this *dōjō* there is the Aiki Shrine where several festivals take place and this is also significant for those who practice *aikidō*, as it is for myself. That is why I think that the shrine along with this *dōjō* is important. However important we may think that it is, if people do not come here the existence of this *dōjō* will not continue. Therefore, I think that our job is to maintain and transmit correctly this *aikidō*. The Iwama Dōjō is one of the two *dōjō* which the founder established. The Tokyo Dōjō and the Ibaraki Dōjō. This *dōjō* being the one in which there is the Aiki Shrine. As such, it is an important *dōjō*.

What were the reasons for O' Sensei building a dōjō in Ibaraki?
The home town of the founder is a place called Tanabe in Wakayama Prefecture, a region dedicated to fishing and agriculture. It was in such place that he grew up. The fundamental things for life are first of all food, just as all living creatures need. Therefore the ideal of agriculture was very strong. Additionally, the religious devotion towards the *kami*.

The Tokyo Dōjō was built in 1931. When the war escalated, the area of the Tokyo Dōjō was burned and destroyed. Also people who attended practice passed away. Under these circumstances, destiny lead him to acquire land here in Iwama in Ibaraki. Here he could pursue agriculture and his devotion towards the *kami*. In this land in Iwama he lived according to 'bunō ichinyo' and the base for living, which is eating food, through agriculture. The founder followed this particular path of agriculture as he perfected *aikidō*. Through the practice of *aikidō* he worked towards the fulfillment of society. The founder himself had a very deep religious devotion, but what he recommended was to simply do *aikidō*.

> **❝** *Japanese martial arts are a way of one's practice for oneself, it has been a way for many years. Since the times of samurai*

02.
Yukitoshi Tatsugi

6TH DAN, AIKIDŌ, IBU

Chapter 2
INTRODUCTION

Yukitoshi Tatsugi Sensei, is a 6th *dan* instructor of *aikidō* at the International Budo University. I am including this interview with Yukitoshi Tatsugi, to highlight how extensive the Aikikai style is, with hundreds of very capable *aikidō* instructors not only in Japan but abroad. Through the International Budo University, Japanese and foreigners have the chance to study *budō* and practice traditional martial arts.

This was my second visit to the International Budo University which is located in Chiba prefecture, near Katsuura City on the southern coast about a two hour train ride from Tokyo. Founded in 1984 by an entrepreneur Dr. Shigeyoshi Matsumae, it is a major sports school and research institution for *budō* studies and sports science. Through its policy of working with the *budō* federations to encourage the internationalization of *budō*, IBU has a large number of foreign students. One such student is Baptiste Tavernier from France, who attended the university for many years and lives close by in Chiba with his Japanese wife. He is my assistant during my visits to the university filming the various *budō* classes and interviewing instructors. I scheduled such a class with Yukitoshi Tatsugi during a three day stay in Katsuura City to visit the uni-

The main *dōjō* at the International Budo University

versity. During this visit I would also be filming with professor Takashi Uozumi, who I interviewed a year earlier to discuss Eugen Herrigel for my Japanese archery movie, *One Shot. One Life.*

Even though it is a relatively short two hour train ride from Tokyo, I always look forward to traveling by train and given enough time, I would choose a two day train ride over a three hour plane flight every time! Because of this constant traveling I was an early user of audible books especially with the launch of the iPhone. So I settled into my routine of looking through the train window and listening to a book, which is the limits of my multitasking. I was listening to *47 Ronin* by Joan Vinge, a newly published version of this classic story. Billboards for the movie *47 Ronin*, starring Keanu Reeves, were on the walls of every train station in Tokyo and rekindled my interest to revisit this true account of a band of *rōnin* (masterless *samurai*) who avenge the killing of their lord. That is until I watched the movie. It was awful in my opinion. I had already downloaded the book from Audible and so I gave it a go. Fortunately as is often the case, the book was far better than the movie.

When you travel in Japan you usually need to book a hotel or *ryokan*, a Japanese inn. Staying with friends will usually require sleeping in the living room and sharing a small bathroom. Not ideal when the walls are paper thin! It's not your friends fault. The luxury of having a spare bedroom for visitors is rare in Japan. On a previous visit to the university, I stayed on the campus in the male dormitory. This meant sleeping in a bunk bed and a long walk the next morning to the student cafeteria for my coffee. I did not relish repeating that stay. This time I asked Baptiste to find a guest house with one demand, a coffee maker that I could use!

The International Budo University campus is spread across about a dozen buildings and in a single day you can do a lot of walking. The most prominent building with a sharply pitched tiled roof holds the two main *dōjō*, one floor being a 400 size *tatami* mat *dōjō* for judo and the equally large *dōjō* for *kendō* on a second floor. There are a number of smaller *dōjō* for *karate, aikidō , jūdō, kendō, kyūdō, naginata* and *shōrinji kenpō*. When I meet martial arts students who have little interest in other styles except the one they practice, I think of this special university and the many martial art styles together on one campus, and I wonder in awe at the treasure that is *budō*.

Compared to the main *dōjō*, the *aikidō dōjō* was far more modest and on my visit there were twelve students. When you meet Yukitoshi Tatsugi Sensei you immediately sense his passion for the martial arts.

Yukitoshi Tatsugi Sensei 2014

THE INTERVIEW

Can you tell us how you got started in martial arts?
I started training in martial arts with *karatedō* in high-school. I was training in *Shitō-ryū karate* during my school years. Then I started *aikidō* when I was at a university. I have been very lucky to happen across many

very good instructors in this time, like the one named Okada Osamu. So I started my *aikidō* practice from that point in time. This year, it has been 30 years since I have started training in *aikidō*.

How did you start teaching at International Budo University?

It was a turn of fate that made me come back here to my old *budō* school, in which I presently give instructions to my pupils. I was not very good at general 'western sports' like baseball, basketball or volleyball that are popular at school and university.

I am good at Japanese *budō*. Beside *aikidō* and *karate* I have also been training in *iaidō* and *kenjutsu*, that is to say, *Ono-ha Ittō-ryū* and *Yagyū Shinkage-ryū*. So this is the reason I say that I am good at Japanese *budō* and the best place for me is the International Budo University.

Which technique do you think is the essence of aikidō?

Basically modern Japanese *aikidō* was created by gathering *jūjutsu* teachings, which were brought together by Morihei Ueshiba Sensei. A big influence in *aikidō* was from the *hanmi no kamae* (oblique body stance), which was taken from *kenjutsu*. So this is important technique. Other technique that were important to Ueshiba Sensei were *irimi* (entering with the body; whole body approach) and *tenkan* (turning conversion, switching). It is these three points that I give an attention to during practice.

As far as important technique are concerned, there is this one called *ikkyō* (first teaching), where after your enemy attacks you with *shōmen uchi* (hit to the front of a head) or *yokomen uchi* (hit to the side of a head) his arm is restrained then pinned. It is a basic *waza* but I think that it is an important technique. I have this student who has become a police officer. He told me that *ikkyō* was the *waza* that was quite useful when restraining a culprit. So, *torimono* (holding down), which is important in *jūjutsu* as well, is a movement that I give the most attention during practice.

What is aikidō? Some practitioners use the word 'harmony'?

It is really hard to translate technical words in *budō* to English. There are words like *aiki* (lit. corresponding energy) and *awase* (to match), which are used in sentences like '*ki wo awaseru*' (lit. to match the energy). When you translate this to English, it means 'harmony' but I believe that the nuance might be a little more different. So this is a Japanese word that represents a technical aspect, which is hard to translate into

Yukitoshi Tatsugi

another language. For example *'Gorin no sho'* (The Book of Five Rings) by Musashi Miyamoto has been translated into English many times but there is this term he uses *'makura no osae'*, which is translated as 'holding down a pillow' but the real nuance is very different from this translation.

In the same way I think using the word 'harmony' to represent *aikidō*, is not really correct. The founder said that *'aikidō* is *'ai'* but translating *'ai'* as 'love' might call for more discussion, but I feel it means something like 'love for mankind'. Harmony in *aikidō* is about practicing against a partner but Ueshiba was kind of waiting for a partner to synchronize with him.

I would like to show you a *waza* that demonstrate this harmony. We will train some basics of *aikidō* now. Here I have my partner perform *katate-dori* (one handed grab). At the beginning it is taught in a sequence like this: first *katate- dori* (single hand grab), then *irimi* (whole body approach), and finally *tenkan* (switch turning). If it is done fast, my partner grabs my forearm while I'm turning, forcing him to synchronize to my move. It might be that these movements like this should be called *'chōwa'* or harmony. I think this is unique to *aikidō*. The partner is the attacking side and I'm a side that performs the move. The partner moves to the place I had moved from. I think this is the idea which the founder arranged as 'harmonizing'. When there are presentations done by 8th dan instructors, it might look as if they are dancing and performing some throws in the middle of it. This is what we learn during practice and it was encouraged by Ueshiba Sensei. I think that he arranged ideas like this and it created modern *aikidō*. This is only my opinion of course.

In some countries martial arts is a business. How is it in Japan?
Japanese martial arts are a way of one's practice of oneself, it has been this kind of study for many years. Since the times of *samurai* it is considered one's own practice. A *samurai* was hired by a feudal domain so he practiced by himself to be of the best service to the lord, his employer.

Basically it is a self-study. While in the past one could be given land or money for military exploits. But generally Japanese *budō* are about training oneself. There is not much thinking about it as a means of making economical profit. Certainly, after the 1964 Tokyo Olympics one can make a living thanks to the popularity of *budō*, like some of the professionals. There might be even people getting prizes in competition, and it is not that I completely deny them but originally Japanese *budō* could only have been stated as 'training oneself'. This kind of ideology

Yukitoshi Tatsugi Sensei teaching at the International Budo University

can be clearly seen in the teachings of *Kamiizu Ise no Kami*, a founder of *Shinkage-ryū*, who lived in the 15th century.

Today I believe that there are almost no Japanese *budō* practitioners who think of it as a means of hurting another person or using it to win in a fight. Our practitioners in our *kendō* and *jūdō* clubs are very strong but there is not one who would think like that. If you ask them why are they doing *budō*, probably most of them would answer that they want to pursue this path of training oneself.

As you can see, it is very distant from business and I think that Japanese are probably poor at making a business out of *budō*. In foreign countries the culture is different and if you take *budō* there it will assimilate, and some of the people might be doing it professionally which I do not deny, but it should be remembered that *budō* first is about training oneself.

I make my own living as an anatomy or biology teacher at the uni-

> **" A big influence in aikidō was from the 'hanmi no kamae' (oblique body stance), which was taken from kenjutsu. So this is important technique...**

versity, so I consider *aikidō* as an addition to my work. But there is no such case that I would take money from my students, not even during seminars. That is because I also learned *budō* for free and was not charged by my teachers. All my *sensei* and *senpai* taught me for free. One of the reasons for that is that they wanted me to precisely pass on the teachings. I am passing on their ideals so I do not think of *budō* as a business.

But because this is a *budō* University I am being paid for what I do. However I do not teach to train professionals. I have about ten students annually enrolling for teachings, to whom I want to pass on not only the techniques but also the ideals so that they will correctly teach children from their provinces. That is one of the reason I teach *aikidō*. That's why I think that if one is making profit from *aikidō*, but all the while remembering about those things, it's fine.

What else is different with your classes at the university?
There's one more thing I would like to add here. I think that demonstrations can be pompous. Sometimes these demonstrations might end up looking like an action movie which will decrease the quality of *waza*. I sometimes feel that demonstrations abroad are a bit too flashy but I cannot deny it since Japanese *budō* was taken abroad to places of different culture to Japan.

So it changes from the technique you are teaching in the dōjō?
I believe this happens. It is the reason why in *aikidō* there are no matches. To say the truth it separates one from what he was training for and because of that there are is no tournaments in *aikidō*. If one puts too much concentration on demonstrations, one might adjust his skills to presentation and end up creating *waza* that are impossible or not effective. We take precautions and do quite simple practice. So if one likes flashy things, our demonstrations or daily practice might look unattractively

simple. Basically Japanese *budō* is made of simple elements and it is what I thoroughly practice and teach with my students.

You trained in karate, which is has many styles, is there a similar situation in aikidō?

The interesting thing about Japanese *budō* is when you have a *soke* (head of the style) and *honbu dōjō* (headquarter of a school), a place where we can all practice together. Sometimes we do different practice but thanks to the spirit of Ueshiba Sensei we can get on well with each other. *Aikidō* still has such traditions. Ueshiba Sensei is close to everyone's heart, regardless of where you practice. We were recently discussing this at a study seminar. The next head of the school is going to be the son. We all are growing together. Moriteru Ueshiba our current *Dōshu* has a son, Mitsuteru Sensei, and he is being helped and brought up by everybody and apparently that is the way of creating a head of a school in *aikidō* and I feel it will be so in the future as well. Originally Japanese *budō* is like that, for example *Shinkage-ryū* and *It tō-ryū* have continued for 200 years thanks to this system.

> " *Among the many disciples that Morihei Ueshiba Sensei, the founder of aikidō taught, Gōzō Shioda Sensei was thought of as a sort of child prodigy*

03.
Susumu Chino
8TH DAN, YŌSHINKAN AIKIDŌ

Chapter 3
INTRODUCTION

Yōshinkan Aikidō has an interesting history which mirrors a situation that a number of Japanese martial arts found themselves at the end of the Second World War. In the post-war period of American occupation of Japan, the martial arts were heavily censored, especially those that promoted '*bushidō*' or warrior spirit. This was the ancient moral code of the *samurai* and used with effect in war time, to prepare Japanese soldiers for death. In post-war Japan, *Kendō, jūdō*, and *naginata* were abolished in schools and outside the education system, the fighting aspects of *budō* were downplayed in favor of promoting spiritual development.

In *aikidō* the pre-war technique of *aikijūjutsu* taught by Morihei Ueshiba, were changed after the war, with some 'harder' elements removed. Gōzō Shioda, an *uchideshi* (live-in student) of Ueshiba for over eight years, found himself at odds with the peace time situation in post-war Japan. The war had toughened his resolve to teach the style of *aikidō* he knew, that of pre-war *aikijūjutsu* taught by the founder. However, Gōzō Shioda had to wait until 1955, when he established *Yōshinkan aikidō*, before he could teach a style with the self defense aspects he felt were being ignored. The truth is, that after the war, the original *Aikikai Honbu Dōjō*

Susumu Chino Sensei teaching at the Yōshinkan Honbu Dōjō

was not being used, and the founder, Morihei Ueshiba was spending most of his time farming in Iwama. The only choice left to Gōzō Shioda was to create his own school. His timing turned out to be perfect.

In 1952 the occupation of Japan by the U.S. military came to an end and the occupying forces returned home. Japanese martial arts began to flourish as *dōjō*'s reopened, including the main center for Budo, the *Dai Nippon Butokukai* in Kyoto. Plans were also made to build a new center for the martial arts in Tokyo, The *Nippon Budōkan* which would open in 1964 in time for the Olympics. *Yōshinkan aikidō* quickly developed a large following helped by a strong teacher specialization training or '*senshūsei* course' that Gōzō Shioda created. Today it is the second largest *aikidō* organization in the world. Each year The All Japan Yōshinkan Aikidō demonstrations take place in Tokyo at the Komazawa Olympic Park General sports ground on October 3rd.

I received approval to attend but upon arrival I was told by a representative from the *honbu dōjō*, Teppei Yanagihara, who informed me, in excellent English, that my filming would be limited due to the heavy presence of the Tokyo police department, in particular, members of the riot police squad who train in *Yōshinkan aikidō*. I was instructed very politely, not to point my camera toward a long table on the edge of the arena floor, where about twenty police officers were seated. With images of riot police beating me to death, I was careful throughout the day to stop my lens from pointing anywhere near that particular table!

I would meet Teppei Yanagihara Sensei again at the *Yōshinkan Honbu Dōjō* where he helps Japanese and foreign students get through the *senshūsei* course. It is a one year intensive full time course, training eight hours a day, five days a week. I arranged to spend a day at the *dōjō* and interview the head of the *dōjō*, Susumu Chino Sensei.

The *honbu dōjō* is located on the second floor above a shopping street in Takadanobaba near Shinjuku, Tokyo. The previous year, I rented an apartment in Takadanobaba for myself and film crew when I could not find a reasonable rate in Shinjuku or Shibuya, my two favorite neighborhoods. Looking up to the *honbu dōjō* from across the street, you can watch *aikidō* students practice through the large plate glass windows. I was sure I must have walked along this street before and this is a good reason to always look up when you are walking along the streets of Tokyo. You never know what you could be missing!

Susumu Chino Sensei 2014

THE INTERVIEW

Can you introduce yourself?

I am the *shihan* of *Yōshinkan aikidō*. My name is Susumu Chino. In the year Shōwa 60 (1985) I entered as a common member, a student, and I trained with the 21st generation of the *senshūsei* course and the following year I became an employee.

Can you talk about the history of Yōshinkan?

In the year Shōwa 29 (1954) the first *Sōgō Enbu Taikai* (Comprehensive Budō Demonstration Tournament) after the Second World War took place. There, Gōzō Shioda Sensei received very high praise. In that demonstration, he received the support from many of the members who insisted that he should open his own *dōjō*. Thus, the following year, Shōwa 30 (1955), he established the first *Yōshinkan aikidō dōjō*. That was the start of *Yōshinkan*.

When it started, the *dōjō* was in Tsukudo-Hachiman. After that there was the *dōjō* in Yoyogi and the *dōjō* in Musashi-Koganei. The *dōjō* in Shinjuku Ochiai was transferred to Takadanobaba, where the *honbu-dōjō* is currently located.

Was Gōzō Shioda the teacher when you joined Yōshinkan aikidō?

Yes. Among the many disciples that Morihei Ueshiba Sensei, the founder of *aikidō* taught, Gōzō Shioda Sensei was thought of as a sort of child prodigy. Shioda Sensei possessed an innate ability. I enrolled in *Yōshinkan* when Gōzō Shioda Sensei was 69 years old. At that time, when he was 69, he would throw robust senior students and big instructors easily.

He displayed a magnificent and beautiful technique. It was like something taken from a story or a movie, where a talented person, an aged old man, short in height, would throw larger opponents all over the place. I felt very strongly that *aikidō* was superb after seeing this with my own eyes. Morehei Ueshiba Sensei, who was in charge of Gōzō Shioda Sensei, was slightly shorter in height, and even then he had a fantastic ability. I often heard that he was a splendid master of *aikidō*.

What is different about Yōshinkan aikidō from other styles?

The characteristic of *Yōshinkan aikidō* that is different from other *ryūha* (schools), is the emphasis we put into *kokyūryoku* (breath-power). I believe that the great importance that Gōzō Shioda Sensei put into this, is what led him to create the *Yōshinkan* style. Currently, there are various styles of *aikidō* being practiced. Among these, I also think that Gōzō Shioda's *Yōshinkan* really places importance on the practice of basics.

The way of standing, adopting the posture, the way of moving the body, all these things are carefully taught by closely adhering to the principles. It is important to first consolidate the basic movements, and then construct the techniques upon that. I think that this is the foundations

> **I enrolled in Yōshinkan when Gōzō Shioda Sensei was 69 years old. He would throw robust senior students and big instructors easily...**

on which *Yōshinkan aikidō* is established.

'Breath power' is different from the breathing that consists of simply inhaling and exhaling air. As a technique and a way to handle the body, its main element is to 'center concentration'. From this we get the 'power concentration', that is distributed to the various parts of the body. These 'center concentration' and 'power concentration' components are expressed in our connection to the opponent through 'breath power'. This is used as a technique and does not simply mean using the power of deep breathing. It is an *aikidō* technique called 'breath power' that Ueshiba Sensei executed within his technique. It is important to place emphasis on this power. In order to do this, one needs a proper standing or posture and use of the body. I think that Gōzō Shioda Sensei thought that this was very important and he emphasized this in his teachings.

What are the important principles in aikidō technique?

In order to break the opponent's balance, we must first avoid breaking our own balance. Specially, when one thinks and tries too much to break the opponent's balance, reversely, it is our own balance which gets broken. The balance in the opponent is broken naturally as a matter of course. I think that it is fundamental to be able to control oneself in order to be able to unbalance the opponent. There are various schools and styles of *aikidō*. I think that many people have the impression that *aikidō* is only about letting go of the strength and moving softly. That kind of movement cannot protect us from an aggressive assault from an opponent. I think that this is often the view.

It is a fact, Morihei Ueshiba Sensei had a very soft technique, but this is because Morihei Ueshiba Sensei had achieved such a state of mind. In order to achieve this and a make it practical, I think that it is important to emphasize the 'breath power' as a base. The continuation of that is the attainment of soft movement.

In order to manifest the power like that of Morihei Ueshiba Sensei

Susumu Chino Sensei demonstrates *tenchi nage*

one must first have the basic *jūjutsu*, and through continuous and pro-longed practice, this mysterious power can be obtained. Such techniques can be performed. It is not just relaxing the body and mimicking move-ments. I think that this is very difficult to know just by looking. I think that it is very important to aim to achieve the movements of a master, but it should not be only the movement, but also the inside content. The posture must be adopted properly, with correct practice. I think that the contents of this practice are more important.

I think that this is difficult to understand unless one explains it. It is difficult to know only by looking at soft movements, and I am afraid that many people think that *aikidō* is useless and that an opponent cannot be put down.

Do you have a favorite technique?
The technique that I like is called *tenchi nage* (lit. heaven and earth throw). This is a technique where the wrist is not bent or twisted, it is a painless technique. This is why the receivers rejoice (laughs). I also like it. It is very simple, yet very difficult, so I think that it is a very *aikidō*-like technique. Yes, I can show to you later.

I understand Yōshinkan is practiced by the Tokyo police?
Since the year Shōwa 35 (1960), *Yōshinkan* has been taught to various patrolling police departments. The *budō* called *aikidō* is very important

for arresting criminals. Since then it has been about 29 years since the *aikidō senshūsei* course system started. About 10 selected members from each riot police squad are strictly trained here at the *Yōshinkan honbu-dō-jō*, training as specialists. This takes place every year, and this year we had the 50th oath taking. Sturdy and special policemen who hold *dan* grades in *kendō* and *jūdō* acquire the *aikidō* techniques, so in the future they will stand as bodyguards. There is also a training period in order to acquire license for instructing female police officers. Upon completion, they return to their respective groups. These are the activities that take place at *Yōshinkan*.

I see you have a class today for very young children?

There are various occasions where the young can experience *aikidō* for themselves. It is difficult to transmit the merits and interesting points of *aikidō* only visually, so taking various opportunities we have them experience it directly in a class. There are special courses and personal experience classes, which are classes that you can try for the first time to see if you enjoy *aikidō*. Here they can experience what is fun and interesting in *aikidō*. These things take place from little children to the elderly.

Do you conduct any seminars aimed at foreigners?

Every year in autumn there is a Comprehensive Budō Demonstration Tournament. The following day there is a compulsory training meeting at the *honbu-dōjō* in order to confirm the attendants technique. Additionally, we send people from here abroad so they go to various branch *dōjō* and conduct seminars and so on. Also, some practitioners from abroad come here to practice. The technique is consolidated and unified through these exchanges. This is how it proceeds.

Outside the dōjō, how has aikido affected your life?

There is a phrase that reads *'aiki soku seikatsu'* (lit. Aiki is daily life). It means that *aikidō* is not something only to be practiced inside the *dōjō*, but also that our daily lives outside the *dōjō* are equal to *aikidō*.

This implies that one lives outside the *dōjō* with the same intention as practicing *aikidō*. As a result, various things are achievable, such as a mental attitude towards stressful situations.

I think that through *aikidō* it is possible to acquire things such as the way to confront those situations, without fear. What *Gōzō* Shioda Sensei was aiming towards was world peace. He was active all over the world as his objective was for the world to become peaceful through *aikidō*. We all practice *aikidō* to strive for that same goal of world peace, even if it is but a small contribution.

The feeling and essence of building harmony is preserved and very present in *aikidō* and in *kata*. By practicing hard to acquire this, we become good friends, avoid conflict, and build harmony in a very proactive manner. We undergo our activities believing that by spreading this way of practice to more people, it is possible to achieve a more peaceful world in the not so distant future. I would like for as many people as possible to please understand this. Specially, young people, I would like to have them come here to practice together.

> **"** *This is not the strength of the hands or the body, but strength all over the body, like a flowing river, pure. A pure flow, that is the spiritual power of aikidō*

04.
Tsuneo Ando

8TH DAN, YŌSHINKAN AIKIDŌ RYŪ

Chapter 4
INTRODUCTION

I first saw Tsuneo Ando Sensei at the annual All Japan Yōshinkan Aikidō Demonstration held in Tokyo at the Komazawa Olympic Park sports complex. He was one of the judges, sitting at a long table at the front of the main auditorium.

Later, I watched Ando Sensei perform a demonstration where he faced multiple opponents. At one point I am sure I counted five attackers rushing toward him. Within two seconds, three were laying on their backs with one or two more attackers about to follow them, whirling through the air. At any moment I expected to catch sight of a wire holding Ando, and he would fly off, into the roof space above, like a scene from the movie, *The Matrix*.

While these demonstrations look well rehearsed, nonetheless they show us the artistry of movement in *aikidō* and the spatial relationship between attacker and defender. While *aikidō* has its critics who say it does not work in a real fight, my experience is that in the street you usually face multiple assailants. Bullies rarely work alone. In this scenario, *aikidō* excels, switching direction with perfect timing and dominating the space regardless of how many attackers. I often refer to *aikidō* when

Tsuneo Ando Sensei at the All Japan Yōshinkan Aikidō Demonstration
Photo: Jon Braeley

discussing movement and distance in *karate* practice.

It was fascinating to watch Tsuneo Ando Sensei for the first time because prior to this, any discussion of *aikidō* and especially Yōshinkan style, would elicit, "Have you been to see Tsuneo Ando Sensei? or "Oh you must meet Ando!" His reputation had grown immensely in *aikidō* circles around the world and he was being compared to Shioda Sensei in technique and looks, being slight in build. I had already received permission to visit his *dōjō* in Urayasu City, just outside Tokyo, close to Disneyland. During a break in the demonstrations I sought out Ando Sensei's personal assistant, Jim Dawes to discuss my visit to film at the dōjō. Jim is *uchideshi* or full time apprentice to Ando Sensei and at the age of 37, was on his way to becoming an accomplished *aikidō* instructor.

The history of Tsuneo Ando Sensei begins when he was born on Shikoku island in 1956 and attended the local Tokushima University to study engineering. It was here that he joined the university *aikidō* club, reaching 2nd *dan* in *Aikikai aikidō*. After leaving the university for employment, he realized the life of a salary-man was not the life he thought he wanted and he turned to *aikidō* for an alternative. He made the decision to become *uchideshi* at the *Yōshinkan Honbu Dōjō* under Gōzō Shioda Sensei. Ando Sensei remained in this position for the next 14 years until he attained the rank of *shihan* in 1993. In 1996 he opened his own school in Urayasu which he named *Yōshinkan Aikidō Ryū*. Tsuneo Ando Sensei currently holds the rank of 8th *dan* in *Yōshinkan aikidō*.

Tsuneo Ando Sensei 2015

THE INTERVIEW

Can you introduce yourself?
My name is Tsuneo Ando. I am from Ehime Prefecture in
Japan. I am 57 years old.

What is your history in aikidō?
About *Aikidō Ryū*, my school where I am teaching today, was established
in October of the year Heisei 8 (1996). Before that I had started *aikidō*
in the university and then I got a job in a company but after a year and
one month I quit my company because all I really wanted to do was *aikidō*. Then I enrolled in *Yōshinkan aikidō*, and after 14 years and I half I
decided to become independent and open my own school.

I studnied under Gōzō Shioda and when he passed away I became
his successor. He taught me many things. One of my precious memories
is when we traveled the two of us together. It was my first time abroad
going with him for an exposition in the U.S.

Why did you choose Yōshinkan style of aikidō
In general, the *aikidō* of *Aikikai* is the martial art from Ueshiba Morihei
Sensei before the war. *Yōshinkan* is post war *aikidō*. I tried both of them. I
think that *Yōshinkan aikidō* has a very good educational system. Also, the

Aikikai aikidō has an educational system, and it aims for further things for those who can develop it. So there are good things in both systems. The training here and the training in the *Yōshinkan honbu dōjō* is very much the same. I also taught in the *honbu dōjō*. There are certain differences which depend on the individual, and I also teach those.

Gōzō Shioda said "Strength comes from 'breath power' (kokyūryoku). Can talk about this?

Breath power refers to *tanden* abdominal breathing. All the power comes from there and from there it flows into the extremities and outward to the opponent. This is not the strength of the hands or the body, but strength all over the body, like a flowing river, pure. A pure flow, that is the spiritual power of *aikidō*.

I will also add that 'power concentration' comes from right posture and originates in the spirit. If one doesn't concentrate, it doesn't occur. Body and mind are one. The instruction to build the right postures comes from the mind. If one just thinks, then this happens. However, if one concentrates then the posture is constructed like a single line. This can be done. This is fundamental and very important.

Can you explain the phrase 'Way of Harmony' when you talk about aikidō?

In *aikidō* we do not hurt the opponent. It's not the way of confronting the enemy, but to become one with him. The real winning comes from getting into good terms with the opponent so that there is no conflict. That is why *aikidō* is called the way of harmony.

There are no forbidden techniques in *aikidō*, but there are certain techniques that could hurt the opponent. The technique we prefer to practice are those which are beneficial for both ourselves and the opponents. One must become one with the opponent. One must not try to impose it. One must integrate with the opponent.

I saw your demonstration against four attackers. What is your method?

When one is attacked by various opponents, one must keep in mind from which direction they come. One must then separate them in time so that they eventually approach one by one. One creates this situation, and then confront each one in an order. It's the same thing as work, you

Tsuneo Ando Sensei teaching at Yōshinkan Aikidō Ryū
Photo: Jon Braeley

establish an order and priority for each task and tackle them one by one. Then it goes smoothly. One must read and organize the timing at which the opponents come toward you.

Do you see any differences between Japanese students and foreigners?

I don't think there are differences between the students in Urayasu and in foreign countries. However, here in Urayasu there are slightly more females. *Aikidō* is not only about being strong. The strength of *aikidō* is not such that it is disliked by females. It's a type of strength that doesn't ward off, but makes one want to practice against that strong person. Different person types can practice together so there are no distinctions in size or strength. This is inviting for females. The current shape of *aikidō* is this.

What has aikidō given you personally, outside of the dōjō?

By doing *aikidō*, I am living my everyday life. I think this works directly along with technical improvement. For example, sleeping too late. That's a bad start for the day. Similarly, if a technique starts off bad, it won't go well. One must determine which kind of living one wants to have and then act accordingly every day one by one. This is also *aikidō* technique. I feel that practice has given me this, and that this is the good thing of *aikidō*.

> **"** *When one is young your moves are full of strength. Sometimes too much strength. Sensei told me to get rid of this excess strength*

05.
Morio Higaonna

10TH DAN, GŌJŪ-RYŪ KARATE, IOKGF

Chapter 5
INTRODUCTION

Morio Higaonna Sensei is considered one of the most important *karate* masters alive today. As the founder of the International Okinawan *Gōjū-ryū karatedō* Federation (IOGKF), he was instrumental in preserving and spreading *Gōjū-ryū karate* around the World. You can understand my frustration when my first efforts to schedule an interview with Higaonna Sensei met with failure. I realized the officials running the Okinawan *Gōjū-ryū* Federation had placed an insurmountable barrier around Higaonna, who had recently been recognized with the title of Intangible Cultural Treasure of Okinawa, Japan's highest award in martial arts.

I did receive one offer by email, from a USA 'representative' that promised to put me in front of Higaonna Sensei if I paid a substantial fee. I declined. I make it a rule not to pay for interviews, except in special situations such as a donation to a monastery. I did have one friend who visited Higaonna Sensei in Okinawa but he passed away. Without this introduction, I was left with few options. Rules of etiquette in Japanese martial arts steadfastly forbid me from showing up at Higaonna Sensei's *dōjō* without an invitation, and this never entered my mind. I had resigned myself to failure, when some six months later, a remarkable concurrence of events took place. I was in Japan to attend the 37th *Kobudō Taikai*

The author with Higaonna Sensei in the *Budōkan* changing rooms

(ancient martial arts demonstration) at the *Nippon Budōkan*. It was early February and a major snowstorm caused myself and my assistant Juan Diego Fonseca to arrive late and in a hurry to start filming. We received our media credentials, and quickly made our way to the arena floor.

The first demonstration, the archery school of Ogasawara, was in progress as I began setting up my camera equipment. By the time I looked up to begin filming, the next demonstration had started. It was Okinawan *Gōjū-ryū karate* led by Morio Higaonna Sensei. It was so unexpected I stood rooted to the spot. "How could I have missed this" was my immediate thought. By the time I recovered from the shock, Higaonna and his team were leaving the floor. I was determined not to miss the opportunity to talk to Higaonna Sensei as we searched the changing rooms that line the perimeter of the *Budōkan*. I wondered what rule in the book of Japanese etiquette would I be breaking by ambushing Higaonna Sensei in the changing rooms. It took ten minutes of frantic searching before we came upon him and his two assistants preparing to leave.

In my unbridled enthusiasm to introduce myself, I failed to notice Morio Higaonna had only one leg in his trouser pants. I stopped dead in my tracks, his two assistant staring at me. Higaonna nonchalantly continued to pull on his pants. Embarassed, I stepped back, apologized, and waited for the 'cultural treasure' to finish dressing. We then exchanged bows and with my improprieties forgiven, I finally had a meeting with Higaonna Sensei, even though a changing room was not the place I had in mind. He listened intently as I explained the reason for ambushing him, and my plans for the seven episode film series, Warriors of Budo. As we talked, his assistant reminded him they needed to leave for the airport. Unruffled by this news, Higaonna let me finish my request to film at his *dōjō* and even answer a few questions. He then produced a card and wrote his telephone number on the back. Handing it to me, Higaonna said "I look forward to seeing you at my *dōjō*. Please call me."

I left the changing room holding the business card as if it was a rare butterfly. As I stared at Higaonna's mobile telephone number I consoled myself that my rudeness justified the result. Then I noticed the program of the *kobudō taikai* sticking out of the side pocket of my camera bag. In my rush to get to in the arena floor, I had forgotten about it. I pulled the program out and on the glossy front cover was Morio Higaonna Sensei.

Morio Higaonna Sensei 2014

THE INTERVIEW

Can you talk about your early years of karate practice?
When I was young, that is to say when I was about 14 or 15, my father was teaching *karate* to one of his friends in a six *tatami* sized room and I was watching him. He was with him all the time teaching him *kata*. In

today's terms, these were the *Pinan* (also *Heian*, lit. 'peace and tranquility') *kata* from *Shōrin-ryū*.

At the time I thought to myself, "*karate* is wonderful, it has such impact, speed and power." I certainly felt I wanted learn it. My father didn't say a thing back then. This friend of my father's started to instruct me in *tsuki* (thrusting punches) and *keri* (kicks), and the basic movements.

That was the reason why, when I reached seventeen years of age, that I went for lessons with my first Sensei, Tsunetaka Shimabukuro, who lives close by around here. I went to him and learned *karate* for about a year. Tsunetaka Shimabukuro knew both *Gōjū-ryū* and *Shōrin-ryū*. The *karate* he taught me was the basic *kata* from *Gōjū-ryū*. The *kata* is called *Gekisai dai* (lit. attack and shut closed, large; conquer and occupy, large).

After this first year, I continued practicing *karate* when I was at Business High School at the end of my first grade. I trained about three hours each day at the end of school, but Shimabukuro Sensei told me to learn at the dōjō of the founder of *Gōjū-ryū*, Chōjun Miyagi, since the *dōjō* was close to my home. He said I could learn very good *Gōjū-ryū* at this *dōjō*.

It was 1959 when I went there and Chōjun Miyagi Sensei had already passed away. The second instructor at the *dōjō* was An'ichi Miyagi Sensei, and so I started to receive instruction from him. From that point in time I thought *karate* was wonderful. During my school years, I trained every day – three hours during school and two to three hours at the *dōjō*. Basically, I was training five hours or more each day at that time.

Can you tell us the history of this *dōjō* where you teach?

My *dōjō* which we are standing in now, was built in 1981. Before this I was in Tokyo and after graduation I was asked to become an instructor in a large *dōjō* belonging to some Okinawan people which was in a place called Yoyogi, a district next to Shinjuku. It was 1959 or the early 1960's. This was a few years before the Tokyo Olympics when the city was very busy. I was teaching *Gōjū-ryū karate* to some students while training myself in this *dōjō* in Tokyo. I would go back to Okinawa in the Spring and Summer. After graduating high school I worked in a bank for one year. I was too busy with work so there was not much time to do *karate* practice. I then decided to stop working at the bank and concentrate on my *karate*.

I came back to live in Okinawa in 1981 and to build this *dōjō* at my home. There are many *karate dōjō* close by in Okinawa. The famous *dōjō* of Higa Eichoku Sensei is only about 100 meters away from here. So I wanted to build this *dōjō* and so I asked Sensei about their opinion. They said something like 'Do it Higaonna, who's going to do that if not you? I've been encouraged by them and then I opened this *dōjō*. For example, my own *senpai* - the *sensei* who has a *dōjō* nearby, Shōshin Nagamine Sensei, Yūchoku Higa Sensei and Ōsatsu Sensei have all visited here to my *dōjō*. My seniors also came. I received congratulations from them.

Chōjun Sensei was a second-third generation. You can see on this photo here in the *dōjō*. I learned from Miyagi Sensei beginning in 1947 and this lasted six years. We practiced every day, morning, day and night. He taught me in great detail, my sensei An'ichi Miyagi. He succeeded the brilliant technique of Chōjun Sensei and I have succeeded from him, training every day, morning, day, and night. This was a person who had truly acquired the essence of *Goju-ryu*.

I'm deeply grateful towards my own *sensei*. Even today I think "Thank you *sensei!*" All I have is a feeling of gratitude.

How have your karate skills evolved since those early days?

How has my *karate* evolved? It does not stop evolving. The *budō* I have learned from *sensei* is something that I can do my whole life. When one is young your moves are full of strength. Sometimes too much strength. Sensei told me to get rid of this excess strength. I was told to do '*kime*' (a final and decisive action) without excessive effort so it would create no recoil. He taught me many details such as this. For example, take a technique like *tsuki* (thrusting punch), there is a root to its power. He told me to get hold of that. In the inside, one should use his *tanden*, (lower abdomen, center of energy) and on the outside use the bottom of the feet and the muscles of the back. In the arms when you use the triceps here while you are doing a punch. I was told to take hold of these various locations of power. It's not only about doing a punch because you have strength, but it's about momentarily releasing all your power with your muscles. One should aim for this.

But I am still green. *Waza* (technique) are endless. The more you train, the larger becomes the number of things you must pay attention to. It's always a kind of challenge with *karate*. It's not perfect, and there is still not enough training.

Can you talk about your every day practice?

I will talk about training in the past. As I told you before in the times of

Chōjun Sensei we would have trained outside. Unlike nowadays were we usually train indoors, we used to train outside, among the nature and in a natural environment.

If it was raining we would go to the *dōjō* and the initial *rei* (formal bow) would be done in *seiza* (formal sitting). Otherwise, when we were outside we would do our bow standing up.

It started with the bow and then we did warm up from the tip of my toes through the knees, then next, my arms and torso and finally the neck which is the closest to a brain. This warm up is made to make you stronger in many aspects, medical, technical, physical and mental.

Chōjun Sensei learned about anatomy from a student of his who was a doctor, you know. The science called post mortem in which you open up a body to see why a person has died. Thanks to that doctor, *sensei* learned about the connections in the human body – the nervous system, muscles, tendons, organs and their locations. How they connect and where they connect.

Therefore his warm up included this medical aspect. That's why we were told to breathe with our *tanden* (lower abdomen) so that the thoracic diaphragm would move. There are three types of breathing, the chest, the abdomen and *tanden* breathing. To draw out your strength you have to breathe with *tanden*. If both the inner and outer powers unite – one will be able to create tremendous power.

I was always told to spin my fist like this (punches while turning forearm counter-clockwise). The opponent will fly that way if it's executed with power. I was told to find this punch that would make him drop to the floor. So I believe this technique is so that you will be able to create powerful punches and kicks.

If I do my warm up alone, it takes me about an hour. The movements in the warm up are made to match what we know about medicine, technique and the body. You have to use your movement, the legs and dodging to avoid an attack, so all those things are included in the warm up moves, which are very rational.

And we do *kata* in *Sanchin* (lit. three battles). *Sanchin* is *jō* (higher), *chū* (medium), *ge* (lower) – *ichi, ni, san* (one, two, three) – *Sanchin*. And there is the power of breathing, the physical strength, and mental strength. These are the properties of *Sanchin*.

There is also an interpretation of *Sanchin* of heaven or the universe, meaning nature and humans who should train in harmony with nature.

Morio Higaonna

Visiting students sit in *seiza* before class begins. Photo: Jon Braeley

So we have '*san*' meaning one, two, three, and '*chin*' meaning battle. It is written using the character for 'battle', '*sen*' (in Japanese). To battle as in combat. By battle you can understand it is a fight with the breathing, with the abdominal breathing. Like a kind of challenge. And those roots, the 'roots of power'. So you use concentration, the breath and the 'roots of power' (points to soles of his feet). You cannot do a proper *kata* without keeping those three elements in balance. *Sanchin* is called the center of oneself. In the past Kanryō Higaonna Sensei learned only *Sanchin* for five years, no other *kata*. *Sanchin* everyday. Of course you also train your unbalanced body with some tools that we have (pointing to strength exercise tools). And in *Sanchin*, by proper *tanden* breathing you make your organs stronger by correcting their inner flow.

Using wooden tools and the *makiwara* (lit. rolled straw; in karate, target for punching practice) make your outer arms stronger. You cannot create a balanced body without training of the inner and outer side. It the same when punching the *makiwara* – if you do one hundred punches with your right hand, you should do two hundred punches with your left hand since it's usually weaker.

Some karate practitioners say that Sanchin can be unhealthy?
There are people who think so. But one must experience *Sanchin* and by doing it properly a person will get stronger. There are some *dai-senpai*

(great senior teacher) like Ura Soki who made it to 103 years old and another who I believe has lived 94 years. The second person to show me *Sanchin* was about 88 or 89, and it was correct. His breathing was correct, so by doing correct *Sanchin* one can live long.

I must warn you that it can be dangerous if one wants to show off. Breathing out should be long. Being tense in your torso with disregard to the lower parts of the body, without correct *tanden* is dangerous. One must concentrate on the *tanden* and not in the muscles. There are people who just show off. That's dangerous. Correct *Sanchin* can be healthy.

I am 75 years of age and I still practice *Sanchin* every day and afterwards I practice technique. If you do correct *Sanchin*, you will live long. If you do incorrect *Sanchin*, it is bad for your body. It's because oxygen doesn't go to your head, it goes only here (points to lower abdomen). If one gets dizzy, it is a sign that the *Sanchin* is not correct.

Have you created your own keiko (practice) and way of teaching?
As for my own instruction, I do it as I was taught. Beginning with the warm up, then using the wooden tools and then doing *Sanchin*. I also include the moving of the feet or *suriashi* (sliding feet). This I do thoroughly for about 30 minutes.

The movement of the legs is important to practice. One slides the feet as if polishing the floor. Not jumping like this (steps, raising the feet). One can move swiftly like this with *suriashi*. In the case of *Gōjū-ryū*, there is a calmness, a stillness to the movement of the feet.

For example, when a punch or strike comes, you have to move with speed. Your knees must be flexible and the feet should be like cushions so you can avoid strikes. If you practice correct training you can gain correct *karate*. In fact it isn't very different from training in the past. Nowadays life is just as harsh and you have to work in order to eat. In the past if one had enough food, one could train for many hours. Many of us practiced for five or six hours every day. After working in a bank for one year, I left and began training all day under Chōjun Sensei. Sensei was a professor but his *karate* training was very hard. He made us do about 1,000 squats every time we trained. The father of the current governor of Okinawa, Mr. Nakaima, was one of the students of Chōjun Miyagi. He was made to do 1000 squats every day. He was a monster! A person of real endurance.

Sensei was like "Do the punch one hundred times! Do the kick one hundred times!" (*Laughing*). When I go to Europe I do things like that

Training with heavy iron 'geta' shoes for powerful kicks

sometimes. But not all the time. There were times like I would say "Do kicks for an hour!" Once I remember in training we did about 7,000 kicks. But the hardest was *shikodachi* (lit. squared groin stance; low straddle stance) for an hour. Your legs tremble and I have done this stance until I was staggering around and unable to walk. When you do this kind of training it can feel really good. I remember in the Netherlands the students were hugging each other saying "It's so good when it's over!"

These kind of punches and kicks are simple technique that we use in hard training together. Everyone is covered in sweat. What I like about going abroad to teach, is that although the language and way of thinking and customs are different, there are no borders to separate us. We all do the training together.

Now there are some Russian students here at my *dōjō*, and although I cannot speak Russian, when we practice together they can still understand me. They see with their eyes. Hear with their ears and feel with their sweat. Mostly Russians can understand at least some Japanese. But we can understand each other without using words. In times like that I feel that *karate* is wonderful – and that's because we can immediately become friends and we can go anywhere in the World.

Gōjū-ryū name is termed 'hard and soft', Where is this from?
Chōjun Miyagi Sensei was the first to name the school *Gōjū-ryū* in the

5th year of Shōwa, in 1931. Before this time, it was just referred to as *karate*. The one who named the school was Chōjun Miyagi.

The Shōwa Emperor held ceremonies in the *Meiji Jingū* (Main Shrine) in which all kind of Japanese *budō* practitioners participated. Shinzato Sensei went to such demonstrations. He had tremendous strength and the other *budō* practitioners, impressed asked 'What *ryūha* is this?' Because there were no schools of *karate* at that time, he probably told them something like *Nāfa-dī*, meaning *Naha-te* (lit. fist of Naha, named after the city). So when Shinzato Sensei came back to Okinawa he told everyone what had happened with the Japanese. Chōjun Sensei then said that *karate* should continue as a Japanese *budō*. He recited a line from the *Kenpō hakku* (lit. Eight passages about kenpō), a poem contained in the *Bubishi* (lit. Treatise on Military Provisions) where it says *"Hō wa gōjū o donto"* (lit. "The method is hardness-softness being inhaled-exhaled"). *Gōjū*, meaning hardness-softness is prepared with the breathing, and then this *gōjū* is expressed. This is how it was established.

What is the biggest difference between karate in Okinawa and the mainland (Japan)?

There are many differences in the *kata* (forms). Our basic technique are the same but in the *kata* there are the biggest differences. For example *Sanchin kata* is obviously different. When I was teaching in Thailand I could clearly see that.

There are some differences in the technique, the timing, the power, the accuracy of each technique and so on. For example, we call this movement *nuku* (to pull out). We do it like this, like pulling out a spear... gently. I have seen others do this move as if it was stuck and there is no need for such excessive power.

Another example is this movement (blocking a punch with arm). In the case of Okinawa it is done like this (short relaxed circular swing of the arm-fist). We use this technique against a strike or punch, defend here (high) and attack groin (low). As a strike approaches, catch this incoming attack with a movement of the hands like a whip. It's like a whip action and catching the punch with it. One swings the arm like this, without strength (swings arm in a circle by his side).

There is this type of punch called *sunzuki* (short/close thrusting punch). There is *toozuki* (distant thrusting punch) and they are used for different situations like this (punches short to stomach then long range

> **" Chōjun sensei always said that the real karate is the one that wins without fighting. Not fighting is the ultimate karate. But that's not to say there were no fights!**

punch). Another example in close combat, we can use this kind of spin punch (turns wrist). And if you do an upper cut-kind of punch you do this (circular punch). To do this I have to train my wrists. It's not about muscles – it's about using the wrists. So we need to use training tools for this.

What is your opinion of Sport karate?
Competitive sports in *karate* are fine. I think of *karate* competitions as a step along the way to achieving something higher. Children and young people like to compete against each other. It's only normal. However in competition one probably does have to take the initiative and attack first. In *karate* as they go up that step, they will reach a different place. Then they should think about continuing karate practice their whole life.

What is the most important point when facing an opponent?
You mean the most important when fighting? Running away! (*Laughs*). But really, in other words you should not interfere. There is this saying we use, '*karate ni sente nashi*.' In *karate* there is no first strike. In practice this can be seen such as all *kata* start from *uke* (receiving position). That's one of the most important spiritual values of *karatedō*.

One should talk and make peace, without fighting. Chōjun Sensei was said to be able to avoid a blow from behind before it came. It was as if he had eyes in back of his head. Nevertheless, Chōjun Sensei was in many fights during his life. Once having a fight with five people at once. He was very fast. This Kanryō Sensei was fast as well, and he used weapons such as a type of Chinese sword. He used the *bō* (long staff) and other weapons which train you to understand distance. That's the most important, to know the distance.

Maai (distance) and the eyes are important. And timing. During training we will use large movements but in real combat you would not do that. Only in training one does large *sabaki* work. In the *Gōjū-ryū*

Morio Higaonna Sensei teaching at his *dōjō* in Okinawa

system technique should be done with large movements at first. It's the same with drawing with a pencil – you have to do broad strokes at first. At first punches or strikes are done in a large way as well. But the important thing is to produce all your strength in the moment of the impact.

At first we use large movements or use large technique but then later it becomes smaller. For example this large circular block becomes a smaller circle. This is also like this big at first (shows a circular double block from *Gekisai dai ni)* but afterwards this movement is kept closer to the body. You do not detach your arms. One avoids making it like this, overextended (arms leave the body). At first beginners do things like that, making the moves very large, but they will understand how we do this after we make an explanation.

In mainland Japan we talk about bushidō and 'samurai spirit' in martial arts. How is it in Okinawa?
Bushidō (samurai code of conduct)… is an influence of mainland when you talk about *samurai*. Here on the Okinawa islands, by '*bushi*' we originally meant people who trained fiercely in *karate*. So it is said like '*bushi* Higaonna', '*bushi* Kanryō'. *Bushi* was a term for people who were an expert or a master. Like 'Miyagi *bushi*'. This was not used for people who were not training in *karate*. It was like a title for people who trained all the time, '*bushi* miyagi' and so on.

I remember this when I was little. '*bushi* Matsumura', '*bushi* Kanryō', '*bushi* Miyagi' - I think those three were called '*bushi*'. Matsumura Sensei of Shuri-te (lit. fist of Shuri, named after the district in the city of Naha) was well educated and intelligent as well as he was excellent at *karate*... He has been to China.

There was a sense to add education to *karate* training. For example Kanryō Sensei didn't take much education, however he has done much training. Chōjun Sensei was very intelligent - he studied medicine himself and so on. It's called 'bunbu ryōdō' (lit. the dual way of scholarship and martiality). The reason there is *karatedō* now is because Chinese ideology was transmitted. For example *kenjutsu* has changed into *kendō*, *jūjutsu to jūdō*. This is an example of Japanese wisdom. It's a wonderful wisdom to attach '*dō*'.

'*Dō*' in this sense means '*kokoro*' (one's heart). The idea of *bushidō* is non-existent in Okinawa but there is the 'spirit'... This makes you courageous. Chōjun Sensei fought quite a lot and once there was a fighter, a boxer who was big and the *sensei* used his *waza* to protect himself and defeat him. So about this *bushidō*...there is something similar in Okinawa.

You can also say it's a kind of victory without fight. Chōjun Sensei always said that the real *karate* is the one that wins without fighting. Not fighting is the ultimate *karate*. But that's not to say there were no fights!

In the old days, disciples of Kanryō Sensei went to this bar where there were always fights. Here we call it '*kakidameshi*' (also, *kakedameshi*; lit. testing through contact; close range sparring), similar to the concept of '*tameshigiri*' (lit. test cutting). It's a practical training. First you learn in school like children and then outside there is this practical education.

One goes there and there are often fights with people who had been drinking. If he runs – you don't chase him. If he faces you, then you fight. Another good point is, as Chōjun Sensei told us – you don't say the name of any person with whom you fought. In fact, you don't even mention that you fought. Chōjun Sensei told us that we can fight as much as we want but we cannot name the person or talk about the fight.

There are lots of fights in Okinawa. But only with your body, no weapons were used. We do *kata*-centered training and basic sparring but because we don't do real fights in the *dōjō*, there is *kakidameshi* outside. There are lot of episodes like this.

As for *bushidō*... some people could have had that mental attitude. Not being scared of your enemy. Of not needing anything. And the attitude of eating only as much you need. And same with the training as well. Not desiring for a position in hierarchy or a desire for being graded. My *sensei* was like that. Only *keiko* (practice). And if he could live on – that was enough. Doing *karate* was all he needed to be happy. That's the spirit in the case of Okinawa.

What effect has karate had on your everyday life?

About the influence of *karate* on my life? Well I know Japanese *budō*, and I also go to many countries and see their martial arts. I still have many things to learn. I'm mostly grateful to my students, to the parents, and to the *sensei*. I say thank you to them with much gratitude. It's thanks to them that I can do *keiko* and it makes me happy to see the students grow. It makes me happy to see them acquire new *karate*. Watching my students doing *keiko* encourages me to do *keiko* as well. That's the reason I continue to practice *karate* today.

> **" The first thing you must know is that Okinawan people are not Japanese people. They are people of Ryūkyū**

06.
Tetsuhiro Hokama
10TH DAN, GŌJŪ-RYŪ KARATE

Chapter 6
INTRODUCTION

Tetsuhiro Hokama *Kyōshi*, 10th *dan*, is a very interesting *karate sensei* and as soon as I knew that I would be traveling to Okinawa I started to make plans to visit him. I had one compelling reason. He is the founder and curator of a *karate* museum, dedicated to all things *karate* and *kobudō*. I could not wait to visit.

As the gatekeeper of the history of Okinawan martial arts, Hokama Sensei is the perfect choice. Now a 10th *dan Gōjū-ryū* instructor, he has spent his life in the study of *karate* and the history of the Okinawan martial arts. He was born in Taiwan in 1944 and both his parents were of Okinawan decent. Like most students of *karate* in Okinawa, his teacher was a family member, in this case, his grandfather Seiken Tokuyama. Hokama graduated to formal *karate* training with a well known instructor, Sekō Higa who was a student of Chōjun Miyagi (1888-1953), the founder of Gōjū-ryū *karate*. The *dōjō* of Higa Sensei was legendary with many students going on to become instructors. It was here that Tetsuhiro Hokama was introduced to earlier martial art styles with roots in China and to *kobudō*, the old Okinawan weapon styles.

By 1977 Tetsuhiro Hokama was awarded the rank of *shihan*, running

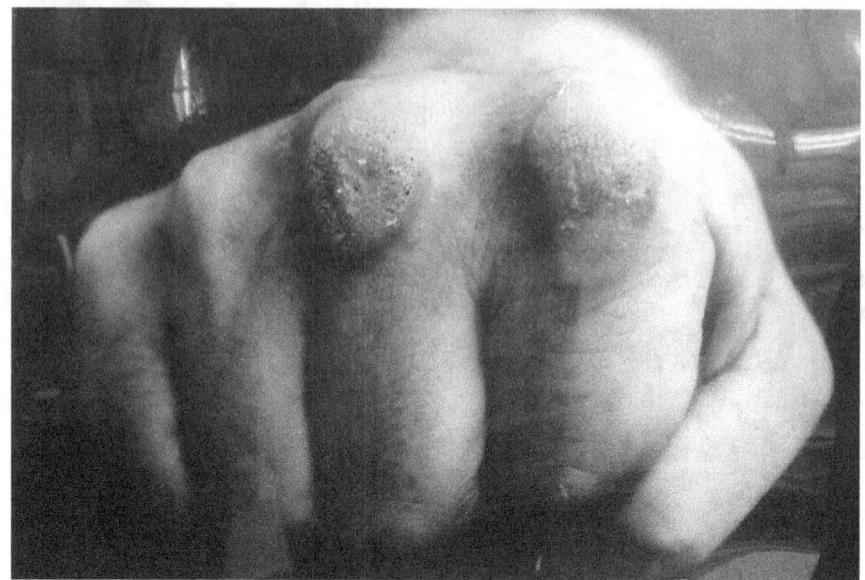

his own *karate* schools and the secretary for the All Okinawa *karatedō* Association. Today he is president of the Okinawa Gōjū-ryū Kenshi Kai *karatedō kobudō* Association.

We were staying at the Best Western hotel in the capital city of Naha, and arranged to spend the day with Hokama Sensei at his *dōjō* and museum, which is about a forty five minute drive North East to the town of Nishihara. The official name of Hokama's museum is the 'Museum of Ryūkyū Martial Arts' and is on the second floor of a large detached corner building, which houses his *dōjō* on the ground floor. Tetsuhiro Hokama met us at the door dressed in an impressive brightly colored woollen *kimono*, worn like an overcoat over his *karategi*. The ground floor is an impressive *dōjō* with plenty of space for a large class and with it's high soaring double height, you can swing a long staff or bō without worrying if you are going to shatter a light fixture. The museum is a second floor gallery and can be reached by stairs from the *dōjō*. After the introductions, we relaxed and drank some wonderful hot tea with our host and then made our way to the museum on the second floor where we would record our interview.

When I stepped on to the second floor my first thought was how I would fit all the hundreds of artifacts and display pieces into my documentary! I could have spent all day searching among the many display items. The museum is crammed from floor to ceiling with all things martial arts, from posters and photographs, weapons, training equipment, diplomas and documents and old artifacts from various *dōjō*, most of them from Okinawa. Greeting me at the entrance is a large black and white poster of a fist with the two heavily calloused knuckles. I made a note to ask about this in my interview. The walls are covered in more photographs showing the history of *karate* through past masters. The weapons of *kobudō*, mounted on walls and in showcases have been gathered from all over the World and are worth the small entry fee alone. And the priceless part of your visit is having Tetsuhiro Hokama walk around with you, telling you the rich history of *karate*.

Tetsuhiro Hokama Sensei, 2014

THE INTERVIEW

What were the mains schools of Okinawan karate to develop?
Very well. In the beginning there were no *karate ryūha* in Japan. In the old days, there was only *karate* here in the *Ryūkyū* Kingdom, you call Okinawa, and it was a different country from Japan. In Japan there was *jūdō, kendō, naginata, aikidō*, and so on. There was no *karate*. It was first taken there around 1922, at the time of Gichin Funakoshi Sensei, as well as the time of Motobu Kochi Sensei.

In Japan there were several *ryūha* in *kendō, jūdō and naginata*. But in Japan, Funakoshi Sensei was asked which *ryūha* there were in Okinawa.

Sensei replied that there are no *ryūha*. For example, what is done in Naha is called *Naha-te*, what is done in Shuri is called *Shuri-te*, and so on. It was used as *kobudō* so it was understood simply as *kobudō*. How ever, if there are no *ryūha* then it would be inconvenient in Japan, so various *ryūha* were determined. I can explain further.

What is called *ryūha* schools did not exist in Okinawa in the past. In Okinawa, *karate* was referred to as '*te*' (hand) as in 'empty hand'. However, in Japan, *jūdō, kendō, naginata , aikidō,* and so on, all have schools. That is why when Gichin Funakoshi Sensei took *karate* to the mainland in 1922 he was asked about which *ryūha* it was. In Okinawa there were no *ryūha*, but *Naha-te, Shuri-te, Tomari-te, kobudō*… However, this was difficult in Japan. Because there were no *ryūha* so *Naha-te* became *Gōjū-ryū karate. Shuri-te* became *Shōrin-ryū karate*, as in 'small forest', 'little forest', or 'pine forest', and this later changed into *Shōtōkan. Tomari-te* and *kobudō* were also transmitted like this. So it changed from '*te*' to *ryūha*, and nowadays it has changed to *karatedō*.

Is China's influence in Okinawan martial arts still in evidence?

Yes, there is still influence from China. In the year 1609, Satsuma, present day Kagoshima, attacked the Ryūkyū Kingdom and caused its fall. At the end of the 1800's, the abolition of feudal domains and establishment of prefectures took place. So, around the year 1870, this became the Okinawa Prefecture. Originally, Okinawa is not the place of origin of *karate*. It came from the Mesopotamian civilization through one route by India, then China, and then to Okinawa. Another route is from Mesopotamia through the silk road, passing through India, then to Indonesia, Thailand, and then to Okinawa through shipping or sea routes. Both routes mixed at Okinawa as the binding point.

Therefore, the *karate* from Okinawa was nourished from China. It received nourishment from the martial arts from the area of China and India and although *karate* is an original work from Okinawa, it was greatly influenced by China and South-east Asia. For this reason, *karate* is based on mimicking animals. There is the fist of the tiger, the fist of the snake, the fist of the monkey, the fist of the elephant, the fist of the crane, etc. They all mimic animals. This is how *karate* increasingly became systemized and eventually became *karatedō*. From that modern time onwards I think that it has not received much influence from China. However, it originally received a lot of influence.

Tetsuhiro Hokama

> **In Japan, Funakoshi Sensei was asked which ryūha (schools) there were in Okinawa. Sensei replied that there are no ryūha...**

There is quite a lot of influence from China. It originated in the Mesopotamian civilization and was then taken to India. In India, several masters like Bodhidharma invented various *karate* and then these were transmitted to China, for example, the Shaolin Temple. That is one route. Another route is from India and through Indonesia, then Taiwan and up to Okinawa, through a maritime route.

These are the two routes which meet in Okinawa as a meeting point. Thus, *karate* in Okinawa was formed as a mixture from martial arts that came from China and South-east Asia. Okinawa was like a melting pot for all of these and from that point of view the recent *karate* is originally from Okinawa. However, it has received a heavy influence from China. In modern times there is no such influence anymore, but in things such as the names of the *kata* and so on, there is influence from China. However, ever since that time I think that it changed quite considerably.

Can you talk about the history of Gōjū ryū?

Gōjū ryū was originally the 'fist of the crane' from Fujian province in China. Various techniques based of mimicking animals were transmitted to Okinawa such as the 'fist of the crane' and 'the fist of the tiger'. At first, these were created in Fujian province in China and then transmitted to Okinawa, and also emissaries from Okinawa traveled to China and learned them.

These were also accredited Chinese envoys to Okinawa, as well as sailors. There were various types of transmission routes. Among these, it is historically known that *Gōjū-ryū* came in 1392 along with the 36 families from China who emigrated to Kume Island. From a historical point of view it can be said that it originated around this time, but of course, the history is much older than that. The first *sensei* from that time was called Yabu, which became Hokkama.

Then came Araki Seisho, and next came Higaonna Kanryō, who was followed by Chōjun Miyagi, and after him Higa Seiko Sensei, and then we are under Higa Seiko Sensei. Fukuchi Sensei and I are under Higa Seikio Sensei. *Gōjū-ryū* has been passed on as one line. From Kanryō Higaonna and Chōjun Miyagi various ramifications take place. Now there are eight groups which form *Gōjū-ryū*. This is the flow of how things went here in Okinawa. When it went to Japan it was passed on as *Gōjū-ryū*.

How did karate travel from Okinawa to mainland Japan?

Shōtōkan was originally taken as *Shuri-te* to Tokyo around 1922 by Gichin Funakoshi Sensei. There, he taught it at various universities in Tokyo such as the University of Tokyo, Chou University, Waseda University, Keio University and so on, and when he was asked what *ryūha* it was, he said that it was *Shuri-te*. However, it was not understood what he meant by that. By attaching the name of a location *Shōtō* became *Shōtōkan-ryū*. However, originally there was no such thing as *Shōtōkan-ryū*. Similarly, if one goes back down the path of the origins of old, there also isn't such a thing as Okinawa *karate*. Of course it depends on which point in time and which location you look at it from, but *Shōtōkan* is *Shuri-te*.

Can you talk about the use of weapons in Okinawan budō?

The *kobujutsu* (old martial techniques) of Okinawa are based on scarcity culture, meaning the culture of wood, the culture of stone, and later the culture of iron. Every country in the world has created its weapons from what they have readily available in the land.

Where there is wood, these are made of wood. Where there is stone, these are made from stone. If there is bronze, these are made of bronze, and so on. Where there is gunpowder, then firearms are made. In the case of Okinawa, it had scarcity and thus it adopted the culture of wood. It made things such as *nunchucku*, staffs, *tonfā* and so on, from wood. Later came iron and it was also integrated.

In the case of Okinawa, there were no resources to create such things as firearms. Canons and guns work with gunpowder, but the weapons here are different. Okinawa has a culture of spirit without those things. It was poor and thus it developed its *bujutsu*. Therefore, everyday tools, fishery tools, agriculture tools, these were the kind of objects that were taken as weapons. This is particular to the Okinawan culture.

For example, Eskimos use animal bone for building shelter and

Tetsuhiro Hokama Sensei discusses early Okinawan weapons

skins for dressing. There, they have stone, ice, animals... They cannot dig things from underground, so they can only use what they have around them. That is why they build the igloo from ice and make tents. Likewise, every culture creates its weapons from what they had available.

Can you show us some interesting things from your museum?

I have attended as an instructor to seminars in more than forty countries from around the world, so I have weapons from various places. For example, I have some weapons from Russia, soviet weapons(pointing). The ones in the bottom of the room are from China, New Guinea, Indonesia. These weapons are from India. Some weapons from Bali Island, Indonesia. These weapons are from around there. These are Philippine, and these from Thailand. You can see that they have two handles. The ones here are *tonfā* from Okinawa, and the two-handle *tonfā* are from Thailand.

These here are Chinese made of bamboo, and next to them *tonfā* from Indonesia. These are used in Philippine *eskrima*, also called *kali*. The ones in this area are all weapons from Okinawa. Staffs, hoes, sickles, *sai*, and so on.

Can you talk about the poster with callousing on the knuckles?

This picture is from my friend, Yabiku Masakatsu Sensei and sadly last year he passed away. He was a policeman, and he was very strong at punching the *makiwara*. He was from *Uechi-ryū* but changed to *Yabiku-ryū*. He lived in Yaeyama Island. He was my senior and my friend.

For example, in the next photo you cannot notice any marks after Bruce Lee hit the *makiwara*. On the other hand, after Yabiku Sensei hit the *makiwara* you can clearly see the marks on his knuckle bones. As for Bruce Lee, he used the *makiwara* to build up muscles in certain parts of his arms and just conditioning his hands. In the case of *Uechi-ryū*, one puts muscle on the shoulders, while for Bruce Lee he put muscles on the arm. Therefore one can see that the training method is different. I think that this is a good characteristic so I put both photographs here to demonstrate and compare. The *makiwara* in Okinawa is used to forge the fists into weapons. I think that's the main characteristic.

Can you tell us about these large stones, I have seen them before?
This is called *chikaraishi* (lit. strength stone). This stone here is from the 'yui' (communal work) of Okinawa. You understand what I mean? In the lean days, people plowed the fields, planted sugarcane, and when homes got damaged by typhoons, people would repair them in exchange for goods and services. Next time that one had a problem, one would also get help in exchange, and so on. This is how it was carried out. The stones were placed in front of the community center. There the strong people of the town would dare each other about who could carry it more times and bet. "I can do it 10 times", "I can do it 15 times", "Alright, let's see about that!". They brought things like meat, vegetables and fish and the one who won would get them.

However, this did not mean that they could take the food home with them. They would put them in a very large cooking pot called *shinmēnābī* (in Japanese: *shimainabe* or *shinmeinabe*; lit. four layer hot pot). This means that it was a cooking pot made from 4 layers of cooking pots hammered together. One would fire these big cooking pots and put the meat and vegetables, and then everyone would sit around the pot and eat together. Even today this continues and people gather around it to meet and create good relationships. In the villages in Okinawa people still do this. They gather together in occasions like funerals or celebrations, like when first moving into a house. They will bring lumber cut from the mountains, and when there is damage from a typhoon help each other out. Okinawa is a place where human relationships are very strong, and

'*Chikaraishi*' stones are used by Higanonna Sensei to condition fists

in this context these stones played a role. It is not just a mere stone, but through it people came together. It is a stone that builds culture.

I have seen these stones in the dōjō of Higaonna Sensei, so they are also used for karate training?
Yes the stones also serves for *karate* training. Some people train by hitting them, but that was not the original way to use it. It was for people to befriend. The stones were companions for the people. They played a fundamental role in the daily lives of Okinawans. I find it very sad that this culture continues to vanish. This is what is called '*yui*' in Okinawa. It's just a stone, but this stone has a soul and it is like a *kami* (spirit, deity).

However, for the sake of practicing *karate*, I believe it is good to strike them. So *chikaraishi* are put to use in the Okinawan *karate dōjō* to condition the hands or arms by striking them.

What is unique about Okinawan people and their culture?
As a researcher in National Studies, I am a teacher of Ryūkyū history. It you want my answer from the standpoint of Anthropology, the first thing you must know is that Okinawan people are not Japanese people. They are people of Ryūkyū, who came originated from the meeting of various cultures as Australian aborigines, Indonesian, as well as Chinese

and Philippine, who met in Okinawa as a common destination. You can see this mix in the Okinawan people today. In Okinawa there are lots of old bones dating as much as the Peking primitive man, Neanderthal, or the Java primitive man

Lately, we have been able to observe the DNA and learn from the relations of origins through mitochondria, and also compare their age through carbon-dating. Carbon 14 has a half-life of 5,730 years, so it is possible to measure the age through this. From these things, we know that Japanese mostly came from the Korean peninsula and the mainland, and to some extend from Hokkaidō and the area from Russia. In the case of Okinawa, they came from the south, what is now Taiwan, Indonesia, Vietnam, or also Australian aborigines. The DNA shows a convergence from this direction with Chinese.

About the culture, well the vowels as 'a, i, u, e, o' are originally not Japanese language, but Sanskrit. The way to compose the syllabic sounds with consonants and vocals (gives examples) is a variation from Sanskrit. Japanese language, take for example the word '*momoiro*' (lit. peach color, refers to pink). In Okinawan language, the vowel reaches only to the 'u', so '*momoiro*' is said '*mumuiru*' in Okinawa, as there is only 'ma, mi, mu'. In Japan it goes until 'ma, mi, mu, me, mo'.

It is a culture where there are three degrees of conjugation. Its comparatively different, but from the variation of vowels and the conjugations we know that there is a relationship like sisters. It is not a parent-child relation, but rather as sisters. That is why Ryūkyū language must become independent of Japanese language. Similarly, Ainu language is its own. It is not Ryūkyū dialect, but Ryūkyū language. Many scholars refer to it like this, but this is a mistake. By my explanation, Ryūkyū Language is different from Japanese language. But still, there is a sisters relationship.

For example, gold is called '*kugani*' in Okinawan and in Japanese it's called '*kogane*'. Last year is 'kozo' in archaic Japanese and 'kuju' in Okinawan. There are grammatical similarities with the Japanese language, and words from about 1,000 years ago are somewhat similar.

> **" Since I was a child, when I became conscious about my surroundings, I saw we had a *dōjō* in my home. My grandfather and father were both practicing karate**

07.

Ippei Yagi

8TH DAN, MEIBUKAN SOHONBU KARATE

Chapter 7
INTRODUCTION

There are approximately four hundred martial arts schools in the island of Okinawa and these are based upon five main styles of *karate* such as *Gōjū-ryū*, *Shōrin-ryū* and *Uechi-ryū*. *Gōjū-ryū karate*, founded by Chōjun Miyagi is one of the most popular styles around the World and a strong reason why so many foreigners visit Okinawa to train.

I chose to visit a *Gōjū-ryū* school that, like the old ways of teaching, is a family run school called *Meibukan karate*. The students are mostly from the surrounding areas. Unlike mainland Japan, *karate* in Okinawa has always been focused on very small groups of students and in the early days of *karate*, it was not uncommon to find only the teacher's family members and close friends as the school's students.

The school was founded in 1952 by Meitoku Yagi Sensei, who was a senior student of Master Chōjun Miyagi. Meibukan *karate* are proud of their heritage and teach *karate* using the old ways, in the days when technique was passed down through family members to student. Meitoku Yagi Sensei also founded the Zen Okinawa Kobudō Renmei, to continue and promote traditional Okinawan martial arts.

My interview is with the grandson of the founder, Ippei Yagi Sensei and took place at the *honbu-dōjō* in Naha, Okinawa.

Ippei Yagi Sensei, 2014

THE INTERVIEW

How did you get started in karate?

We are the Gōjū-ryū Meibukan Sohonbu (Original general headquarters) Dōjō. Meibukan was established by my grandfather, Meitoku Yagi. Chōjun Miyagi Sensei was the one that had created *Gōjū-ryū*. His was the first *karate* school established not only in Okinawa, but also the world. As for our philosophy, we are the *dōjō* that continue the tradition of *kata*. The *dōjō* was opened in 1952, in this location. It was a traditionally, Okinawa-style Japanese building, which was renovated 30 years ago.

Since I was a child, when I became conscious about my surroundings, I saw we had a *dōjō* in my home. My grandfather and father were both practicing *karate* as if it was natural. Although it was tiring, they were very strict and practiced with their mind and body, everyday. I never asked myself "why are we doing this?" If you were born into my family, then it would mean that *karate* is your family profession. My parents told me that practice is made to train a person's heart, so I trained without question.

Can you tell us about your school's affiliations?

I cannot say anything in too much detail due to time, but the Traditional Okinawan karatedō Promotion Association is made of four large orga-

> ❝ *If you were born into my family, then it would mean that karate is your family profession...*

nizations. At first there was only our federation, the Zen Okinawa *karate* Renmei. The president of the Promotion Association is a prefectural governor. There are four vice-presidents, all of whom are presidents of other large organizations. Meitetsu Yagi, my father, is a president of the organization that has the longest history – Zen Okinawa *karate* Renmei. They are unifying *karate* in Okinawa so we can call everyone *karate* practitioner from around the world, and there is a plan for a *karatedō Kaikan* (*karatedō* Meeting Hall). I've heard that this is an organization that aims to prevent fighting or arguments among the various *karate* schools.

What is the difference in your Gōjū-ryū style and other schools?
There are many *ryūha* (schools) today aren't there? It is said that martial arts came from China but originally there was *karate* named '*ti*' (in Japanese: *te*; lit. hand) on Ryūkyū Islands, which was meant to defend Okinawa. It is written as 'hand' but in local dialect it is pronounced '*ti*'. *Naha-ti*, *Tomari-ti* and *Shuri-ti*, three of them. Then martial arts came and mixed with '*ti*' – this became '*te*'. The school that entered *Naha-te* is *Gōjū-ryū*. If we speak in detail, *Naha-te* and *Tomari-te* are *Shōrin-ryū*.

There are detailed differences, for example in some there are grappling *waza* and in *Gōjū-ryū*, *sokutō-geri* (lit. feet-blade kick) are strong. Also in *Gōjū-ryū* the breathing techniques are *suparinpei* (lit. one hundred zero eight; 108), *seipai* (lit. ten eight; 18), especially basics, *Sanchin*, there are many of them. Anyway, *waza* are different depending on the region where a school was founded. There are also some safety measures so we don't fight with each other.

Do you train in weapons?
I occasionally instruct in *kobudō*, that is, *nunchaku*, *kama (sickle)* and *bo*, but only to our black belt or higher level students. Originally there is a meaning of 'empty hands' in *karate*, right? And originally it wasn't meant for attacking but only for defending yourself, so it didn't need weapons.

Ryūkyū kingdom was often attacked by outside countries. *Kobudō* started because our people had to use the equipment they had in their hands, while being attacked. So we teach *kobudō*, and it is like the story of the *shamisen* (three-stringed instrument), so it is not forgotten.

There are times only *kobudō* is practiced. Old masters have been telling since past that *karateka* can even wield a pencil as a weapon, right? Eyes, throat, or can avoid a punch and stab like this. That's why we aren't particular about weapons, because a pencil or even a fork will make a weapon. If there is a multitude of opponents, it is easier with a weapon to defend yourself.

Can you tell us about your daily training?

Time is precious, so each practitioner should do a warm-up on his own, before we start the class training, so when the time for practice comes, we start immediately. At first we do all the breathing and *kata*, like *Sanchin*. In the past, in order to train oneself *karateka* would put effort into his endurance. Nowadays we have soccer, baseball, basketball. Competitive sports. So now we have to show competitive *kata* or some students will leave. So this means when there is kata competition to be held, we will do *kata* practice. Also if there is *kumite* competition, then we will practice more *kumite*. This is what we do.

There are times in what I call the 'off season', when we go back to mostly basics. I have students who I have been instructing since their childhood, and spirituality that's important, to go back to basics. If one struts along proudly because he's strong, well it's not good. If one is weak and their friends or family are threatened and one gets beaten, then that's not good as well. One has to be able to save the ones he loves or defend himself, and one has to be strong. And bragging about one's strength is bad. The basics are about the human being, their mentality.

Can you talk about Sanchin and what are the benefits?

You know *zazen* (sitting *zen* meditation), what the monks do in meditation? The ideogram for 'standing' can be read as 'ritsu'. It is called *ritsuzen* (lit. standing *zen* meditation), to show its importance in *karate*, it is in the basics. When one breathes out, he can use his inner power. If you use only strength in your punches it is not as good as punching with the use of breathing, using your whole body. In order to unify it all, there is breathing.

Even though you do not attack, you breathe in, and when you punch

you breathe out, and in the moment of impact, you breathe out completely. This creates the most power. It will have less effect if your punch
is strongest before reaching the target and if your arm is bent at the el-
bow. To maximize the punch you need to harmonize it with breathing. It
all can be learned through *Sanchin*. Those are the basics that make taking
another step easier. One has to train the balance of his body in order to
go further. So it's complete basics, along with breathing technique.

What are the main benefits of karate to you?

In my opinion, *karate* is about endurance. It's about enduring training.
One gets beaten by the teachers everyday, and sometimes little ones are
training while crying, but they still attend classes don't they? Firstly, there
is practice of *waza* in order to protect oneself and also training to become
stronger. Only by going to the *dōjō* do their hearts become stronger. They
might think "oh, I want to play baseball with my friends" but they continue
coming. Just take a look at the problem of bullying - if there is child that's
weak, through *karate* training he eventually is able to decline to fight or
not, and he becomes more confident.

I train *karate* every day – when I fight, I'm strong, but I always avoid
fighting. By training every day, there are many things that get stronger,
but I have one more thing to say. By training every day, kicking and so
on, limbs get stronger and they don't hurt their legs and joints. Every-

thing is good, breathing, practicing makes one stronger, one won't hurt himself. But I think that becoming mentally stronger is the most important of all. I think that's the best case.

Kids like to compete. Does sports karate effect your school?

I'm concerned that I might become scolded for answering this, but *karate* competitions do have an effect on our school. I know that baseball and other sports take away young people. Students only have a certain amount of time in each day for sports. However this is the same with *karate* and I think as a way of popularizing *karate*, I believe can be a good thing.

At first we were against allowing students to go to competitions but in the end it was permitted and some of our students started winning. We have a traditional *dōjō* and our opinion was to keep students together as a class to practice the same *karate*, but lately we are letting them go to competitions that show how strong they are. When they compete and become successful, I have seen they also want to go back to the *karate* basics. I also know some *karate* students who travel to different countries doing competitive karate, and they start to research about the roots of *karate* and this brings them here to Okinawa. I think this can only be a good thing. Of course there are many schools in Okinawa that do not promote or like their students to enter competitions.

> **"** *There was not a day with-
> out thinking about karate
> technique. In order to be
> a good karate competitor,
> as early as starting from
> breakfast, I was thinking
> about training*

08.

Masao Kagawa

9TH DAN, JKS SHŌTŌKAN KARATE

Chapter 8

INTRODUCTION

Masao Kagawa, 9th dan, is the Chief Instructor of Japan *karate Shōtō* Federation (JKS). He had cemented his reputation as one of the World's top *karate* competitors in the two decades before our interview in 2003. In the 1980's he won every honor in Japan, including first place *kumite* in the 1983 All Japan Championships, a competition he would dominate for the next decade. He would also win multiple *kumite* and *kata* championships in the International Shōtō Cup and World Games.

Like a number of great *karate* masters, Masao Kagawa was a graduate of Teikyo University, which was home to one of Japan's best *karate* schools. From there, he joined the Japan Karate Association (JKA) instructors course in 1983, under the guidance of Masatoshi Nakayama and Tetsuhiko Asai, who were the bearers of the *Shōtōkan karate* legacy. At the JKA, Kagawa would train alongside two of the best *karate* competitors in Japan, Masahiko Tanaka and Mikio Yahara. You could not ask for a better martial arts pedigree.

Three years before our interview with Kagawa Sensei, many years of political infighting within the JKA ended with Tetsuhiko Asai splitting away and forming the Japan *karate Shōtōkai* (JKS). Kagawa left the JKA and joined the group led by Asai and became the JKS chief instructor.

Kagawa Sensei teaching a children's class at the JKS

My interview would take place at the new JKS *honbu-dōjō* in Sugamo, a small suburb of Tokyo. The splitting apart of the JKA was the talk of the martial arts world, but I made a decision not to ask Kagawa Sensei about this. My opinion is you don't waste time talking about politics when you have the World's best technical *karate* exponent in front of you.

Sugamo is not where you would expect a *karate* headquarters to be, but in the aftermath of leaving the JKA, I think time was a factor for the JKS to find a home. It took some time to find the door to the *dōjō* which was unmarked. Our only clue was a lady walking outside with two girls wearing *karate* uniforms. The two young girls should have been a clue to what lay in wait for us. I expected the JKS to arrange a black belt level class during our visit (which is in fact what the JKA did by scheduling an instructors class for my filming). But when we entered the *dōjō*, boys and girls were preparing for class. Their parents in attendance, seated by the side of the wooden floor of the *dōjō*. Was Masao Kagawa Sensei going to teach a children's class during our filming?

The only black belts were two *senpai*, and one introduced himself as Kyle Helou. He had moved to Japan from the U.S. two years to enter the JKS instructor program which had a reputation of being very tough. Kyle confirmed that Kagawa Sensei was going to teach the kids! I was very surprised. Ten minutes later Kagawa Sensei entered the *dōjō* and introduced himself. He was very friendly but also business like, making sure we knew where we could film and he explained to the children's parents about our presence. Class began after formal bows and I was further surprised that a *senpai* did not start the warm up, but instead Kagawa Sensei took the warm up, showing incredible stretching ability. The boys and girls ranged from about seven years of age to fourteen years and as Japanese children do, they remained stoic the entire class, with perfect *dōjō* etiquette.

At one point, Kagawa Sensei was teaching *mawashigeri* or roundhouse kick and using Kyle for a training partner. I heard the crack and saw a brief flash of pain across Kyle's face as Kagawa's kick landed across his ribs. It was done without fuss but I knew Kyle was hurt and this was born out after the class when he told me that a trip to the hospital may be needed. Nevertheless, he insisted that he join me for a drink after I completed the interview with Kagawa Sensei. Kyle did pass the instructor course and is currently the chief instructor at the JKS *dōjō* in Lebanon.

Masao Kagawa Sensei, 2003

THE INTERVIEW

In what way has your karate changed today from JKA style?

When I was a competitor, I wanted to be the number one *karate* competitor, and there was not a day without thinking about karate technique. In order to be a good *karate* competitor, as early as starting from the breakfast, I was thinking about training, practice, technique, and training for technique day and night. My life was nothing but *karate*.

Now, as a *karate* instructor, my focus is to raise good *karate* students as well as good competitors. I think about how I should be teaching, how to make sure my students understand *karate*. And, now my *karate* practice and teaching is a pleasure.

Japan Karate Association (JKA) is basically *Shōtōkan*, there is no major difference between them and us. However, Japan *karate Shōtō Renmei* (JKS) is also *Shōtōkan* but JKS practices new styles that are implemented by our *karate* chief instructor, Asai Sensei. And similarly, the JKA also have different kinds of techniques and basic practice that *Shōtōkan* doesn't have.

You achieved great success in competitions, how did your training in the *dōjō* help make this happen?

I learned the basics of *karate* exclusively at the beginning, as if that is all there is to *karate*. I learned the technique, the movement and speed extensively. In addition, I have trained myself to raise my physical aspect since I have small body. In *karate*, the technique is used in the barest of moments and therefore, just having *karate* technique is not enough. You need to have the ability to see the future. To anticipate. Also, I have trained specifically on my ability to make my technique faster than my opponents.

I would also mention, that I learned the technique of movement, that is, the movement to stillness, and from stillness to movement. Here I am talking about the faster technique that acts in the split second that comes naturally. I trained for this. You assume a posture of defense, yet you are not defending and you stay still using a natural posture of *karate*. This is *karate*! You are relaxed but your mind is aware and it is very sharp. With this method you catch the slightest movement of your opponent.

My best attribute is that I am good with the counter-attack. In *karate* there is the precept of *Sen no sen* (defend and counter-attack during the opponent's attack), *Sensen no sen* (anticipating the opponent's attack, and attack in advance as the opponent's move initiates), and *Go no sen* (defend an opponent's attack, and then counter-attack). I developed *Go no sen* that is most appropriate to my body and my characteristics and because of this, only I can do this technique correctly. And I practice this technique as often as possible and I have been fighting with this method ever since.

Kagawa Sensei teaching *mawashigeri* (roundhouse kick)

Are there any specific technique you use for competition?

I have been practicing *karate* to always face a challenge, and this means I put myself in some stage of an extreme situation. Because of this, I am never satisfied unless I have an extensive *karate* practice. This kind of practice gave me stronger technique, a stronger will, and the ability to act faster and wiser than my opponent during the fight. Through my *karate* training I make this come out naturally. Through my everyday *karate* practice I find new technique or make changes to technique that become available to me when I am in the fight. Without this practice, there are no technique that will come naturally to me during the fight. I must place myself on the edge. Gather all my energy when I am training and finally develop the better technique to win.

What advice would you give to students entering competitions?

There are many strong *karate* competitors, but little of them understand *karatedō*. You need to understand that winning is not only the target in a *karate* life. From *karate* you learn a better way of thinking, better character, manners, respect, and sense of propriety. In Japan the *karate* competitor must be a well polished competitor who gains respect regardless of winning or losing the fight. It can be hard to be a good *karate* person, especially when one has lost the fight.

But *karate* was created in Japan. This *karate*, now known through

Masao Kagawa Sensei teaching in the JKS *honbu-dōjō* 2003

out the World, was born here in Japan. Therefore, the *karate* competitor from Japan must have good character, good manners and better technique and let the non-Japanese competitor wonder where that comes from? The young non-Japanese *karate* competitor would learn from this. The Japanese competitor feels a responsibility for winning the fight, but just winning does not gain people's respect. It is important that people admire and respect a Japanese competitor regardless of winning or losing the fight. For this to happen, we practice *karate* and learn our way of life from *karate*.

Can you give me an example of this philosophy?
Yes, I can explain this way. If you have seventy percent energy, you should not try to fight with one hundred percent energy; your full energy of seventy percent is fine. If you only have only sixty percent of your energy, you fight with all of your sixty percent energy. You will feel disappointed if you try to fight as if you have more energy. You need to be satisfied if you have fought with the full use of sixty percent of your energy. It is fine to lose, if you have fought with all the energy and technique you have.

You accept the loss of the fight and acknowledge that the opponent was stronger than you. The competitors who are generous, have a good character and a good heart will grow and flourish. The competitors who

> **The reality is that technique is the matter of a split second. You do not see flashy movements in the skilled karate competitor**

are dishonest will not. Apologize If you did something wrong and listen if someone gives you advice. You must focus on what you do, because the people who do not focus do not grow. You should have good focus, good character and put all your effort in practice and in competition.

A student who only makes an effort when an instructor is watching, does not grow. I train my students with the hope that they will be a global type of *karate* competitor, who have a world class spirit, would have respect in *karate*, and have the knowledge and style as a *karate* person. To have world class character, and be the *karate* competitor who can challenge to be the world champion.

Karate may be an Olympic sport. How do you feel about this?

It is a shame that *karate* may change in the style and the rules, since it will become a part of the Olympics. But it is not preventable since *karate* will be a sport of the Olympics. In my mind, I feel one half of me is sad and other half accepts the change. My hope is that at least the *karate* will be the number one sport in the Olympics. And, I will put in my effort and cooperation so that *karate* can be the number one sport in the Olympics. So I acknowledge and accept the changes of karate because of the Olympics.

Since some of the original technique and rules of *karate* are not made for the Olympics, they must be changed. The original art of *karate* was made for defense, to protect oneself and your family. But the original style and the rules of *karate* are not suitable for the Olympics, and therefore, must be changed.

I feel the new rules will be strict and make this harder for Japanese competitors. The *karate* associations must change the rules in order to understand the *karate* technique, but there are various opinions against the amount of points that is given to various technique. Again, we must accept the change in order to join the Olympics.

The real *karate* person is not the one who uses big movements and large flashy actions. In real *karate*, this technique does not win points. You have to have knowledge of *karate* in order to catch the opponent's quick technique without hesitation. The big movement or eye catching action will work for those watching who are unskilled, but the reality is that technique is the matter of a split second. You do not see flashy movements in the skilled *karate* competitor. That is why you must practice the basics extensively, master the technique, and be able to use the technique in matter of a split second and not think about winning points.

Do you teach or help to develop karate outside Japan?

Yes I do, even if there is something I have to do in Japan, I will go overseas to practice as well. If I hear a request or call, I am glad to go overseas and practice with foreign students. This allows me to discover new technique, and teach my *karate*. I have a responsibility as the coach of the Japan National Team at the moment. But in the future, my hope is that I would go out even more to other countries and have a training camp and teach foreign students.

What has karate given to you outside of this dōjō?

I would not as happy as I am now, if there was no *karate* in my life. However I must say that as a *karate* person I guard myself against desire. Everyone has desire, to want things of various kinds. But through practicing *karate*, you learn to rethink. You learn to restrict yourself and to reconsider against your desires or wanting. You find out the better way of your life, it is not just the technique of *karate*, but you learn to apply the better judgments you have learned through karate practice. *Karate* can be the guard against unnecessary desire in your life. That to me is the meaning of *karate*. I would like to write a book and introduce the true meaning of *karate* spirit sometime in the future.

> **❝**
> *I have come to believe that I have acquired shizentai (a natural state), but even so, I feel nervousness with the idea of not being able to do it*

09.
Tatsuya Naka
7TH DAN, JAPAN KARATE ASSOCIATION

Chapter 9
INTRODUCTION

Tatsuya Naka, 7th *dan*, is a full time instructor at the Japan *Karate* Association (JKA). He began training in *Wadō-ryū* style *karate* and switched to *Shōtōkan* style *karate* when he entered Takushoku University. After graduation in 1986, he continued his *Shōtōkan karate* training by enrolling in the JKA Instructors Course and after completing this in 1989, began teaching full time at the JKA Honbu Dōjō.

Naka Sensei can be called a modernist in his approach to *karate*. His *karate* is ever expanding and his thirst for knowledge has never left him since he was a young student. Today, his Youtube channel, Kuro-obi World, with over than 600,000 subscribers, showcases his travels across Japan and China in his quest to meet other great martial arts masters and explore their art. Kuro-obi World, is a nod to his famous 2007 movie, Kuro Obi (Black Belt), where Naka showed his mastery of *karate* and an immediate penchant for acting. The movie was a great success and paved the way for a second movie with Tatsuya Naka, titled 'High Kick Girl' released in 2009.

Beside teaching daily classes at the JKA Honbu Dōjō, Naka Sensei is on a quest to research the history of martial arts around the World. His easy going manner and charismatic movie star demeanor makes him one

Author Jon Braeley with Tatsuya Naka Sensei. JKA Honbu Dōjō 2015

of the JKA's most popular instructors. This makes Naka Sensei an obvious reason why the JKA asked him to manage their Public Relations division.

The evening before my visit to the JKA, I was sleeping soundly under a warm futon in an apartment near Setagaya, a few minutes west of Shibuya. I had arrived the day before, from the blue skies of a warm and balmy Miami Beach. Little did I know that outside a thick blanket of snow was silently falling on Tokyo. In the morning when I left to go across Tokyo to the JKA dōjō, the city was in the grip of a blizzard with heavy snow making a simple road crossing treacherous. Nonetheless, my thoughts were on the meeting with Naka Sensei and I shrugged off the biting cold and driving snow.

My interview with Tatsuya Naka took place in the small visitors room in the main offices on the ground floor of the honbu dōjō. It was the same room I met Masahiko Tanaka Sensei, for an interview that

Tatsuya Naka

took place exactly twelve years before. However, I found the personalities of the two instructors could not be more different. While I found Tanaka Sensei to be intense, projecting a menacing figure, Naka Sensei was relaxed and playful. I put this down to a generations gap of the JKA instructors. We also interviewed Toshihiro Mori Sensei, 9th *dan*, of the Japan Karate Association, at the same time as Naka Sensei and include this interview immediately afterward.

Toshihiro Mori Sensei and Tatsuya Naka Sensei. JKA Honbu Dōjō 2015
Photo: Jon Braeley

Tatsuya Naka Sensei, 2015

THE INTERVIEW

The 'Best Karate' books by Masatoshi Nakayama were my first martial art books. Did they also influence you?
The story of JKA is also a story of *Shōtōkan karate*. In Taisho 11 (1922), Funakoshi Gichin Sensei from Okinawa introduced *karate* to Japan. His disciples gathered after the war to create JKA. Therefore, JKA is the succession of *Shōtōkan karate*. Continuing with what I just said, Funakoshi Sensei brought *karate* from Okinawa.

Nakayama Sensei made it easy to transmit and spread to the world with a much more educational and physiological approach. He compiled *karate* in easy to understand ways and published a book called *Dynamic Karate* which was available in English. This book is well known in Japan and it helped promulgate *karate* around the world. In Japan this book was published as a series called *Best Karate*. In the past Japanese *karate* was practiced by watching and following. Then it was made easier to be understood by westerners by Nakayama Sensei, who taught that it would be difficult to promulgate around the world in that way. So thanks to that labor by Nakayama Sensei, *karate* became widespread.

What are the main characteristics of Shōtōkan karate?

About the characteristics of *Shōtōkan karate*? It is dynamic, straightforward, speedy movements, and strong. It uses muscles that are not used in everyday life to give more power and speed to the techniques. This is the *'kime karate'*, which is characteristic of JKA *karate*.

Why do you think Shōtōkan karate it is so popular?

About sixty or seventy percent of *karate* in the world is *Shōtōkan*. JKA headquarters is the mecca of all the practitioners of *Shōtōkan karate*. Therefore, we have many visitors from abroad. I invite everyone to come here to Japan, to the mecca that is JKA, and train for your further development.One of the reasons for this success is the *kenshūsei* program (induction training for interns) of the JKA. It has helped spread *Shōtōkan karate* over the world with the *kenshūsei* system. It is a course to produce professional *karate* instructors.

The instructors who graduate from this course then go around the world and help promulgate the JKA, the *Shōtōkan karate*. Not only Japanese, but also foreigner members have learned this course. Since it is taught in Japanese language, it is also required to understand Japanese, as well as to be at least 2nd *dan*, and have at least 2 years to fulfill the course. Sometimes it might take more time. It is a very difficult and strict world in the *dōjō* of the JKA, so it might require to extend the course 1 or 2 years. There are currently no foreigners in the program.

Do you think samurai spirit is still part of Japanese culture?

Yes it is. *Samurai* spirit is not only about being strong, but also about living correctly. You must always have correct manners, a good mind and tell no lies. Also you should never give up. This spirit is engraved in the heart of Japan. Not only Japanese, but also foreigners can understand the *samurai* spirit as a valuable world culture.

Naka Sensei at the Instructors class, JKA Honbu Dōjō 2015

What are your views on karate as an Olympic sport?

About *karate* being an Olympic sport, there are both for and against points. As for myself, I think that if *karate* enters the Olympics it will gain importance, but on the other hand, I have a strong fear that the best qualities of Japanese *budō* might be at risk. This is especially because of the current rules in *karate* competitions.

I think that the good things that *karate* as a *budō* contributes to the World could be lost if it is viewed only as a sport for winning medals.

Can you talk about your film career?

Until now I have participated in three films. The first film was *Kuro Obi*, which is really the first *karate* film to be released in Japan. The producer, Nishin, wanted to make a traditional *karate* film and he came to me. I thought I was only going to be a consultant on the movie, but he insisted that I participate. At first I refused but he persuaded me with his passion and enthusiasm. *Kuro Obi* became popular and the public's voice that wanted to see more *karate* films was heard. Responding to that, we made a second and a third movie about *karate*.

At first it was hard to be an actor. For two months before the shooting I attended acting classes. The *karate* parts in the movies are just like my everyday *karate* practice so that was comfortable to do.

What made you start your karate practice?

From a personal point of view, I started *karate* in my first year of school. I had been doing baseball, but then I saw the charm of *karate*. Then I followed that path through high school and the university, and eventually became *kenshūsei* for two years. After graduating from it, I became an instructor here. Every day I live with a strong thought about *karate* at all times. Even today, the same feeling as when I started *karate* remains unchanged. I live my every day thinking about *karate* all the time.

What has karate given you outside of the dōjō?

At first my motivation to practice was to become strong. But that changed little by little as my conception of strength changed. I started to look for the ways in which to develop and my idea of what it means to become strong changed. This implied treating not only my life in the *dōjō* but everyday life as training. All of life's occurrences, not only at the *dōjō* but also outside, are opportunities to grow. I have come to recognize this more recently.

Through *karate* I acquired the concept of learning from mistakes, forging myself through my mistakes, and to develop further from mistakes. This is a coming together of people who look forward to mutual growth and development. Easily said, it is to become a human being who can be useful to others. That is the direction I want to follow.

When I was younger, I used to become stressed before a competition months in advance, to such a degree that people around me noticed I was nervous. How can you be with *shizentai* (a natural state or posture)? Really, the only way is to have self-confidence. And in order to do that, one must do lots of *keiko* (practice), and then everyday life also starts changing for the better. I have come to believe that I have acquired *shizentai*, but even so, I feel nervousness with the idea of not being able to do it.

> **"** *The things that we learn from imitating sensei, these are ultimately not our own. In order to make these technique our own, one must separate oneself from that way of learning*

10.
Toshihiro Mori
9TH DAN, JAPAN KARATE ASSOCIATION

Toshihiro Mori Sensei, 2015

THE INTERVIEW

What is the difference in Shōtōkan karate from other styles?
The *Shōtōkan karate*, that is, I should say the JKA *Shōtōkan karate*, is based upon the concept of *Ichigeki-Hissatsu* (one attack certain kill). This teaching was introduced into karate by a *sensei* from Okinawa called Sokōn Matsumura who learned *Jigen-ryū kendō* from Kagoshima. The JKA *karate* has this concept into it, *Ichigeki-Hissatsu* that originated in the *Jigen-ryū*.

This is the characteristic of JKA *karate* which is *Shōtōkan*. We often express this characteristic as *kime karate*, which means *karate* that concentrates all the power into a single focus. This is *kime karate*, which is the characteristic of JKA *karate*.

We always do *kime* to defeat ourselves. We are always striving to do this during practice. Through this and technique we can also win against an opponent. We are constantly doing this during actual practice. This is JKA *Shōtōkan karate*.

We do not include *nagewaza* (throwing technique) in our training class. I think that in the past throws to the ground were used to a certain extent, but not today.

What advice would you give to new students?

About how to practice *karate*? Training so that they are able to acquire a good *karate*? Well first of all, one must listen carefully to the *sensei*, and understand what he is teaching you. Listen very carefully during class. Then you must consciously try to apply those things into your practice. One must practice *kihon* (basic technique) always with consistency, starting with the foundations. Such as the way to stand (posture), the way to strike, the way of receiving (blocking), the way of kicking. It is important to acquire all these things one by one, correctly.

Can you explain how this basic training works in one's practice?

Well I need to add that it's important that one should not get fixated in the shape or structure of the technique. If this happens, it becomes difficult to actually use the technique. It could be said that one gets stuck in this structure This has to be tore down at a certain point. Tear it down and you become able to use the technique.

In other words, one learns what the teacher says, and also by observing the senior and junior students, and you learn by copying, by imitating. This is important. Then one also becomes able to use the technique.

However, the things we learn from the *sensei*, the things that we learn from imitating *sensei*, these are ultimately not our own. In order to make these technique our own, one must separate oneself from that way of

> **"**
> *I did keiko (practice) at school, then I would travel to the dōjō to do more keiko. Afterward, when I got home, before going to sleep, I did some more keiko...*

learning, and create our own technique in which we become skilled at. One must make an outline of our own ideal technique. In the case of *karate*, this flow is called *Shu-ha-ri*, meaning to protect, then tear apart and then separate. This is the three progressive steps in the pursuit of your improvement.

How important is kata training in JKA karate?

The most representative *kata* of *Shōtōkan karate* are the *Kanku dai* (lit. observe the sky/emptiness, large version), *Bassai dai* (lit. breach the fortress, large version), *Jion* (lit. mercy and gratitude) and *Enpi* (lit. flying swallow). These four *kata* which Funakoshi Sensei always performed, are also the *kata* that we always train in daily class.

The reason why these four *kata* were chosen is because they represent the important characteristics of *Shōtōkan karate*. This four *kata* display *ichigeki hissatsu*, which I talked about before, and in addition the free movement of the body. They were created to conform to simulate several situations, and they teach how to respond to each of those situations.

Can you show us an example of this point here?

Yes, as I was saying before, there is a strike based on the *Jigen-ryū* from *kendō*, which is the *oizuki* (chasing thrust punch) strike. It maximizes the power to beat your opponent in a single blow by concentrating all one's power instantly. All of your power is put into this single concentrated attack so that if lands it will certainly defeat the attacker. This is the characteristic of the *oizuki* technique from JKA.

Can you tell us how you got started in karate?

My parents practiced *karate* and I learned from my father and that was my first motivation. I started in first year of school. I have always continued training in *karate* ever since that day. I did *keiko* (practice) at school, then I would travel to the *dōjō* to do more *keiko*. Afterward, when I got home, before going to sleep, I did some more *keiko*. Practicing was always so much fun, so I was always practicing. And I am still enjoying it so much.

What has karate given to you personally outside the dōjō?

I always come across teachings from *karate* in my daily life. I think that the most important teaching I received is the relationship between technique and my self-confidence. The connection between oneself and *karate* technique. From this, something great certainly begins to take root and grow. Strength is born out of this.

I have learned this from *karate* practice, that if one wants to achieve something in society, and become one with this idea, then a good result will follow. This I have learned through *karate*. In our lives, to become one with the things that we think and believe in and put them into real practice. This is the path that I have walked until now. And I will continue living my life this way.

> **The single most important thing for us is the single attack, ichigeki hissatsu or "certain kill in a single attack"**

11.
Mikio Yahara

10TH DAN, SHŌTŌKAN KARATE
WORLD KARATENOMICHI FEDERATION

Chapter 11
INTRODUCTION

Mikio Yahara Sensei needs little introduction to *karate* enthusiasts. While one of the most accomplished Japanese *Shōtōkan karate* masters in the World, it is his 'bad-boy' reputation that has kept him in the headlines for the last three decades.

Born in 1947, Mikio Yahara joined the Japan Karate Association straight out of university as a *kenshūsei* or junior instructor. In the early seventies he quickly notched up an impressive record of major tournament titles over the next ten years. However, while he always reached second or third in the All Japan Championships and the JKA World Championships, the winners podium often eluded him.

It is said that Mikio Yahara could not get on the right side of the JKA referees and the judges, with his "win at all costs" philosophy and what could only be described as flamboyant *karate* style. On a number of occasions in competition he was disqualified for taking the fight too seriously or *shinken shōbu (lit. victory or defeat using live blades), meaning* a real fight.

There are numerous story's of Yahara's exploits as a young black belt on the streets, mingling with *yakuza* mobsters and getting into real fights. A story he has not denied is that he once turned up for a major compe-

tition with a knife wound! In the daily classes at the JKA he was often admonished for his unwillingness to make concessions to his training partners. He would attack and defend as if his life depended upon it, which often ended with someone receiving medical treatment.

Regardless of Yahara's single mindedness to win, he was respected by many of his peers at the JKA including Nakayama Sensei who once said of Yahara's fighting style as "In the heat of the fight, his style can leave those watching breathless."

At the end of the nineteen eighties, he left the JKA and went out on his own, where he could practice his own style of *karate*, a martial art he loved so passionately. I remember visiting the JKA in the mid nineties and I saw Mikio Yahara listed among the current and past instructors. I asked my Japanese friend what it said next to his name and he replied, "expelled."

In the year 2000, Mikio Yahara realized his dream and established his own school of *karate*, the Karatenomichi World Federation (KWF). This would allow him to spread his single *karate* philosophy that a fight is won with *ippon* (single full point) - the ability to deliver a single killing blow. This was central to what he termed budō *karate*, that had a disregard for sports *karate*, that he considered hamstrung by rules and technique that is compromised.

In 2014 I visited with Mikio Yahara at the *karatenomichi* headquarters in downtown Tokyo. I found him to be quite humble. For example, during the interview my audio assistant suffered a malfunction in the recording and on returning to my apartment in Tokyo, I found the audio of the entire interview unusable. I was mortified. Yahara does not suffer fools, and it was with some nervousness that I contacted him to explain the problem and request a second interview which I assured him, will be much better quality. I knew I had to appeal to his sense that all things must be done with perfection as the goal. He granted a second interview for the next day and even though he was not teaching, he wore his *kara-tegi* (uniform) at my request. For this he got my respect.

A year later, I posted a short video trailer on Youtube which featured Mikio Yahara. In the comments I was sad to see a few subscribers label him a "thug" and a bully. One comment alluded to Yahara's own confession that he fractured three ribs of his opponent during his 8th *dan* grading test. I have witnessed *karate* masters, who have also injured opponents. This is neither done on purpose or by mistake. It is *karate* the traditional way. It is *budō*.

Mikio Yahara Sensei, 2015

THE INTERVIEW

Can you please introduce yourself?
My name is Yahara Mikio. I am currently the head instructor of the World Federation of *karatenomichi,* or we say KWF.

You use the term budō karate, can you define what you mean?

I think it is probably different depending on what one is talking about – *bujutsu karate* or *budō karate*. *Budō* is a process, a 'way' which one takes in order to reach one's goal. *Bujutsu*, on the other hand is a set of skills needed to defeat an opponent. Those are the two types, with two different meanings.

The difference between what you call sports *karate* and with *budō karate* is that sports *karate* is a game in which fighting takes place within a set of rules in order to win points. *Budō karate*, as I just said before, is to defeat an adversary with a single attack in order to protect oneself. *Budō karate*, is to defeat an opponent with *ichigeki hissatsu*, meaning "certain kill in a single attack." *Budō karate* is the way one trains for this purpose.

What is the difference between Karatenomichi and the JKA style that you practiced in the past?

The roots of my *karate* is the JKA. When I was really young, I trained a lot with JKA. Following that, I looked at the parts of *karate* which JKA were lacking to me. For example, the way of moving there is sports like and the sparring is like a game. I took the JKA *karate* and divided it more delicately into smaller parts. Dividing the body in parts and limbs like the arms, legs, and hips joints, to see how to make full use of them in order to defeat an opponent.

I think that parting from what is JKA *karate* and focusing it more into the direction of how to use it to defeat an opponent is the main difference between our KWF *karate* and the JKA.

Can you talk about the JKA Honbu Dōjō and your reputation for tough training?

I have changed since the times when I belonged to the JKA. The times have changed. In my JKA days, well in fact, ever since I was a young, I had a fixation for JKA *karate* and I that is why I started *karate* practice as soon as I could. For that sake, I moved from the Shikoku countryside to a university in Tokyo. As for my reason to come to a university in Tokyo? My real objective was not studying but rather practicing *karate*.

At the beginning it was a different age and daily practice was a very strict, very difficult, and very painful. Nowadays, if you just receive a little scratch it is enough motive for legal demands and other problems. Back in those days, every day I thought "I am going to die today", or "I will

Mikio Yahara teaching at the KWF Honbu Dōjō 2015

die tomorrow." I trained within that extreme state of mind. Now when I look back at those memories it is with nostalgia and I remember having fun when I was training.

So how did your bad boy reputation get started?
Well back then, for my own *karate*, I studied the movements of animals, especially beasts of prey. When facing an opponent, in order to defend oneself there can be no mercy. With that feeling, regardless if the opponent was a white belt or black belt, or being bigger or smaller than me, I fought them all with the same feeling. That feeling was that the opponent must be defeated.

Naturally, some people around me got injured, and from that people started saying that Yahara is a scary person, or that he is a demolisher. These kind of names were among the rumors and gossip that spread. Apparently, that is the origin of various names that people use to refer to me.

What is your philosophy behind the Shōtōkan of KWF?
Karate which we are pursuing at KWF must follow *ichigeki hissatsu*. What this means is that for the sake of protecting ourselves successfully, we must defeat the adversary in a single blow. If the opponent attacks and we are unable to defeat him in a single movement, then if he follows

> **Back in those days, every day I thought "I am going to die today", or "I will die tomorrow". I trained within that extreme state of mind. Now when I look back at those memories it is with nostalgia.**

his attack we will be done for. We will be defeated.

In order to follow *ichigeki hissatsu*, when we are facing an opponent, we must move earnestly so we can defeat the attacker with one blow. We must develop our flesh and bones into a weapon capable of doing this. This means our whole body, the joints and the muscles, and we must exercise them with the single objective of focusing them all into a single point. If we achieve this we can produce great destructive power. This is the *karate* of the KWF. In other words, it is best described by *ichigeki hissatsu*.

I get the feeling you were a samurai in a past life?

I do not know about my own previous lives, but my ancestors were *samurai*. There is record of the activities of my ancestors going back to about 600 years ago. Even today, the records in the town where I was born still exist. I believe that from this, my father and mother also have *bushi* (*samurai*) origins. Yes we are *samurai*, no doubt.

And the Samurai spirit or bushidō, does it still exists today?

Regarding present day Japan, I personally believe that the spirit of *bushidō* has almost completely faded away. Modern generations today haven't got *bushidō* in them, have they? The spirit of *bushidō* was originally a teaching from ancient China, from the person named Confucius. That person's teaching, what is called Confucianism, is the basis for many things in *bushidō*, they came from the teachings and spirit of Confucianism.

For example, *bushidō* is respecting our elders and our superiors. It is respecting our family and respecting our ancestors. It originated from this spirit. For instance, if I am walking along the street together with my teacher, I must not go alongside with the teacher. Rather, I must retreat three steps back and allow him to walk in front. I must be very considerate and be careful not step over his shadow. We must take care of the people above us. This is one example, to retreat three steps behind and avoid stepping on their shadow. It is also said that the way of *bushidō* is found in death. *Bushidō* applies towards our family, towards people important to us, and in the past, to our lord. In the latter case, to have the disposition to give our lives for the sake of our master or lord. One must have this mental and spiritual readiness. This is *bushidō*.

Can you give me an example of this bushidō spirit in karate?

Yes I can, in the phrase, *'Niku o kirasete, hone o kiru.'* This is an expression that generally means "let him cut your meat, but break his bones" which I have made into my personal motto and represents one of the most important basics of the KWF *karate*. This really is *budō*. For example, when fighting an opponent, a barrier of fear can be created between you. Because of this barrier of fear, one cannot leap forwards. If one is afraid of an enemy's *waza*, of being hit or killed, he will run away. If one is conscious of this, they become stiff, almost unable to move.

When one attacks, he should not care if he's hit, kicked, wounded or if he has his flesh cut. If one receives, say, a punch or a kick from the opponent, it does not matter if it hurts, or if one bleeds, or even it causes you to have a bone broken. One must go beyond that. You should have the mental attitude to go forward and to go through, breaking the enemy's bones in order to defeat the enemy that is strong. Furthermore, one goes for breaking the bones that are deep inside the meat. One must penetrate with movements that originate from this mentality. That's the spirit of *'Niku o kirasete, hone o kiru.'*

In ancient times there was a saying "Being under the falling blade is hell itself. Let's plunge into it, let's plunge into it. Paradise is also found there." Let me try to explain this to you. Suppose that the adversary swings at us with a *katana* (Japanese single-bladed sabre). Getting scared makes one unable to move. If we cannot move we will be cut through. Against a falling sword we must rush into the enemy. We must plunge deep into the adversary's *katana*. This is where our chance to save ourselves lies. This expresses the technique and spirit of "Let him cut your meat, but break his bones."

But I would like to add to this. Regarding what I just said, and this is not only me but I think it is true for all the serious *budō* practitioners. There is *Shin-gi-tai* meaning "Spirit, technique and physical strength." Even if one possesses the spirit, it is not enough if one does not have the technique to defeat the opponent. Even if one possesses both the spirit and the technique, if our body is ill or is in a state where it cannot fight, then this is also insufficient.

The body, the spiritual, mental power, and also the techniques to defeat an opponent. It is necessary to have all of these virtues. Together, they are called *Shin-gi-tai*. I think all three of them are important.

How important is kata in today's karate practice?

Regarding *kata* in *karate* and how important it is in modern day *karate*, it is necessary to first know about its history. Nowadays, some people of the modern era think that *kata* is nonsense and unnecessary. In a combat game that is all about getting points within a certain set of rules, speed and timing is everything. *Kata* is different from this. The *karate* and *kata* of the past is very simple.

This simplicity is due to the fact that the way of fighting of the past was very simple. For example, an adversary comes to grab us so we receive that and decide the outcome. In modern combat sports there is absolutely no need for such a thing. In *kata*, all the necessary technique that can actually be used for the purpose of defending oneself are contained within the *kata*. This is the reason why *kata* is given such importance by the people who practice *karate* as *budō* and as a means to defend themselves.

Modern people today know *karate*'s movement only in terms of *kumite (sparring)*. From their point of view, *kata* is nonsense. They think it is a relic of the past, and this is not true. *Karate* starts and ends in *kata*, is the truth. Because the truth is a basis of *karate*, and *kata* are basics. But today's *kumite* is all about speed. For that kind of people *kata* are relics of the past. To train true *bujutsu* there is no other way than *kata*. *Kata* contains both knowledge of attacking and defending. I think that this is where the difference between sports and *karate* lie. The difference between *budō* and sports *karate*.

Would you say you have a scientific approach to karate?

A scientific approach? Everyone has the same flesh and bones. Some way or another, through *karate*, one can transform this flesh and bones into a weapon. For this purpose, there are calculated movements of the body and legs, that one repeats to get their best potential. When this is done with the joints, then these can be used as springs. Muscles and joints that work like springs. These are calculated movements.

For example, analyzing to which extent one should rotate the hips, or how to bend the ankles. These calculated movements can be used to understand the way in which the body parts are linked together. Upon this, strong technique can be built and this is what I research. You could call this a scientific approach.

After talking I now understand why you formed the KWF?
One's mentality and body must become one or it will not work. Distance and timing are part of our skills, right? Although one can have a good *waza*, it means nothing if there is no willpower and mental strength to make good use of it. On the other hand, if you have only mental strength and no skills you will become reckless. Mental strength will be attained if one learns correct skills. By having both - mentality and physical strength - one will be able to fight.

Every man has the same human body. To create good *waza* one should learn the best way of moving, creating strength, the way of creating power, and it will become evident for oneself. KWF is an organization that researches and makes practical use of such aspects. KWF uses and controls as a weapon the power that is unleashed after accumulated to the limits in one's muscles. KWF's characteristic is creating power from contraction and expansion of muscles and joints. I would like to show it at the *dōjō* today during practice. From my experience I'd say that when thinking 'I must win' one gets carried away and when thinking 'I will lose' one cannot go forward. So *'Niku o kirasete, hone o kiru'* is not created. One's ability can change with repetition of defeating, being wounded and wounding, doesn't it? When one has a confidence in one's strength he won't think about winning or losing. His body will move naturally. One's mind will become thoughtless and a body will move before thinking about it, thanks to numerous practice. So there is no unnecessary thought. There is nothing. I think that is *mushin*. People in the past were obviously scared before going to battle, so in order to become calm they washed their bodies under waterfalls, did *zazen* and many other things to gain *mushin*. Only having a lot of experience is not enough. Gaining confidence will lead to natural *mushin*.

The single most important thing for us is the single attack, *ichigeki hissatsu*. This means, without fail, bring an opponent down with a single movement. This sensation can be described in Japanese with the saying *'ichigo ichie'* (an instance only encountered once, or popularly known as once-in-a-lifetime encounter). There is only one chance. If we lose this one chance, there will not be a second chance.

For example, when we meet an important person to us, this could be the last moment we will share with that person. Once we part then we will never meet again since it is probable that we will die. Therefore, we must give utmost importance to the instant of our meeting. A single instant. It is the same in *karate*. Chances are instantaneous and we must not let them escape.

When we say "Let him cut your meat, but break his bones" or "certain kill in a single attack" it also has the feeling of "an instance only encountered once". This, I think, is the essence of the *karate* that I aim for and that is the aim of KWF.

The techniques of modern Wadō-ryū were composed by gathering the characteristics of several schools and blending them into one

12.
Hironori Ōtsuka

10TH DAN, WADŌ-RYŪ KARATE

Chapter 12
INTRODUCTION

The story of *wadō-ryū karate* is an interesting one to a *Shōtōkan karate* practitioner. *Wadō-ryū* was founded a few years after Hironori Ōtsuka left the *Shōtōkan karate Dōjō* of Gichin Funakoshi.

I was introduced to *Wadō-ryū karate* style in the late seventies, when I attended a seminar in England, by Tatsuo Suzuki, *hanshi* 8th *dan*, who was one of the *Wadō-ryū* founder's most senior students. Suzuki Sensei was living and teaching in the United Kingdom and although his *dōjō* was a long way from my home town, I managed to train with him a number of times. The last time I met with Tatsuo Suzuki was in 2002, when he visited the United States. It was wonderful to relive the training with my old *sensei*. I was always struck by how relaxed and soft he was. He would say "too hard-like wood" when he felt my body during practice.

Because of my relationship with Tatsuo Suzuki, I was especially interested to meet the founders son, Hironori Ōtsuka. In fact, I first met Hironori Ōtsuka at the *budō* demonstration at *Meiji Jingū* (Meiji Imperial Shrine), Tokyo, where he was demonstrating an unarmed defense against a real sword, which had the crowd holding their breath! More remarkable was afterwards, when I asked Ōtsuka Sensei how he practiced this in the *dōjō*, he told me "Oh we don't practice this. It's far too dangerous!"

Hironori Ōtsuka Sensei, 2015

THE INTERVIEW

Can you talk about the history of Wadō-ryū karate?

The story of *Wadō-ryū karate?* Yes, well this year marks its 80th year which is *Wadō-ryū* beginning in the *Shōwa* period. My father learned *Yōshin-ryū jūjutsu* since his early childhood and continued all the way in his life. In the 11th year of the *Taishō* period (1922), *karate* came to Japan for the first time from Okinawa. He went on to learn this *karate*.

Afterwards, about the 3rd of 4th year of the *Shōwa* period (1928-1929), he became independent and started to create the basic theory and techniques for *Wadō-ryū* style. It became an organization in the 9th year of the *Shōwa* period (1934). It was in this time, that I was being born in the 9th year of the *Shōwa* period (1934), during the time just before the Second World War. I have lived since then with the history of *Wadō-ryū*.

And what led Hironori Ohtsuka to create this new karate?

The characteristics of Wadō-ryū are taken from the following *budō*, such as the teachings of Japanese ancient *kobudō*, and *jūjutsu*, *kenjutsu* and also *naginata* among a few others.

By taking away the disadvantages of these *budō*, and being imaginative and creative, he developed the philosophy and techniques of *Wadō-ryū*. At first it was only *karate* and then my father began to integrate *jūjutsu* into *karate*. By integrating the characteristic elements of *karate* like punching and kicking into *jūjutsu* it became a new style of *karate*.

The philosophy of *Wadō-ryū* that I just spoke of, can be compared to the flow of water. Water flows from a higher place to a lower place. It flows along with objects, and if the object is hard, water avoids it and runs past it or around it. If there is an opening, it will trickle through it until the opening becomes wide enough to allow the water to flow more freely. In other words, *Wadō-ryū* is connected with the laws of the heaven and the earth, and of man. We must not oppose the way of heaven, nor oppose the way of man. That is to say, we should follow the natural course of events. This is the way.

All the techniques are also based on the body flowing. What I aim towards is to conceive technique even at the scale of a micron. For this purpose I continue to practice to this day, but I feel that I cannot yet do it the way that I envisage. My predecessor, the founder, lived until he was 90 years old, and until he was 88 he continued to be active, take part in demonstrations and also continue to teach. And all this time, for about 30 years, I would also participate in his training as his opponent, but even now I cannot even come close to him.

Now we are also demonstrating at Meiji Shrine, and for that we watch footage of my predecessor in his early 60s, and late 70s, and also in his late 80's. We do this every time, so when we demonstrate we have the founder as our ideal in mind. I still think that there is still a long way to go in this training crusade.

I watched your demonstration at the Meiji Shrine where you defended against a sword. Can you tell us about this?

Yes. Additionally, we took this practice from *kendō*, or rather I should say *kenjutsu*. Among the Japanese *bujutsu* schools, the most technically advanced one is *Yagyū-ryū*. Before *Yagyū-ryū*, swordsmanship was done in full armor, with helmet and body armor. That is why in those days it was not a big deal to be cut because it was usually slight and not life threatening.

However, in the times of *Yagyū-ryū*, the warrior or soldier replaced the armor with simple clothing, which meant that a cut could be bad enough to cause a hemorrhage that could mean a loss of life. Therefore, body movements were created in order that one could completely avoid being touched by the blade.

Hironori Ōtsuka at the *Meiji Jingū* demonstration. 2014
Photo: Jon Braeley

And you incorporated this technique to defend against the sword?

First let me say that the techniques of modern *Wadō-ryū* were composed by gathering the characteristics of several schools and blending them into one. For example, the *kodachi* short sword of the *Toda-ryū*. How to use a short *katana* against a longer one. That is the use of the *kodachi* of the *Toda-ryū*. Then there is also the use of the blade from the *Yagyū-ryū*. We often do this using real swords when performing demonstrations, but have never practiced in the *dōjō*, because it is quite scary.

Therefore we always perform without such rehearsals or training. The blade is very sharp, so when we do it habitually one can see what you could call the "ultimate truth." There really is such a thing. That is why we do not practice this, and we perform this without rehearsal.

The sequence of the technique is predetermined but if one just goes along with the sequence one can get hurt. Even if one does not make a mistake, it is possible that the partner will make a mistake. Likewise, if the partner does not make a mistake it is possible that we will make a mistake. That is why, even though the set of movements are defined, in the very instant of actually doing it we remove these from the mind. We do it so that we can respond according to the distance and timing of the partner in that moment. If this is not done this way it is very dangerous. This takes a few years to achieve! At first one is too conscious about the sharpness of the blade, but eventually, after a lot of practice, the edge of the blade stops from being fixed in our gaze. We are not alone in this kind of practice. Among the other schools of Japanese *bujutsu* like *kenjutsu*, there are *shinken shirahadori* (lit. drawn live-blade taking; bare-handed blade grip) techniques, which is the evasion and parrying of the naked live blade and also disarming techniques. But I would add that it is unusual for a school like ours to do this technique.

And what techniques do you use for this practice?

Well, the first most important thing is *maai* (distance) and *kiai* (intention). *Maai* and *kiai* depend on the length of the opponent's blade. Using the distance of a spear against a short blade would be too far away, and on the other hand, using the distance of a *katana* against a spear would be too close. The distance is in relation to the weapon of the opponent. Then there is timing. Depending on the approach of the opponent one must either take the initiative (*sente*), respond to his action (*go no sen*), or take a preemptive intuitive action (*sensen no sen*).

The trinity of essential points of *kendō* consisting of *Ki-ken-tai icchi* (lit. agreement of spirit, sword and body as one) mind, body and technique must also simultaneously arise. When the opponent attacks, cutting, in that very instant, distance, *kiai*, the trinity of mind, body and technique, and additionally, body-management, must all emerge immediately and unconsciously.

And the drills we watched, ippon and sanbon kumite?

The *karate* nowadays is mostly practiced as competition *karate*. It is not true *budō*. The truth is that the original Okinawan *karate* was not *budō* either, it was for practical reasons. In Japanese *budō* there is no such thing as defense. *Kendō* and *jūdō* are like this. It begins with a cut. It begins with an attack. In *jūdō*, there are locks, throws, and grappling. One does not want to be cut or thrown or locked, and that is why we do learn defensive movement. Okinawan *karate*, however, always begins with defense. This can be seen in *kata*. I will break this down into steps. In step one, the opponent attacks. In step two, we execute a defensive move, and if we strike on step three the opponent will also strike. However, *aiuchi* (simultaneous striking) serves no purpose. For that reason, our method is not step one, opponent attacks, then step two, we defend, then step three. It is not this. If the opponent attacks in one, we strike back in one, we evade and strike simultaneously.

> **"**
> *We practice to always avoid wasteful technique, wasteful power, and wasteful movement. Then after we have considered these, the three most important things are speed, weight perception and the use of the hip*

So this is the Wadō-ryū concept of 'sente', to take initiative?
Yes let me explain. In maths one plus one is two, right? One plus two is three. However, our math works differently like this, one plus one is one, one plus two is also one, one plus three is also one. What this means is that in a single count we execute three techniques simultaneously. That is the utmost characteristic of *Wadō-ryū*.

What is the differences between Wadō-ryū and other styles?
As you know, *karate* nowadays is done always using power. According to Japanese *budō*, the worst things you can do, or mistakes are wasteful power, wasteful movements and wasteful technique. If these three, or even only one of these things were present, it doesn't matter if you practice a lifetime, you will never become proficient. We practice to always avoid wasteful techniques, wasteful power, and wasteful movements. Then after we have considered these, the three most important things are speed, weight perception and the use of the hip.

Speed means knowing that a straight line is the fastest way. Weight perception means, for example, having the mental image of what 4kg of cotton and what 4kg of iron are like. The kilogram weight represent the damage, which has a certain density. Cotton being very different to iron. As far as how we use our hips, let me explain. Do you know how a water wheel works? When water strikes the water wheel, it causes the wheel to turn or rotate. Similarly, when the opponent strikes we have it flow past us like a water wheel. It is not that we simply allow an attack to flow past. It is the center of our body which turns. This is what we all aim for when we practice.

How different is Wadō-ryū from Okinawan Karate?
It is Okinawan *karate*. The *kata* that came from Okinawa is the same but

Seiza at the *Wadō-ryū Honbu Dōjō*. Photo: Jon Braeley

they are contradictory. This is why my predecessor had to consider the *kata* and figure them out in his own particular way to make the current ones, the ones we are teaching today. Originally, Okinawan *karate* lacked meaning whatsoever. One would imitate and block and throw and so on, but originally there was really no meaning. I will explain.

When *karate* came from Okinawa, *karate* was only *kata*. There was no transmission of *kihon* (fundamental basics). The person who created the *kihon* we use was my father. He thought that only repeating the *kata* that came from Okinawa was not the best way to practice. Japanese *budō* without exception must have a basic foundation. For example, in *kendō* there is the *uchikomi* (strike repetition) practice, and in *jūdō* there is throwing practice and so on.

Since there was no basic foundation in the karate that came to Japan, the movements for punches and kicks in the *kata* must be figured out by oneself. For example we have four types of punches: *junzuki* (punch with leading arm while stationary or moving back), *junzuki no tsukkomi* (stepping penetrating punch), *gyakuzuki* (punch forward with the rear or reverse arm), and *gyaku no tsukkomi* (a lateral sideways moving *gyakuzuki*). The kicks are added to these punching technique.

We also have the following *waza* (technique): The *nagashi waza* (parrying blocking techniques from *jūjutsu*), *tobikomizuki* (snap punch or jab with leading arm to the head), and *tobikominagashizuki* (a lunging *tobikomizuki* similar to a sword thrust). This makes six technique that are

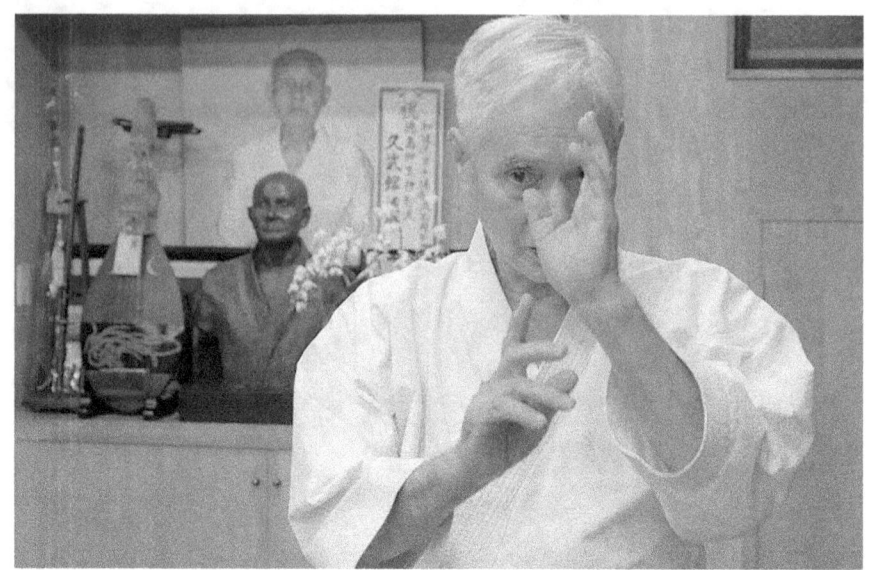

Wadō-ryū karate borrows technique from *kendō, jūdō and jūjutsu*

taught as the basic foundations in *Wadō-ryū*. And then, we have *kata*. The technique we learn as the basics must be used within the *kata*. When practicing the basics, one stands as the center and picture the target of the opponents in all the directions, front, back, left, right, the diagonals, and even up towards the ceiling, and below towards the floor. The basic technique are practiced while always picturing at least ten directions.

Take *oizuki* for example. *Oizuki* is an outgoing technique (stepping forward punch attack). It has no meaning as a response for counter attack. That is the reason why we use *junzuki*. The left strikes to the left, the right strikes to the right. That is the meaning of its name, '*jun*' (lit. order, compliance). The moment when it lands in the left side, the response is to the left, and the same for the right side. We constantly think about which side we must strike, left or right, from this direction we are able to respond accordingly.

We punch and kick to build an unconscious response while imagining an opponent. The basics that we practice must be put into use in the *kata* the exact same way. The *kata* works in all directions, as I said before, front, back, up, down. We practice it imagining or picturing the opponent in all these directions one at a time. When there are continuous movements in a *kata*, there are cases where these movements contradict each other. Here we teach the reason why these contradictory moves are

Wadō-ryū karate and *jūjutsu technique working together*

executed in that particular way. No one asks why or how do they? We repeat this cycle of why and how, many times, sometimes hundreds of times. This is how we practice.

For example, take a hand towel after training and squeeze it. If it is summer time we can hang it to dry while still a little bit wet, but in the winter it will freeze. That is why we must squeeze until we get the very last drop out. We practice as if squeezing to the last drop every time, so that we are able to progress not only technically but in various aspects. Ultimately, *Wadō-ryū* is the heart of Japan, what is called Yamato. It is the heart of Japan.

Let me explain this way. There is a word in Japan said "*kurai;*" in this context it means high-level or rank, pride, you could say it is "to have class." The objective is to build humans who possess "*kurai*". I will tell you about a well known story regarding this meaning. When I was a student, I heard this from many of my teachers. The emperor was in Kyoto every May. There is a one week long *budō* festival, and my dad participated in this every time. On one of those occasions it was the 10th *Kendō Tenran-jiai* (a competition held with the Emperor as a spectator), the winner was a person called Saimura. Everyone congratulated him, but he looked disappointed and angry and he replied "What is there to congratulate?". But the people insisted that they congratulate him because he had won the competition. To them he replied "Today I fought only to win, nothing else". The crowd replied, "Well, it is because you fought to win that you won, is that not so?". Saimura answered, "No. Regardless of victory or defeat, one must display a loss or a victory that manifests itself as "*kurai*." It is this that will leave a deep lasting impression in the audience."

You see examples of this in the Olympic games. After winning, the competitor will stand in a pose to receive congratulations or admiration from the audience. Recently something happened that they stopped doing this in *jūdō*. When seen from the point of view of the spirit of Japanese *budō*, these winning postures are made disregarding the opponent's feelings of sadness and desolation. One cannot achieve victory by oneself. It is because there is an opponent that one can be victorious. That is why we must express gratitude towards the opponent. A person who does this will demonstrate "*kurai*". This is what is called the spirit of *budō*.

> *There is something called the Ryūkyū-buyō (dance). The 'otoko odori' is a dance which certainly has inserted some basics of Okinawan karate*

13.
Taeko Ebata
KINGAI-RYŪ KOBUDŌ, OKINAWA

Chapter 13
INTRODUCTION

I met Taeko Ebata at the annual demonstrations of traditional *budō* that take place November 3rd in the gardens of the *Meiji Jingū* in Tokyo. The event where I accompanied Ōtsuka Sensei. If you are not familiar with *Meiji Jingū* or Imperial Shrine, it is located in a large park of the same name and links with Yoyogi Park, between Shinjuku and Shibuya in Tokyo. *Meiji Jingū* is by far one of the best attractions in Tokyo, and was built in honor of Emperor Meiji and his wife, in 1920. The grounds of the shrine are home to two wonderful *dōjōs*, the *Shiseikan Dōjō* and a large *Kyūdōjō* adjacent, which holds the All Japan Kyūdō Championships, usually on the same holiday, November 3rd.

A five minute walk takes you to the main lawn where the *koryū* (classical martial arts) schools perform demonstrations which goes by the official title, *Meiji Jingū Kobudō Enbu* Taikai (lit. Meiji Imperial Shrine Ancient Budō Demonstration Tournament). The crowds start to arrive early, about an hour before the first demonstrations which usually begin around 10 o'clock in the morning.

I was struck by Taeko Ebata's small size, which was made more startling by what she was wielding. She was holding a large, heavy looking tool, shaped like a pickax but with a wide blade and a thick wooden

A lesson in Ryūkyū-buyō (dance) with Taeko Ebata

shaft. This is the *kuwa* or hoe, and is an Okinawan farming tool that could easily serve as a weapon if required. A popular belief is that the *kuwa*, and many other farming tools, became weapons for the peasants under the harsh rule of the Satsuma *samurai* when Japan took control of Okinawa. This *kuwa* was almost the same height as Taeko Ebata and looked to be the same weight as her, yet she was moving it around with gusto. She was warming up a short distance from the demonstration area and so I decided to approach her.

I waited patiently until Taeko Ebata took a break and I could introduce myself. I was putting the *Warriors of Budo* series together and planning the trip to take us to Okinawa, part of the Ryūkyū Islands. An important part of my mission to the birthplace of *karate*, would be to document the ancient culture of Okinawa that was responsible for the martial arts to flourish. Taeko Ebata is an expert in *Ryūkyū-buyō* (*Ryūkyū* dance) and the early fighting art of *Ryūkyū tūdī* (lit. Tang Dynasty (China) hand/fist; also *tōde*), which developed into *karate*.

I knew Taeko Ebata would be the perfect person to help me, but would she be in Okinawa at the same time as my visit? We talked for as long as possible until she was called to perform in the demonstrations. I left with a promise from Taeko Ebata that she would do her best to be in Okinawa for our interview and to demonstrate ancient *Ryūkyū* dance and *kobudō*. It would be almost six months after our first meeting that we met again, this time in Okinawa, at the *dōjō* of *Kingai-ryū karate* where Taeko Ebata teaches her ancient fighting arts. Prior to our meeting and interview, I was able to film traditional dance of the *Ryūkyū* Islands which gave me something to compare what Ebata Taeko would be doing in her demonstrations of *Ryūkyū-buyō*.

Taeko Ebata did not let me down and her demonstrations that day in her *dōjō* in Okinawa were captivating. I had not seen the martial arts looked at from a point of view held by someone like Ebata who was trained in Okinawan classical dance. Ebata was also enjoying herself and this spread to me and Baptiste Tavernier and his wife, Naoko who were with me. Thank you Taeko Ebata we had so much fun!

Taeko Ebata Sensei, 2014

THE INTERVIEW

Can you introduce yourself and give me some history of yourself?
My name is Taeko Ebata. This is my ninth year in the *Kōdōkan*, in Okinawa. In this *dōjō*, *Kingai-ryū karate* and *kobudō* practice takes place. However, the headmaster passed away 13 years ago so *Kingai-ryū* instruction is currently not being taught here. One of his disciples is now in Tokyo, and we receive instruction from him, time to time.

Regarding *kobudō*, it is my main focus. For example, I practice using agricultural tools as a weapon most of the time. I will talk about my *kobudō* practice and the traditions of Okinawa. There is some- thing called the *Ryūkyū-buyō* (*Ryūkyū* dance), which I have been doing since I was a child, from nine years old. There are both '*onna odori*' (womens dance) and '*otoko odori*' (mens dance). The *otoko odori* is a dance which certainly includes some basics of Okinawa *karate*. In the past age of the *Ryūkyū* Kingdom, there was '*koten-buyō*' (lit. classical dance) and also the '*shomin-buyō*' (ordinary people's dance) performed by people in the countryside which are both '*megara*' style dancing. *Megara* dancing moves along matching the music; one arranges the dancing by oneself. This is the Okinawan dance, and also the Okinawan '*ti*', in other words, the Okinawan *karate*. One explanation is that it was transmitted in this way. As for myself, I am not knowledgeable enough to know everything, but when performing *otoko odori* from *Ryūkyū-buyō* one can strongly feel that there is *karate* included in it. It is an indelicate way to say it but, the naturalness and the way to use the hips, and so on, are common to both. As one learns this, one can also use it efficiently in the dance.

Can you talk about your own kobudō practice?

I will explain about the weapons. I think everyone knows about the *tonfā* and *sai* used in *kobudō*. As for me, my weapon of preference are the *kuwa* (mattock/hoe) and the *eku* (Okinawan style oar) and I use them for presentations and demonstrations. This came into use when the Satsuma took control and people had to look around for things to use such as agricultural tools such as this. As for the people of the sea, they used the *eku* as a weapon for fighting. Everyone used what they had readily available around them. This has been continuing for several hundreds of years.

Do any of the weapons have Chinese origin?

That is right that Chinese weapons are used in Okinawa. For example, the *sai* is basically of Chinese origin. There are other things resembling this that can be found in China. This is an Okinawan *kuwa*, but in China they also have something very similar. For example this *eku* is particular to Okinawa.

Can you talk about the dance you just performed?

What I danced just before was the '*Hatoma bushi*' (verses from Hatoma Island) dance. There is classical dancing, which is dancing performed in the royal court. The common folk dance what is called '*zō odori*' (mixed dancing). The dance I did now is a *zō odori* called *Hatoma bushi*. This dance is performed within the scenery of the seashore. In movements such as this one can see that there is *karate* included. Also in this one, where this wide opening of the legs is and image from *karate*. All these dances have elements from *karate* in them.

This reminds me of kata in karate?

The dance that I just danced now is a prayer for well being and health. It contains elements that I see from *karate* in various places. For example, this (turns and blocks with two hands) and I see things like this (stomps the feet while punching with two fists). It has elements from *karate* such as these.

This is also true for *kobudō*. For example, (performs a punch *oizu–*

Taeko Ebata is a master of the *kuwa* (hoe), used as an Okinawan weapon

ki), but like this with the hips pushing to the front. These things are also implemented in the dancing. These are some similar aspects between the Okinawan dancing and the Okinawan *karate*.

As far as the dance, people with a good sense of rhythm and pitch can do it even if they don't usually do it, like *zō odori* and "*minyō*" (folklore music). However, old songs that have low mourning singing and pace are difficult. Classical dancing must be studied carefully. The ones which are danced in groups are such that anyone can do them. School children do them as club activities. E*isā* (folk dancing from Okinawa) was originally danced in the august *Obon* as memorial service for the dead. However, it spread over the world and now it is done like a festival. But traditionally, it is a dance for memorial service during *Obon*.

Does everyone dance eisā?

In school and high school everyone does it during sports festivals. There is also an *eisā* competition which takes place two or three times every year, with a World Tournament in Okinawa. Everyone loves Okinawa so they like to come here from all over the world to watch or participate.

Now everyone creates their own groups defined by similar interests or age. High school student groups, adults only groups, school groups, everyone. There is always a gathering of people that you can join. It is like *awa-odori* (another folk dance from the mainland). Everyone defines the dance by themselves and performs it.

So there are always new dances?

Yes, every time there are more new dances. There are new songs so people device new dances to go along with them. In the last weekend of January in each year, there is an event called '*Mori no nigiwai*' (lit. Bustling prosperity of the woods) organized by the Japan Tourist Bureau and it is here that every Okinawan art is performed. For example, the girls who are now singing like idols, there is also valet with Okinawan music, the old *megara* dancing. There is also *bōjutsu* and *kobudō* demonstrations. With this initiative from Japan Tourist Bureau, one can get a general idea of the Okinawan culture. It is done for two days. I participate every year. Many people participate, around 2,000. It seems the only place where they organize something like this is Okinawa. In Hokkaidō and so on they do it once every 2 or 3 years. Based on this one gets the feeling that Okinawa is truly the 'islands of performing arts'.

Do you perform kobudō?

Well each year it can change and currently I present *ryumu*. Until the year before the last I was in the *kobudō* but some people are taking a break and now other groups are performing. There are actually so many of them. These also keep on appearing. It is quite interesting.

Your hairstyle - is that a weapon tied in your hair?

This in the hair, it is called '*katakashira*' which is a type of traditional top-knot. This style was used by men officials like *samure* (Okinawan equivalent to *samurai*) in ancient times. When it is a wooden piece stuck here in the knot, it is usually associated with a peasant or common people.

There are differences marked by color, gold or silver. This was used by the *samure*. Actually when performing this dance one should where a normal wooden one since it is peasant dance. On the other hand, when doing classical dance one must were this as a *samure*.

Women wore this for their appearance but they also carried their protective *mamori-gatana* (lit. amulet *katana*; small, concealable blade). They could reach for it and use it for stabbing an attacker.

> **If one seriously wants to gain deep knowledge about *jūdō*, one should not limit oneself to think of *jūdō* as only a competitive sport**

14.
Naoki Murata

8TH DAN, KŌDŌKAN JŪDŌ

Chapter 14

INTRODUCTION

In terms of the history of Japanese martial arts or *budō*, the *Kōdōkan*, serving as the *jūdō honbu-dōjō*,, ranks as the holy grail for a documentary of the martial arts. The *Kōdōkan* represented the vision that the founder, Jigorō Kanō shihan, had for *jūdō*. From the moment I decided to document the martial arts, I wanted to step inside the *Kōdōkan*.

Kano Sensei had a formal training in *Jujutsu* and became a highly qualified instructor. As his training and teaching progressed he realized that he was defeating his opponents with his superior understanding of throwing techniques. His methods encompassed "maximum efficiency with minimum effort", a phrase he adopted. He named his martial art, *jūdō* in the belief that he had found "the way".

Just as important as the creation of *jūdō* itself, Jigorō Kanō, as an educator, was able to place *jūdō* into the schools and make it part of the curriculum. He did not stop there and under his guidance, *jūdō* became the first Japanese martial art to gain worldwide recognition outside Japan. In 1909 he became the first Asian member of the International Olympic Committee and saw *jūdō* become an Olympic sport.

The idea for the *Kōdōkan Jūdō* Institute started in 1882 with ten students and by the year 1900, membership had risen to a thousand stu-

Jon Braeley visited the *Kōdōkan* in 2003 and waited 11 years to return

dents. The *Kōdōkan* we see today, was built in 1958 and at eight floors in height with practice halls of 1300 mats, it was the envy of all the martial arts schools in Japan. One little known fact is the previous home of the *Kōdōkan* was taken over by the Japan Karate Association, which became a legal entity in 1957, just before their founder, Gichin Funakoshi passed away at the age of 89 years.

My first visit to the *Kōdōkan* took place in 2003 just before the start of filming of our first documentary release, *The Empty Mind*. The *Kōdōkan* is easy to find, located in Bunkyo Ward, near the downtown area of Tokyo close to the Tokyo Dome. In fact, as you exit the nearby train stations, there are signposts in English pointing you to the *Kōdōkan* - a rarity in Japan and an indication of the importance of this institution. My appointment was to discuss the inclusion of *jūdō* in our documentary and find an appropriate instructor and spokesperson to interview. As with all appointments in Japan, I made sure to arrive five minutes before our scheduled time, in this case, ten o'clock in the morning. In fact I was outside the *Kōdōkan* a few minutes before this, so I could check out the bronze statue of Jigoro Kano and read the inscription.

Beside our meeting I was hoping to take a tour of the *Kōdōkan* and see for myself the wonderful training facilities and the museum and library. From the lobby I was taken to the visitors reception room on the ground floor, which was a large well lit room with touches of art-deco

Naoki Murata

decoration. The ceiling was high and long pendant lights hung low over the polished hardwood large table in the center of the room. A young lady brought in glasses of water as I waited, along with my assistant, with a great deal of anticipation for this meeting.

Then an event happened which was beyond my imagination. An earthquake occurred somewhere in Japan. I did not know where but Tokyo was feeling the consequence. The large conference table appeared to vibrate on the tile floor, emitting a slight noise and the glasses of water shook, just enough for me to notice the water moving. Then the pendant lights swayed, and knocked against each other without breaking. I stood up and grabbed my backpack. I could hear people moving in the lobby outside and we joined about a dozen employees walking quickly through the doors to the street in a very orderly calm way. I did not see any students and thought perhaps that it was too early for *jūdō* practice.

Most of the employees took the opportunity to smoke a cigarette and I waited outside for ten minutes before deciding that it may be best to leave, as I could not imagine our meeting would resume. It was my first experience of an earthquake so I skipped the subway train, and took a taxi back to my hotel in Shinjuku. I called my Japanese assistant at her home in Miami, just as she was getting into bed and after apologizing, I asked her if she could send a fax to the *Kōdōkan*, thanking them for the appointment and I would be in touch again. In fact, it would be eleven years later when I returned to the *Kōdōkan* during the filming of *Warriors of Budo* series. This second visit was just as eventful but not life-threatening.

The All Japan Jūdō Federation which is housed in the Kōdōkan Jūdō Institute building was going through a major scandal in 2013, being accused of the inability to govern itself and of allowing corruption to take place. This resulted in a number of high level executive dismissals, including the resignation of the chairman Haruki Uemura. A number of these high level executives are Judoka from within the *Kōdōkan* and the timing for me could not be worse. My requests to film inside the *Kōdōkan* were met with silence, then with refusal by the *Kōdōkan*. This meant no outside camera crews would be allowed to film inside during this time. My answer to them was that by allowing Empty Mind Films inside the *Kōdōkan* at this time would demonstrate to the outside world, they are an organization that is transparent with no secrets to hide. In other words, business as usual.

I decided to wait, but my problem was that time was running out, as the *jūdō* episode would be the fourth installment of the *Warriors of Budo* series. I had two good contacts in the *jūdō* world and put them to work, but still no news. It would be Alex Bennett, founder of Kendo World magazine, that would break the deadlock. He is a leading expert on *budō* and professor at Kansai University in Japan as well as director at the Japanese Academy of Budō. Alex had already agreed to narrate our series and on hearing about our plight with the *Kōdōkan* offered to help. So a week later I found myself outside the *Kōdōkan* with Alex early one morning, discussing our strategy. Alex disappeared inside while I went for a cup of coffee at a small cafe next to the Tokyo Dome. An hour later he joined me with the news. The *Kōdōkan* had agreed on my filming. I put down my cup of coffee before I spilled it, and congratulated Alex, adding, "well third time lucky!" And we both knew luck had nothing to do with it.

Naoki Murata Sensei, 2014

THE INTERVIEW

Can you talk about the history of the Kōdōkan?
The well-known date in which *Kōdōkan* was established is May of 1882. This corresponds to the year Meiji 15. May of the year 1882 is when the *Kōdōkan* was established. The *Kōdōkan* is centered on the man called Jigorō Kanō, and us, his disciples. Around 17 or 18 people gathered to create the *Kōdōkan* of new *jūjutsu* or what become known as *jūdō*.

About Kanō Sensei, he was not originally from Tokyo, but from Kobe in Hyogo Prefecture in western Japan. He came to Tokyo when he was 9 years old. Kanō Sensei had a small build and was weaker than most people normally are. When school finished and it was time to play outside, he was bullied by the other boys because of his small body. He always lost and this made him miserable.

He took interest in studying the *jūjutsu* that existed in Japan, where even if one has a small body, if the right technique is used a larger opponent can be thrown. He started learning upon his arrival to Tokyo. This is when he started university, so that means that he was 18 years old. After studying for 4 years at the university, he came up with the idea of *jūdō*.

Can you tell us the reason why Kanō Sensei created *jūdō*?
Yes, I can tell you about the reasons for Kano Sensei created *jūdō*. At first, he studied *jūjutsu*. However, *jūjutsu* included very dangerous techniques. With the change of era marked by the fall of the *samurai*, Japan entered a so-called period of 'cultural enlightenment' in which there was the intent to include a new culture. Old things, such as *jūjutsu* and the *katana*, for example, became prohibited. *jūjutsu* also fell out of use.

However, *jujutsu* is a really wonderful thing because of how it can forge both the body and the mind. However *jūjutsu* includes dangerous elements. By taking these out Kanō Sensei changed it from a way of killing to a way of building people. In turn, this became a physical education system, in other words *jūdō*, was created. This is what Jigorō Kanō Sensei was thinking when he created *jūdō* based on *jūjutsu*.

What is the mission the *Kōdōkan*?
The objective of *Kōdōkan jūdō* is that by studying the *jūdō* of *Kōdōkan*, you become able to use the power of mind and body, *shinshin* in Japanese, to its highest degree of efficiency. This is our way of thinking. For students to acquire this way of thinking of aspiring to maximize the power of mind and body is our main objective.

This is what you mean in the phrase 'seiryoku zen'yō'?
This scroll of calligraphy is written 'seiryoku zen'yō'. It is only four characters but it expresses the deep spirit of *jūdō*. I will explain this by looking at the meaning of each character. The uppermost two characters read 'seiryoku'. In English this means the body and mind energy. Physical and

Calligraphy of Kanō Sensei, 'seiryoku zen'yō', meaning maximum efficiency

mental energy. Then '*zen'yō*' means the most efficient use of something. Most effective or maximum effective use of both physical and mental energy. During daily *jūdō* practice, if one observes this principle then one is able to throw the opponent successfully. If it doesn't follow this then one is putting too much strength and it does not work out. Day by day during *jūdō* training we study this principle.

Also, once the practice is finished, one must also apply this theory and principle to the outside world in our daily life. Think '*seiryoku zen'yō*' when you talk with your friends, study, drive your car. That is why there is the way of thinking of *jūdō* as the way of humanity. This concept is expressed completely by this '*seiryoku zen'yō*' and we should always think about this.

We also have another scroll on display with four characters. This is read '*jita kyōei.*' This is also one of the principles of *jūdō*. '*Jita*' means oneself and others, in other words, you and me. In English, it expresses mutual benefit. Me and you. The lower two read '*kyōei*'. This means that both flourish. Both become happy. Both prosper. Mutual welfare and benefit is how it is written in English. *Seiryoku zen'yō*, if one uses the power of mind and body efficiently then there will be no harm towards the opponent. The most efficient way is not one in which harm is inflicted, but one in which both can develop. This is what is expressed by *jita kyōei*, which is the ultimate spirit of *jūdō*.

Kanō Sensei thought that the most efficient way to use the power of mind and body in order to achieve an objective is one in which there is no harm or disregard for other people. Certainly, in *jūdō* we practice together making the best use of the strength of mind and body in such a way that we can both mutually improve our technique. By doing this, one can see that after one or two years later, both practitioners have improved, and became better at *jūdō*.

For those who practice *jūdō*, you place *seiryoku zen'yō* and *jita kyōei* into your hearts, and eventually are able to manifest this through your bodies by daily practice. Words alone are not good enough! One must train as to be able to express this with the body. Our *jūdō* also becomes stronger, just like our hearts infuses with *seiryoku zen'yō* and *jita kyōei*. We are then walking the way of humanity, and enjoying good relationships, with everyone building a world of mutual prosperity. This is Jigorō Kanō Sensei's ideal. We practice to fulfill this ideal. When the maximum power of mind and body are put to use efficiently, it is called *seiryoku zen'yō*, and the result of this is *jita kyōei*. Our intention is to always have in mind the spirit of *jūdō* as described by *seiryoku zen'yō* and *jita kyōei* when we are practicing *jūdō*.

And where does the word Kōdōkan come from?
The name *Kōdōkan* is written in Japanese using three characters. I will explain its meaning by dissecting the meaning of each. The '*Ko*' in *Kōdōkan* means 'to teach' or 'to lecture.' '*Dō*' means 'way.' It is the same *dō* as in *jūdō*. The meaning of the *dō* in *jūdō* is the "way of people", or the way which people must traverse. It also implies other meaning such as "main principle" and "ethics".

This is for *dō*. Then, '*kan*' in *Kōdōkan* means 'place,' 'home,' 'building,' among others. Therefore, the meaning of *Kōdōkan* as being composed by these three characters is 'the place where the way is taught', or 'the hall where the way is taught'. If seen like this, then it is implied that *jūdō* is the way of people.

Kanō Sensei created the belt ranking system in martial arts, yes?
The era of *jūjutsu* is the era before *jūdō*. At that time there was no *dan-kyū* (grade-level) system like now, but there was a distinction between stages. Advancing from one stage on to the next took large amounts of time. Kanō Sensei observed that because of this, the students lost interest, so he made the time between this intervals shorter. This is what

later became the *dan-kyū* system, like progressing up a ladder. By having smaller divisions the motivation to advance to the next level generated the interest to continue.

In various martial arts in Japan, beginners are identified with the color white. In Japanese culture, white means that there is nothing. The *jūdō* uniform has an immaculate white appearance. Regarding the color of the belt, it is also white in the beginning, meaning that one still doesn't know anything. After acquiring a *dan* degree, as opposed to not knowing, one wears a black belt that represents that we are experienced. So yes, I believe that this started with *jūdō*.

Why do you think jūdō spread so successfully outside Japan?

This is an excellent question, as to how *jūdō* became so successful globally. This is my personal opinion. I have not been to all of the many countries that practice *jūdō*, but I have been to over a dozen of them where I have seen that they have traditional combat sports, or how it is often referred to around the world as "martial arts". I believe that in *jūjutsu*, which came before *jūdō*, all the techniques from all this martial arts around the world can be found. *Jūdō* was originated from *jūjutsu*, Therefore, I think that in *jūdō* one can find the techniques that are also found in the worlds many combat sports. So, for the people around the world, it is as if they were doing their own countries' techniques, but wearing a white *jūdō* uniform. *Jūdō* can include many of the techniques of the various combat sports of the world.

The people around the world can use them directly like that. That is one reason. The second one is the fascination and the mystery that we have when we see small people throw larger opponents. Another reason is that Jigorō Kanō Sensei was very proficient in English so this permitted him to travel abroad, mainly to Europe but also to the United States, and explain the theory and principles of *jūdō* personally, as well as do demonstration about technique. These are all reasons for the success that *jūdō* has experienced around the World.

And does this include jūdō practiced as a competitive sport?

In general, even when looking at the same thing, the way of thinking about it and what is seen can be different between the Japanese and the rest of the world. Likewise, some things which people abroad overlook, the Japanese cannot permit. This difference in thinking about the tech-

The main *dōjō* at the *Kōdōkan*. Photo: Jon Braeley

nical aspects and rules of *jūdō* can cause many discrepancies. We discuss these discrepancies and look for solutions to them that we agree. However, in some cases the solutions that are not in full accordance to what the Japanese would think can be quite a few. As the years pass in this manner, the rules and other aspects of *jūdō* can and do change.

In the case where *jūdō* is practiced as a competitive sport, and as the rules that are used in the fighting change, the form of the techniques also changes little by little. The form and the posture of technique changes. As a result, the technical aspect changes little by little. The rules changes little by little. When one looks back at the starting point of *jūdō* in Japan, one can notice that the *jūdō* practiced today in the world has changed since. I think that the Japanese people feel these changes in *jūdō* more acutely than the people in the rest of the World.

Do you have objects that belonged to Kanō Sensei?

Kanō Sensei's personal belongings are in storage and not in display, but here in this museum we have some of his many brush-written pieces and calligraphy. Here in this museum we also display many of his utensils. We have quite a lot of them. Also, we have his *jūjutsu* uniform from the days when he practiced *jūjutsu*. These are things from about 130 years ago.

I cannot remember the exact date now, but this *jūdō* Museum, *Shiryōkan* (lit. reference library) as we call it, has been here for some 30-some years already, since the time when the *Kōdōkan* was refurbished. It was then that this Museum was constructed.

My role here is to gather the history of *jūdō* and to teach it to people, guide through the Museum and explain the items on display, among other things. Also, as 8th *dan* in *jūdō* I also serve as a technical instructor that includes teaching *jūdō* several times every week.

I also travel abroad to do lectures about the history of *jūdō*, and naturally, on those occasions I use the opportunity to teach the technical aspects as well. I have been appointed to do an all-round type of work for the *Kōdōkan*.

Could you take us around the museum and the exhibits?

Yes. My job at the *Kōdōkan* is to be the curator of the Museum and Reference Library. My secondary job is to explain about the history of *jūdō* to the visitors of the Museum.

This exhibit of a *jūdō* uniform is about 130 years old, from around the time when Jigorō Kanō Sensei was creating *jūdō*. It belonged to one of the disciples. This uniform is very small, as was the person who owned it. His name was Shirō Saigō. This Mr. Shirō Saigō could throw over practitioners of old-style *jūjutsu* using the techniques from the new *jūdō*. That is how people in Japan then thought that *jūdō* was more impressive than *jūjutsu* and it became accepted. This person, Saigo Shiro is important as the one who demonstrated and symbolized the acceptance of *jūdō* as a martial art at this time. So his practice uniform is displayed here. It is likely that if this person had not been there at that time, *jūdō* would have never risen in popularity. In order to praise his merits, *Kōdōkan* has put his uniform on display here.

Here we have a display of historical photographs. Jigorō Kanō Sensei is well known as the father of *jūdō*. However, that was not his only achievement. He was the first Olympic Committee Member to be chosen from an Asian country. The so-called father of modern Olympics, the French Pierre de Cubertein, knew that in order to have countries from the east participate, good relationships should be built. Kanō Sensei's idea of a prosperous cultural society through the spirit of Judo as "*seiryoku zen'yō* and '*jita kyōei*' was similar to the idea of Pierre de Cubertein, in creating a peaceful world through sports. That is why Kanō Sensei was very pleased to be invited and heed the call to meet, and thus became the first Committee member from Asia.

The commemorative photograph of the time when Kanō went to meet Cubertein at the Olympics is on display. It was in the year 1912, at

The grave of Jigorō Kanō in Yahashira cemetery. Photo: Jon Braeley

the 5th Olympic games in Stockholm. Kanō Sensei went as the leader of the Japanese team, taking along with him two players. One was a sprinter, and the other a long distance marathon runner. Unfortunately, neither of them made it to the finals, but Kanō Sensei and the two athletes did succeed in starting up the activities regarding the Olympics in Japan.

At that time, there were still many people who did not know about Japan and Kanō Sensei wanted to show them. He thought in order to do that he could invite people to Japan by hosting an Olympic games in Tokyo. The Olympic committee in agreeing with him, then determined that the Olympic games would take place in Tokyo, and this would be in 1940.

All this activity must have caused a lot fatigue in his body, and on the way back to Japan after the IOC meeting, just a couple days before arriving in Yokohama, Kanō Sensei passed away aboard the ship. We refer to Kanō Sensei as the father of both *jūdō* and the Olympics in Japan.

How close is the jūdō practiced today to the jūdō of Kanō Sensei?

Nowadays, the people all over the world know about *jūdō*. However, this *jūdō* is almost always the "*jūdō* as a competitive sport" and this is only a fraction of *jūdō* as a whole. As a matter of fact, this competitive sport *jūdō* is only one part of the *jūdō* created by Kanō Sensei. For example, *jūdō* originated from *jūjutsu*, *jūjutsu* was *Bujutsu*, and *Bujutsu* are techniques, so there are many techniques that cannot be part of *jūdō as* a competitive sport. The technique that must not be done are precisely those which were *Bujutsu*, or *jūjutsu*, that are practiced for protecting life. Therefore, if one seriously wants to gain deep knowledge about *jūdō*, one should not limit oneself to think of *jūdō* as only a competitive sport. Please do not forget that besides these, there are many other techniques to defeat opponents within *jūdō*.

Jūdō is a "way of people", and what this means is that it is a method which nurtures a heart that strives for mutual development. *Jūdō* is not only a competitive sport about winning or losing, or taking home a gold or silver medal. It is about cultivating the spirit. The spirit of *'jita kyōei.'* *Jūdō* exists for the purpose of cultivating this spirit. I would be very glad is you please remember this important point.

I have traveled to many countries around the world, and I would like to ask all people of the world, of course including Japan, to please do not stop doing *jūdō*. It is a "way", and we think that as such it has no ending. It goes on and on. That is like cultivating our spirit and it has no ending, it keeps going on and on. Today, be better than yesterday, tomorrow be better than today. Be better this year than last year. Do this through a lifetime and improve oneself continuously and you will help others.

This is the gentle 'way' which the person called Jigorō Kanō created. So please, practice while young. If you do other sports, that is also good, but please don't stop practicing *jūdō*. This way, one can arrive at new depths and gain a deeper understanding of humanity. So I would be very pleased if everyone keeps studying *jūdō*.

> *What we aim for is dynamic, magnificent technique. Through this big technique, making the opponent's back contact the ground with momentum. This kind of technique is 'ippon'*

15.
Mikihiro Mukai

7TH DAN, KŌDŌKAN JŪDŌ

Mikihiro Mukai Sensei 2014
INTERVIEW

Can you introduce yourself?

Pleased to meet you. My name is Mikihiro Mukai, from *Kōdōkan*. I serve everyday as an instructor for the students here in *Kōdōkan*. The *jūdō* of *Kōdōkan* is the one which Kanō Jigorō created based on the good parts of the *jūjutsu* which he studied.

What is the difference between Kanō Sensei's jūjutsu and jūdō?

In simple terms, the differences between *Kōdōkan jūdō* and the original *jūjutsu* are that the *atemi* (blows to the body) and other dangerous techniques were excluded so that the daily practice could take place more easily without any of the students suffering a bad injury.

Is there any difference between Japanese jūdō and foreign jūdō?

This *Kōdōkan jūdō* is the one which many outstanding instructors have taught abroad. Now it has also become an Olympic discipline. The competitive *jūdō* in the Olympics has been observed in some detail. I think that in a global perspective, it is this competitive *jūdō* which has become more widely known all over the world. However, from the beginning in

Japan, the *jūdō* which is safe and has the ultimate objective of creating a peaceful human society, is not the one which is focused on winning. I think this is the big difference between us.

This leads to my next question, has international jūdō had an affect on jūdō practiced in Japan?

I think that the methods of practicing abroad which have the ultimate objective to achieve victory in competition have become numerous. Of course, also in Japan the practice which has the objective of winning in the Olympics is widely done. However, teaching towards children is centered on the *jūdō* which serves as self-protection and in the practice of the basics so this practice can be extended long into the future.

Nonetheless, the competitive *jūdō* has had a lot of influence in Japan and in many places kids are training with the objective of winning in competitions. The kids are made to practice very hard, using *jūdō* like adults. Outside Japan, *jūdō* for kids is done entertainingly and easily, so that kids continue practice in the long term. Nowadays, also in Japan we have the kids train entertainingly or else they will not continue in the future. For this reason, Japan has adopted this method of training kids so that the practice is fun and interesting.

Is there a difference in male and female practice at the Kōdōkan?

In comparison to the rest of the world, Japan was quite late in allowing women to participate in competitions. Even here in the *Kōdōkan*, the women's training take place in a different *dōjō* only between girls, but we have a male instructor. Practice takes places only between women. However, what has changed is that in schools - junior school practice is mixed, and here if they so wish, the women can also practice together with men in this main *dōjō* of the *Kōdōkan*.

Are there any striking techniques in jūdō ?
Using kicks and strikes and other movements can cause injury when during daily practice. As dangerous techniques, these have been removed and are not part of daily practice. In competition, these are considered foul-play. However, these are techniques that have been included since long time ago so they are practiced through *kata*. In *kata* practice, kicks, punches, as well as wrist twisting and such things are practiced.

Sometimes I see blue jūdōgi being worn instead of white?
The blue uniform became popular in competitions, because it is easy for the spectators to see, especially if one competitor wears blue and the other wears white. So the blue color uniform became acceptable in competitions. In Japan, there are historical reasons such as the meaning of spirituality and so on that are connected to *jūdō*, so here at the *Kōdōkan* we kindly ask people to only wear a white uniform. However, in special cases like international training camps where practitioners may not have enough white uniforms for continuous days of practice, it is allowed to wear blue uniforms in the *Kōdōkan*. On the other hand, when we Japanese travel abroad for practice and representatives of *Kōdōkan* go to teach, especially in France, we ask everyone to please use their white uniforms.

What is a consideration when teaching jūdō to children?
In Japan, well here at the *Kōdōkan*, we ask the children to center practice around leg techniques. The reason is that if kids do not learn how to use their legs while young, when they grow up its hard for them to acquire the skill. We teach leg techniques because these are not about strength, but rather about correct timing. If they acquire these then in the future when they grow stronger they can make the best use of their bodies and do more splendid techniques.

Can you describe the difference between randori and kata?
In the year 1882, Jigorō Kanō Shihan established *Kōdōkan* and at that

time the main focus was practice of *jūjutsu kata*. Then, practice at *Kōdōkan* was not only *kata*, but also free-sparring also called *randori*. With regard to this *randori*, in spaces between the practitioners, *kata* practice was also conducted. Nowadays in *Kōdōkan* we separate *randori* practice from *kata* practice and conduct them separately. However, the practice inclined towards *randori* with the goal to win at competitions has become very strong and with this a need to go back to basics through *kata*. For this reason, there now is a world championship for *kata*.

A recent newspaper showed a female station attendant use 'seoin-age' to subdue a male attacker - can you comment on this?

Yes this is a good throw and I can imagine that in this situation the station attendant would use this technique. This situation can happen in some cases when a woman is grabbed or hugged from behind by an assailant. As the arm comes around, one holds this arm and pulls the opponent onto your hips, and then rolls and throws the opponent to the front. This is how the technique is done.

Therefore, it is a very efficient technique which allows a woman with a small build or less physical strength to be able to throw a larger or stronger opponent. I am sure the attacker was very surprised.

Young people like to compete. How do you handle students who practice only for competitions?

That is right. Here in the *Kōdōkan*, there are kids who practice mostly for the sake of winning at competitions. Therefore, we do allow them to practice for winning matches. However, here at the *Kōdōkan* it is basic general rule that we do not do practice just for the sake of winning competitions. But in this age, people who practice for winning have increased and therefore the kids now, who practice from 4 to 6pm, are not taught winning at matches.

They are only instructed in the basics of *jūdō*. But afterward they can practice competition technique. Once they finish at 6pm and afterwards, kids who want to win and participate in competitions can stay if they wish and practice for that purpose. That is a little bit more severe practice, and we also teach a little about techniques used to win. However, what I am careful as an instructor is to not teach too much as to allow children to have their own thoughts.

Jūdō at the *Kōdōkan* is about single winning technique or *'ippon'*

How did you start teaching jūdō?

I graduated from the university, and at first I was a high school instructor. I realized that I still lacked studying as an instructor, so I returned to the university for as a graduate student. After finishing the graduate studies, I got employed to instruct at the *Kōdōkan* at the same time as I coached the national team. When I was in the graduate school I was also coaching university students. I am currently also coaching corporate teams. My personal teaching experience goes from children to adults, also including national team members.

I think that many instructors consider teaching children the most difficult. When I was coaching the national team, it was the women's team which I was training, and that was also quite challenging. However, it was a great learning experience for me. One must make adaptations to the way of teaching adults, as well as the way of teaching women. One needs to devise different methods specially for teaching children.

Karate and kendō may become Olympic sports, can you comment?

I know that various competitive sports like *karate*, *sumō*, sambo, among others, want to become Olympic disciplines and undertake actions to do so. Regarding *karate*, there is the Korean combat sport *taekwondo* which is already an Olympic discipline. Recently, *jūdō* came to resemble wrestling very much, and under those conditions it could be thought that *jūdō* would no longer be recognized as an Olympic discipline. For that reason, the IJF, the International Jūdō Federation, revised the rules. As a result, it now seems that wrestling is about to be taken from the Olympics and now *jūdō* is receiving a higher acceptance.

For *karate* to become selected as an Olympic discipline, I think it is important for *karate* to be able to demonstrate clearly what makes it different and distinguishable from *taekwondo*.

With regard to competition, how have the rules changed over the years and what is the effect on jūdō in Japan?

Originally, there were not so many rules. The opinion of the instructor who were performing as a referee at that time was considered very importantly. This is way back, at the time when there was only one referee. That referee was a very high ranking and also old, and thus a person who was respected by everybody. So it was all entrusted to this referee. However, that became unreliable and then it was defined that there should be three referees, as well as video cameras prepared in case where verification was needed.

Even then various problems took place, with some claims that proper judgment was not occurring. Therefore, the way of acting as referee also made some adaptations. Now, in Japan there are three referees and the judgment is based on the opinion of the three. In the International Jūdō Federation, only one referee stands on the mats, while the other two are watching the video. If the video shows any mistakes, then the referee is informed. Same with the rules too, as I said before, grabbing the legs or folding the body while holding on with the head like in wrestling, are different in *jūdō*. Grabbing the legs in considered foul-play and the rule is strictly enforced, so that there is a clear distinction between *jūdō* and wrestling.

Do competitions change the type of techniques you practice?

Everyone, I think especially foreigners, have a strong opinion about scoring points. We *jūdōka* in Japan do not think about scoring points. What we aim for is dynamic, magnificent technique. And through this big

> **"**
>
> *The Kōdōkan has a general rule that we do not do practice for the sake of winning competitions. The kids who practice from 4 to 6pm, are not taught winning at matches. They are only instructed in the basics of jūdō...*

technique, making the opponent's back contact the ground with momentum. This kind of technique is '*ippon*' (winning point).

Additionally, within this *ippon*, the opponent is skillfully maneuvered so that no harm is made to him by the throw. This is the ideal of '*ippon*'. That is why the one doing the throw must have some surplus. The techniques in competition now have become such that one will allow the opponent to get hurt in order to get a point. The *jūdō* that we at the *Kōdōkan* seek is not like that. An *ippon* includes executing the techniques in such way that we protect the opponent from harm.

One of the most effective techniques is *uchimata*. (lit. inner thigh; throw executed by putting one leg between the opponent's legs). With the revision of rules and the prohibition to grab the pants, the technique called *seoinage* (carry over the back throw) which I explained before and is very efficient for women, also experienced a revival as a very effective technique. Before, it was allowed to grab the legs, so when techniques like this throw were done, one could avoid the throw by grabbing on to the opponent's legs. Now it is not allowed to grab the legs so it became possible to perform an *ippon* using this technique. It is a very popular.

Previously, and until recently in Japan, there were two separate sets of rules, those of the internationally accepted and those specified for refereeing by the *Kōdōkan*. For children's' competitions, the rules used were those specified for refereeing by *Kōdōkan*. However, now there is a single set of rules specified by the International Jūdō Federation. Whether this is good or not, we must see how it turns out from now on.

However, this does not mean that the rules set by *Kōdōkan* for refereeing have disappeared. As a *Kōdōkan* person, I think that there is a need for the refereeing rules set by *Kōdōkan* to be revised and presented again to the IJF in order to restore the *Kōdōkan jūdō*.

Do you think jūdō and jūjutsu should be part of police training?

If one looks back to the history of *Kōdōkan*, tournaments between the *Kōdōkan jūdō* and many schools and styles of *jūjutsu* took place. In those tournaments, the *Kōdōkan jūdō* showed overwhelming victories. This is why *jūdō* became part of the police curriculum and now *jūdō* practice takes places for all police forces. I believe that *jūdō* helps to make a strong police that prevents crime, as well as one that knows how to handle it when it occurs.

How close is the practice of jūdō today than the jūdō Kanō Sensei first started teaching?

Our objective as stated by Kanō Shihan is expressed over there (points to calligraphy on the wall) as "*Jūdō* is the way to the most effective use of both physical and spiritual strength. By training you in attacks and defenses it refines your body and your soul and helps you make the spiritual essence of *jūdō* a part of your very being. In this way you are able to perfect yourself and contribute something of value to the world. This is the final goal of *jūdō* discipline".

If the strength that we acquire through *jūdō* is not used to contribute to this world, then this is not the original aim of *jūdō*. Our ultimate objective is to use what we learn through *jūdō* in order to serve a role toward the world. This is why one must apply the things one learns through *jūdō* in your daily life as well. Depending on the country the way of thinking varies. Presently, *jūdō* is practiced in about 200 countries and territories. I think that if it was only a matter of winning in matches, it would have never expanded so much. For example in the United States, there are people who besides practicing attractive sports such as American football and baseball, also train in *jūdō*.

Really, it is not only about winning, but because one can also become stronger mentally or spiritually. Also, one's manners improve. These things can serve a helpful role in our daily lives. I think that *Kōdōkan jūdō* excels in these good aspects. I would like you to please understand *jūdō* this way and for many people to practice *jūdō*. We will also continue the development of *jūdō* by providing the world with what we can while we learn together from each other. Actually, in Japan *jūdō* is considered a very dangerous sport. In a span of 30 years, more than 100 people died. Allow me to speak sincerely. Reflecting upon this, and I do not know if it is true that 100 people have passed away or not, but when we heard the report

Jūdō is called the 'gentle way' but in Japan fatal injuries do occur,
and Mukai Sensei suffers from damaged ears

from the person who conducted this research we though to ourselves that it is a terrible situation. *Jūdō* people gathered to think what can be done to improve safety in *jūdō*. In the last 3 years since then, there have been no casualties and no severe injuries from *jūdō*. But I need to say when competition is so important there is no way to avoid any injury.

Acquire the basics properly and prepare your body well. This building up of the body can be done with enjoyment. The children say so as well. Not only make them train strictly, but to strengthen the body while having fun. At the same time, acquire the techniques to protect our own bodies. On top of all that, one can begin to aspire to participate in competition and win. I think it is very important to build upon the basics.

Just now on the mat, you can see the children are practicing at the back, while practitioners who already are representative players for Japan are training. These two groups cannot be made to train the same way by no means. The children need to train according to what they need now. And *jūdō* practice must be made fun. When the adult level is achieved, one must conduct training which is strict to oneself, aiming to improve. This distinction must be made.

Do you have many injuries? I see your ears are swollen. We call this a cauliflower ear!
As for myself, I have never gotten injured very much. I think this is be-

cause ever since my childhood, the instructors that have raised me have taught the basics very solidly. I have experienced muscular stretches or bone pain, but in those time I have also been taught the ways to cease the pain, how to undergo rehabilitation and so on. In Japan, there is something called the "*jūdō* bonesetter." Of course one can get injured, but one also learns the methods of how to heal those injuries. As for as my ears, swollen ears occur not only in *jūdō*, but also wrestling and *sumo*, among others. In techniques such as the ones we are seeing now, the hands come in contact with the ears and internal bleeding can occur. It would be good if one takes rest when this internal bleeding happens, but as one become a high school student and on, even if the ear is a little bit swollen, one cannot take a rest from training. Then it happens that the internal bleeding hardens, and it becomes like this. My ear on this other side is actually fine.

In our age, in order to become strong we believed that if we did not get this injury we were not strong enough. When the ear got this large it hurt quite a bit, but in order to become a strong *jūdōka* I thought it was good. There are also people who say that in reality, strong people's ears do not become like this. The reason for this argument is that strong people are not defeated. They are always strong so they cannot be held down, and they take care not to get the opponent's arm underneath and so on. I have one good ear and one that is swollen so I can show people with different opinions, either the one ear or the other! It is OK!

> **"**
> *I can honestly say that if it*
> *weren't for this sport and if it*
> *weren't for this Judo club and this*
> *family, it's scary to think about*
> *where I might have ended up!*

16.
Kayla Harrison
JŪDŌ OLYMPIC GOLD MEDALIST

Chapter 16
INTRODUCTION

For the United States, the standout star of the 2012 Olympic Games in London, was undoubtedly Kayla Harrison, who became the first American to win a Gold Medal in jūdō. How she got there is a story that must be told so others may be inspired.

Kayla, from Middleton, Ohio, started *jūdō* practice at six years of age and by her teens started to show great promise as a national *jūdō* champion, winning a number of state level tournaments. At thirteen years, she signed up with coach Daniel Doyle. Over the next three years, as Kayla competed across the country accompanied by coach Doyle, he sexually abused her. Three years later, Kayla finally revealed the sexual abuse to a close friend and the truth came out. Coach Doyle was arrested, found guilty and sentenced to ten years in prison. Kayla was traumatized by this terrible event and went into a deep depression. Her mother sought the help of Jimmy Pedro, an Olympic *jūdō* coach. Pedro visited the family and fearing that Kayla may take her own life, requested she should stay with him and his father Jim, at their training facility in Wakefield, north of Boston, where they could keep a close eye on her. It was here that their work began in rebuilding Kayla, and convincing her that the sexual abuse she suffered

Unfortunately Kayla took the Olympic gold medal back

was not her fault. The Pedro's were able to lift Kayla out of depression and build her self esteem. Slowly they began to turn Kayla's life around and she began training and working toward competition readiness. In 2019, Kayla and Pedro's efforts were rewarded when she won the *jūdō* World championships. In their preparation for the Olympic Games in London, Jimmy Pedro would often encourage her to be fearless, and today, Kayla has founded 'The Fearless Foundation', to help survivors of sexual abuse through sports and education.

Up to this point all my interviews had taken place in Japan, but this story had to be told. I contacted Kayla and Jimmy after the London Olympics and made arrangements to visit the Pedro's Judo Center.

Kayla Harrison, 2014

THE INTERVIEW

You won the World Championships and then the Gold Medal in
jūdō in the last Olympics in 2012. What keeps you going?
A lot of people question why I am continuing to fight because I won the world championships and I won the Gold medal in the Olympics and these were my two goals my whole life. But for me it's an inner drive and it's an inner purpose.

Actually what changed is that I've been injured for the last year and I had reconstructive knee surgery so for myself there's also that feeling of can I do it again? Can I go to the top of the mountain again? I also know from my experience now, that the top of the mountain is absolutely worth it. So all of the pain and sacrifice is worth it and that's what keeps me motivated.

And do you feel more pressure or less, as we approach the next
Olympics in Rio De Janeiro?
Winning the Olympics, that's something that can never be taken away from me. Even if I never win another match I'll always be Olympic champion. I'll always be World champion and I'll always be the first so there's no pressure in that sense. The pressure comes from within myself.

When you have an injury, when you have a major surgery, you really have to go back to the basics and you have to go back to putting one foot in front of the other. Right now that's where I am at and every day I do a little bit more than the day before and slowly but surely I'm going to come back. My goal is to be the best in the World again and to be number one in the World and obviously I want to win a World Championship again. I want to win the Olympics again. So I have got a long way to go to get there, but it's just really focusing on the big picture and realizing that I might have a bad practice or I might have a bad tournament, but as long as I do good on the day, thats what counts.

What changes have you made to your jūdō since the injury?
I think that even if even if I hadn't been injured I would have to make some changes. You can't do the same thing over and over again and expect your opponents to just let you get away with it. There was always going to be some adapting from this Olympics but because of my knee, things are changing in my workout program, and in the techniques I choose to focus on. This time around it's funny because before the Olympics I would train, fighting, fighting, fighting and brawling, but this time around I'm going to have to be a much smarter fighter. I need to go about things in a much more collected way if I'm going to be successful. So there's a lot to think about.

In my life, I feel like everything changes every four years and this time it's been no different. Now I have a big surgery to come back from and I haven't fought in over a year, so there's a lot to do, and Jimmy Pedro and his father are the ones that are going to help me get through it. You know they've always been there as my support system. They've always been the people that I can count on, not just in *jūdō* but outside of *jūdō* as well, so I'm very lucky to have them on my team.

This is why it's not hard to stay motivated right now because you know this is a completely different game to me now. I'm not the same athlete. I'm not showing up here at the Pedro *dōjō*, at the age of sixteen with a lot of potential but no experience. Now I have the experience and we know I have the potential. But I have limitations and I have things that are in my way. I have new road blocks that I'm going to have to overcome.

When you are about to face an opponent is there a fight strategy?
Because there are so many competitions every year and because there are girls that you know are leaders in the pack, Jimmy and I do a lot of video reviews. We look at all of the fighters I'm going to fight and especially the ones that I have trouble with. A good example is the Hungarian competitor that I fought in the quarter finals of the Olympics, Abigél Joó. She had beaten me twice before and I had never beaten her. She's tall and she's a lefty, and she does use *uchimata* which just so happens to be my kryptonite (weakness). But Jimmy and I did a lot of video review and we talked about a strategy because we knew that I would most likely have to fight her in the Olympics if I made it to the quarterfinals. So we worked on this fight every single night and in practice here in the *dōjō*. Jimmy would have guys come out and just do a left-side *uchimata* to me, over and over again.

So yes, there is absolutely always a strategy but that's not to say that I go out there and I just stick with my strategy. I always like to have a set plan for my first exchange with an opponent. So for example, I know that if I go out against Mayra Aguilar (Brazilian *jūdōka* Champion) I know the first thing I'm going to do. It might not be that move every single time, but the very first exchange is important for me to win.

So you are looking for weaknesses in the opponent?
Absolutely, but I'm looking at more than just their weaknesses. I look at my own weaknesses and I figure out where I can get stronger because I can't control what they will do and what they changed before the fight, or how they have grown as an athlete. What I can control how I'm going to change and grow and adapt.

Kayla and coach Jimmy Pedro at Pedro Jūdō

What preparations do you make before a competition?

It's funny that you ask that, because I think that one of the things that sets myself apart from the girls in my division specifically, is my mental attitude towards competing. And I really inherited this from Jimmy Pedro. He and his father are big believers in positive thinking and visualization. I didn't really learn the power of visualization until after I had won the world championships. In 2008, I won the Junior World Championship and it was kind of just all right. I had won the Junior Worlds and it meant I could win at a World level. So I sort of expected in my mind, well after the Junior World Championships, now I should go on to win the Senior World championships. So in my mind I expected to go and win the World championships in 2009, and I didn't. In fact I lost pretty badly and I couldn't understand why that happened. I had trained right and I had prepared right. I did everything right, but I didn't win.

So I went back and I talked with Jimmy and he said, "Well did you visualize yourself winning? Do you think about winning? And I said, "yes I think about it of course. What do you mean? I think about it all the time." So Jimmy said, "but do you really think about it? Do you picture every single step? What it's going to take?" I said, "no not really." And he said "I want you to do that."

And so every day I would visualize myself winning the World Championships. I would visualize my breakfast that day. My weigh in and my warm up on my first match then my second match and then my third match and the semi final match and I would visualize all of it. Even the referee awarding me the match. Then hugging my coach Jimmy and hugging my family. I would picture all of it. In 2010 I won the World Championships and I realized then not only was visualization powerful, but it was a real tool that I could use. My brain had made a pathway so that the day that I showed up my body just knew what to do.

So it was that from 2010 until 2012, every night before I went to sleep I would visualize myself winning the Olympics. I would visualize the perfect day, the perfect match and the perfect moment. I would change opponents, so one night it would be the French girl, the next night it would be the Brazilian girl but I always pictured myself winning and I would smash the girl on the final match. Then I would hug Jimmy and I would see the American flag rise and hear the national anthem and I would feel the gold medal go around my neck.

By the time I got to the Olympic Games, I had done this so many times in my mind that it was like my body just knew what was going to happen. You know it was like athletes call them white moments or being in the zone. I could sense everyone around me was buzzing but I was just a calm, cool, in a collected bubble and I knew I was going to win.

What is your daily training routine?

Well we have two *jūdō* sessions a day. The morning session is a lot of drilling and a lot of technique. We do good warm up and we do a lot of *uchikomi* (repetition drills) and we do a lot of throws. We do a lot of *newaza* (ground technique) and a lot of transitioning, say from standing to the ground.

A big part of our *jūdō* is, firstly, the gripping. We really focus on where we put our hands on the *jūdōgi* (uniform) in order to win. The second part we focus on is *newaza* (ground technique) and Jimmy is very well known for his *newaza*, as well as a lot of my teammates. I won 50 percent of my matches at the Olympics with *newaza*. So we focus on not just *newaza* but the transition from standing to *newaza*. That's a big area where there's a lot of weakness in the rest of the world, so we really focus on that, and we practice it and we drill it and we drill it! Our session at night is mostly all sparring. Sometimes we do a little bit of learning but for the most part we do a lot of *randori* (free sparring). Before I moved to the Pedro's *dōjō*, you could say that I was terrible at *newaza*. And that would not be a false statement. But you know, seven years of getting pinned and arm-barred and choked by some of the best *newaza* specialists in the world has turned me into being pretty good at defense and pretty good at offense.

Has the popularity of MMA and Brazilian Jiu-Jitsu put more newaza into jūdō?

Well maybe. It's a possibility. I think that you know in this *dōjō*, we are not a school that focuses on MMA and we don't train MMA athletes here, but I think that a lot of gyms across our country do. I think more and more your see MMA gyms that have *jūdō* classes and boxing classes and have different classes where they probably do focus a lot on the *newaza* part of it. You can be a great wrestler but still get arm-barred. I think that's what's so great about *jūdō* for Mixed Martial Arts. You can not only stand up and fight, but you know how to win on the ground as well.

I think that there has been a big change in how much time referees will allow for *newaza* now. You know there used to be a time that if you didn't show progress on the ground, it would be '*Matte!*' From the referee. So you have to stand up and start back over. But now they are letting you work. *Newaza* is a part of *jūdō* and they're allowing you to show it or showcase that part.

You know the difference between *newaza* and *tachiwaza* (standing technique) is that if you throw the opponent, it's a half a second but sometimes it takes over a minute to get a pin or to really get sync on an arm-bar, so it's exciting to see that because *newaza* is something we do focus on here. I would add that I think more matches are going to be won on the mat than won standing. Especially because of the new rules. It's getting harder and harder to throw someone for *ippon* (winning point). So more often you're going to have to win on the mat.

You were sexually abused at a young age by your jūdō coach – how did you find the courage to move forward with your life?

This may sound strange, but I don't think that it was courage. I think that it was my survival instincts kicking in. It got to the point where I hated myself. And I hated my family and I hated *jūdō* and I couldn't look in the mirror anymore. I knew that if I didn't say something, I was either going to run away, or I was going to kill myself. And I'm just really thankful that I did say something, and that I was believed. You know it's really scary to come forward with that truth, and I can't imagine what it would have felt like to come forward with that truth and have no one believe

Kayla reliving the trauma of being a victim of
sexual abuse by her first *jūdō* coach

me. So I am really lucky that things turned out the way they did.

So about a month after I had told my mother what had been happening to me, she immediately pressed charges and the FBI got involved. During that time I was a mess. And my mother understood that if I didn't have something to get out of bed for in the morning, that she was really afraid she was going to lose me.

She made a tough decision to get me back into *jūdō* and she really took a leap of faith and trust in Jimmy Pedro and his father with my care. So during this time, I moved up here to Wakefield, Massachusetts and I lived in the athletes house which was less than a mile away from the *dōjō*. *Jūdō* is what saved my life! The Pedro's and *jūdō* have changed my life. They saved my life! I can honestly say that if it weren't for this sport and if it weren't for this *jūdō* club and this family, it's scary to think about where I might have ended up. You can ask anyone who was here at that time. There wasn't a day that went by that I wasn't on this mat crying. But *jūdō* made me mentally tough and helped me to survive and thrive. I faced it head on and I had the support of my team mates and the support of my coaches and the support of my family and I trusted that nothing bad was going to happen to me on this mat. It's because of this that I was able to come full circle and in fact, become Olympic champion, which if you had seen me at sixteen you never would have thought possible.

What advise would you give to victims of abusive relationships?

Well I'm sure that there are a lot of stories that we don't know about, because unfortunately it is something that is still very much a taboo in the world and especially in our society. It's something that people don't want to think about or hear about but it does happen all the time. You know, one in 6 boys and one in 4 girls will be sexually abused before their eighteenth birthday. That mountain that we're talking about is something that I look back on now and you know, I have no sadness in my heart anymore. I have nothing but joy. Because it was a struggle, and there were days when I wanted to quit and there were days when I hit rock bottom and words cannot even begin to describe it. There were days when I didn't get out of bed, let alone brush my hair or my teeth or come to train.

Now, after the recent injury, I'm kind of back to the same place in a much smaller way. I'm just putting one foot in front of the other and that's what I did then and it got me to where I am now. That's kind of my message always to the kids and to the people in a bad situation. If anyone hears my story and that if you put one foot in front of the other, one step at a time and surround yourself with people who believe in you, then eventually you're going to believe in yourself again. And when you believe in yourself anything is possible. I really mean anything. I am living proof of that.

You know if I were talking to a victim now I wouldn't I wouldn't change anything in that sentence. I would say that I know what you're going through right now and I know what it feels like. You feel you will never be happy again. But there is a light at the end of the tunnel and a rainbow after the rain. There is a shiny gold medal at the end of all this pain, if you can just bring yourself to talk about it or tell someone. To get help. There are people who will listen, and there are people who will believe in you. You have just got to be strong enough to find it.

I am now in the process of starting a foundation. You know, I came out with my story publicly, shortly before the Olympics. After winning the Olympics I was just inundated with organizations who wanted me to come speak or share my story or help them. It really was amazing and it still is to this day. There's no feeling like being able to reach out and help someone and tell them that there is a light at the end of the tunnel. But I can't be everywhere at once and what I found through all my travels is there are a lot of really great organizations doing amazing things, but at a small scale. At a regional or local level or a state level. I found there is no

The final second when Kayla Harrison wins the Olympic Gold medal

"Live Strong" for survivors of sexual abuse and no easy place where you can go and donate time or money in an effort to ending this epidemic.

That's what I want my foundation to be. I want it to out last me and outlive me. So one of the things that I'm doing is working on a book with a psychologist. To sort of use my story as a teaching tool. We are going to use my story to say, "this is what you're feeling right now, and this is what it looks like when someone you care about, who is close to you, takes advantage of you."

There is all this material on "stranger danger" and "say no to drugs" and bullying and alcohol but there is nothing that tells our kids "this is what it looks like when someone you love or care about, takes advantage of you." So I want to be in your kids seventh grade health class and I want them to have to read about it, and talk about it and learn about it.

This leads me to the question, what has jūdō given to you?

Well I think that you're looking at it you know. Just what martial arts can do. When I was 16 years old I couldn't look people in the eyes and I wore sweatpants everywhere! I mumbled a lot and I had no confidence. I had no self worth, and with or without a gold medal, I can honestly say that *jūdō* gave me that confidence long before I was a world champion. Long before I was an Olympic champion. Now I'm a strong confident young woman who can look you in the eye and have a real conversation with you about real things and that would not have been possible for me without *jūdō*.

Martial arts brings out the best in you absolutely. It just instills so many values that you're learning, and you don't even realize you're learning at the time. You know these kids (on the *dōjō* mat) are learning all about discipline and all about respecting others and all about what it means to really do your very best and they don't even know it! To them, they're just having *jūdō* practice and having fun. What's so amazing to me about martial arts is that it really is about "Mind and body." It's your whole life and your whole being and you're not just getting your body stronger, you're getting your mind strong and you're learning good values and learning good morals. In my opinion training in martial arts is absolutely the best for teaching you perseverance. You know how hard it is to get thrown and then have to get back up and do it again and again and again!

Can you take me through your Olympic jūdō final?
Jimmy Pedro and I always go through the same routine before a major fight. We have a breathing exercise that we do together before I walk out. So it's breathe in for 7, hold it for 2, then breathe out for 7. It's really just kind of to calm myself and center myself. Then you walk out into the arena and you have to stand right next to the person you're about to try and beat up (laughs). This part is always kind of a tense moment. But I remember feeling completely prepared in the Olympics. I just felt like I was ready. You can see I was ready to go!

When I grabbed her *jūdōgi* I felt extremely confident. I felt like I was in better shape. I felt like I was more prepared. I felt like this is going to be my match as long as I didn't do something crazy to screw it up, that I was going to win. So I scored the first point and I felt good, but my goal was to stay on the offense and continue to attack and continue to just wear her down. Then I came in for a move and I was down on the ground and I had continuation from the ground but really I was just trying to get on the ground so I can Pin her or choke her. They scored it and then they went back to look at it and took the point away.

You know I wasn't very phased by that happening. I was sure that they were going to take the point away honestly. The only concern I had, is that I had grabbed her legs after I hit the mat so I was like, "oh gosh I hope they're not going to disqualify me at the Olympic Games!" That was just a flash of that but then I was like no, lets keep going and stick to the game plan. Continue, continue, continue and pressure, pressure, pressure! And that was really the game plan the whole time. To go out and just work, work, work.

Jimmy is at the match side, and he's telling me along the way maybe where to grab or what to do or don't do. My opponent is big at counters, so once I was up a point, the need to turn my back became less. I didn't need to turn my back as much, and the less I turn my back, is the less chance of getting countered. Then I score second point, and with this point, there's only a minute left in the match and now it's time to get on my bike. I went into a much more cautious mode, whereas before I was just sort of attack, attack, attack. So before the second point I was going full steam ahead, but then it was oh my gosh, there's 56 seconds left in the finals of the Olympic Games! Play smart! Play smart! Play smart! I hear Jimmy telling me "grip, circle move! Grip, circle, move!" Then I hear him say "don't turn your back again! You don't need to turn your back!"

I specifically remember at one point, and there's probably 30 seconds left in the match and I hear, "Kayla…. Kayla Harrison!" And I look over at Jimmy and he's shouting. "You will win this match if you play smart! You will be Olympic champion!" And I'm thinking "okay play smart. What does that mean? What does he mean play smart?" I think that if Jimmy could have crawled out on to that mat he would have tried to win it for me. So then I started to circle - grip - circle - move, until the end.

And what were your feelings the moment you realize you have won the Olympic Gold medal?

Honestly in that moment, it was a reflection of that climb that we talked about earlier. The ups and the downs. The highs and the lows. Every match and every training session. Every bruise and you know every bruise on your body. Every medal that I had won and every tournament I had fought in and all the training camps I had gone to. It was just kind of like, we did it, we did it! It's all worth it! In that moment it was all worth it.

You know how much I wanted her to win that day? I wanted her to win more than anything that day. She had sacrificed so much!

17.

Jimmy Pedro

USA NATIONAL JŪDŌ COACH

Jimmy Pedro Sensei, 2014

THE INTERVIEW

What is your involvement with jūdō Federations?

I am the national coach for USA *jūdō* and was the Olympic coach in 2012, and as such I attend all of the international competitions. I am a part of the IJF coaching commission, so when new rules come out or changes in rules, I give my input as to what I think is correct or what I don't think it's correct. All the coaches collectively have their input as a coaching group, and this is better for the sport. We also work with the referees on the implications of the changes in the rules.

In 2012 USA jūdō had one of their best Olympics while Japan suffered their worst. Any thoughts on this?

Yes, there was a reason for that. The USA team was ready to fight and that process started back in 2005 with selecting the 20 most talented kids in America. Like Kayla, who we groomed for success from when she was 15 years old. USA *jūdō* and myself and one or two others, got together and went through the national roster of all the young kids coming up to see which had the potential, that eight years from now would be on the podium in London. I was sick of the U.S. being the laughing stock of

the *jūdō* world. I remember we were in Italy at the championships, and I said to the team, "I was champion for one reason, I outworked everybody. I expect all of you to be the first on the mat and the last one to leave. When you're on this mat you don't go off for any reason. You're going to do every round and unless an ambulance takes you out of here. I want you on the mat training, because it takes hard work to win". All those kids stayed in the sport for all those years and five made the Olympic team and the others maybe barely missed out.

Now we've got three or four athletes that are at World level. So we need to keep them in the sport for the next four years and we will have more chances at a medal but also bring up others who could follow them, because our champions are not just great competitors, but great role models. They do the right things, they work hard and they're personable. They give back.

***I talked to a Japanese jūdō instructor who said their objective is
to win by ippon. Can you comment on this?***
My objective always in sport was to win. If I have to win through *newaza* (ground technique) then fine, I will win with *newaza*. If I have to win by strategy, then I win by strategy. If I can win by *ippon*, all the better because then I save myself for future matches but ultimately if I got to be World

champion I don't care how I got there (laughs). If the Japanese would rather not have a World Championship title unless it's winning by *ippon*, then thats their choice. I think winning and achieving your dreams and your goals is the ultimate objective, regardless of how you get there.

The truth is, we don't have the number of bodies to train with, and we don't have the financial resources that they do in Japan or in Brazil and in France and most of the other countries. So to think that I'm going to walk out on to the *jūdō* mat, grab a Japanese player with both hands and we're going to float around in his style of *jūdō*, well that's not to my benefit. I have to use my brain and my strategy, my skills to win.

But you know Kayla has her favorite techniques and you know she'll do should do thousands of repetitive techniques so it becomes instinctual. Every athlete has three, four or five techniques that they do all the time and that are their go to moves. The objective is to force your opponent into a situation where you're always in that position where you're executing your best or your favorite moves. The techniques you've drilled thousands of times.

How is the *jūdō* you teach compared to traditional *Kōdōkan jūdō?*

We have a system of *jūdō* here at the school, that is a curriculum that I've written and really based on my *jūdō*, and not necessarily *Kōdōkan jūdō*. It's competitive *jūdō*. I believe that if they learn the foundations at a young age, eventually when are young adults they'll have skills that would be good for competition. And it's based on my *jūdō* and so all my students can do the same techniques that I did when I competed. That's what our curriculum is based on, but of course a lot of the techniques come from *Kōdōkan jūdō*.

It is similar *jūdō* to what the Japanese are doing otherwise, but we have a real focus on the ground game, *newaza* techniques. The turn-over techniques for young students, how to control your opponent and how to roll your opponent. On the adult side we focus more on grip strategy, on the gripping side of the game and *jūdō* that works. *Jūdō* that's affective in competition. It's not just for *kata*, or for demonstrations. It's real *jūdō* I guess. We don't learn techniques just for the sake of saying "Hey we know all these techniques" or just for passing a test, but you can't use in a real situation. We're better off, having students focus on specific techniques that they can do exceptionally well. I'd rather have them know five techniques they can throw everybody with, rather than thirty tech-

> **"**
>
> *We don't learn techniques just for the sake of saying "Hey we know all these techniques". I'd rather have them know five techniques they can throw everybody with, rather than thirty techniques that they can't throw anybody with...*

niques that they can't throw anybody with.

Many schools of thought are that you teach a technique equally on both sides, say a right sided throw and a left sided throw. My philosophy is students then spend half their time doing left sided techniques and half the time on right sided techniques, but the problem is that a student who does 50-50, will never be better than somebody who spends 100 percent of their time on specific technique. That person theoretically is going to win because they're 100 percent stronger on the side they prefer.

Do you feel jūdō has suffered with recent rule changes?

It's been a little bit more difficult in these last four years due to the rule changes, with the inability for grips and inability to grab legs and defend yourself and the rules have changed quite a bit. You used to be able at least defend yourself by grabbing legs now you can't even touch legs. I think one of the reasons was the IJF deciding that it did not want the sport to look similar to wrestling, considering that the IOC needed to get rid of a certain number of sports in the Olympics. Personally I think *jūdō* back in 2004 and 2008 was dynamic. It was exciting. It was explosive. It was a fantastic sport. I feel now, with the new IJF rules for 2016 rules, *jūdō* is not what it used to be. It's slowed down the sport. It's much slower and less emphasis is put on gripping obviously, but they've also taken away a lot of the techniques that are in *Kōdōkan jūdō*. For example, you can no longer do *kata-guruma* and *te-guruma* (lit. shoulder wheel and hand wheel; leg grabs), and so the number of techniques that you can now do in *jūdō* is about half of what you were able to do.

This means that to me as a competitor who competed in the old generation compared to today, the sport is limiting. I don't have as many options technically. What ends up happening now, as a result of all the penalties that are given in the sport, is the person receiving the penalties, says "I may as well just throw caution to the wind and take a chance because I have no prayer of winning!" What happens is they end up getting thrown. They have to take a big risk. What you end up with, is not always the best *jūdōka* wins. It's whoever was more fortunate that day to get some good calls, and didn't have to get forced into doing something they didn't want to do.

Did the Federations think matches were too long for the public?
Yes, I think the thought process was that there's not enough *ippon*. Not enough spectacular throws. The goal was to increase the excitement. Make *jūdō* better for the audience or the television viewers. My rebuttal to that is, "what television viewers?" *Jūdō* is not seen other than briefly at the Olympic Games and maybe a few times in Europe for World championships or in Japan for the World championships. The rest of the world doesn't watch *jūdō* on TV. Only *jūdōka* watch Judo! For *jūdōka*, the matches are always exciting because we understand the sport.

Has the popularity of MMA affected jūdō?
I know that the folks in charge of the IJF absolutely abhor MMA. They want nothing to do with mixed martial arts. They view it as violent and without etiquette and without any class. Without any humanity or compassion. The people at the highest level of mixed martial arts are very nice guys. Very intelligent. Very classy and very respectful of each other. It's a good culture. They're doing what they're doing on television for the show of it. They're just professional athletes training three or four times a day to be the best in the sport. They're not trying to hurt the other guy but trying to win a contest to become a champion.

Can you talk about your preparations for Kayla Harrison?
I'd say that leading up to competitions, practice is pretty intense here. Typically it consists of warming up or conditioning exercises and then it's drilling hard and going over techniques with drills either standing or on the floor and then intense gripping techniques. We do some strategic gripping exercises with multiple opponents coming at you.

On strategy, the most obvious is to take away your opponent's strengths, their best technique. If you can shut this down and make them try to beat you with something else, then the chances are that they're not as good as their second technique, so you've got a better chance to beat them.

Jimmy and Kayla are focused just before the 2012 Olympic final

Most *jūdōka* in the world have good standing *waza*, good standing technique. So if you give everybody their favorite grip, a lot of people can execute their best throws with a favorite grip. So for example, Kayla talks about left *uchimata*, so typically I need my hand either here or on her back, to execute *uchimata*. So for Kayla's Olympic opponent, Abigail, this is her power hand, so Kayla's gripping strategy going into the Olympics was to take that power hand out of play. So for Abigail, if she can't put that hand on her uniform then essentially she can't do *uchimata* on Kayla, and can't score on her. So in the Olympic finals, Kayla shut that power arm down for most of the fight, and that meant she was able to get her offense going. And so that's part of the strategy. So here, my goal is to get that hand on her *jūdōgi* so I can throw her, but she takes it out, so now I have to go with plan B. I have to find a different way to beat Kayla. And she has a chance to get her offense going so the odds are in her favor to win the match.

Heading into the Olympics, Kayla was mentally ready to win. She convinced herself through visualization, through positive self talk right up to that final day at the Olympics. All day long, she was killer Harrison! Olympic champion! Nobody's beaten us today! It was working and she fed off of that energy. The positive energy that said, "I'm going to do it", and even though she hadn't done it yet, she just felt like it was going to happen. She believed it was going to happen and she went out and performed.

This is the visualization methods that Kayla talked about earlier?
Yes. I was an athlete and as an athlete myself, the positive self talk, the visualization was a big reason why I was so successful. But I didn't have that added component of somebody else building me up to be champion. So with Kayla that day I just wanted her to believe that it was possible. Today we're going to be Olympic champion. Kayla Harrison is going to be Olympic gold medalist today. It's going to happen! Let's start the day out right by going out there, take it to this Russian. Yes it's going to be a tough match but you can beat her so let's go get it, and in that first match she won it in the first minute. She came off the mat, I said "see I told you today's is our day."

On to the next one! Three matches the go. Two matches to go. All day it was getting this in her head, "is she tougher than you? Does she want more than you? You want to win this match? You want to win the Olympics? Is she going to stop you? Don't let her stop you! We're going to be Olympic champions and nothing's stopping you today!"

I mean she was ready then. "I'm going to be Olympic champion!" It's that excitement and that energy and that positivity that allows athletes to do it. If you don't believe it's possible, and you don't see it happen enough times, then when that day comes and you get there and you stop, and say "oh I'm trying to be the Olympic champion today" and you've never really thought about it, and not seen it happen, then it becomes still hoping for it to happen.

I believe Kayla saw it enough times in her brain, "I'm going to be Olympic champion, I'm going to be on the top of the podium." When she got to that day, what happened was those brain waves had already created that pathway. So she accepted it and just walked right through that tunnel and her body made it happen. And I believe that's the power of the mind. It had been there before and done it before. It was supposed to happen and it was believable so it became reality. It was not a dream.

I made a documentary with a UFC champion and he dropped a weight class for his return to competition. Your thoughts?
My mentality is that you don't cut a lot of weight and you don't diet and try to drop your weight drastically to get into a lower weight class. I believe that if you have the skill, and you have done the training that you're going to win regardless of what weight you fight at, as long as you're not giving up a lot of weight. You can't be small for a weight class and expect

to win but if you're naturally 165 pounds, then you should fight at 160.

Thinking this way allows the athlete to focus more on getting better as an athlete. When they come to training they're not worried about how much they weigh after practice or how much they're going to eat later or how much water they're putting into their system. They just come to practice, they train hard and they go home. They eat, they go to sleep, they get up to eat again and then train again.

Even now with Kayla after winning the 2012 Olympics, she came back here and she wanted to drop to 70 kilos. She wanted to drop down a weight class and she said the reason was to have a new challenge. She wanted to fight against new people and not face the same girl she competed against in the last Olympics. To Kayla it would be motivation and be a new set of challenges. And she did it a couple of times. She dropped down to that weight class, but I saw it was a constant struggle for her. She was always fighting herself and mentally it's draining. It makes you tired physically. The reality is, she's not as good at the lower weight class so when she came back, one of the things I said was, "You're fighting at 78! There's no talk of 70 kilos! We tried it and it's not going to work, so let's just focus on winning the next Olympics.

What is the most challenging aspect of getting to the top, of winning the finals of a competition?

You've heard of the saying talent is overrated? At least in America, too many talented kids go through the motions of trying to be champion without fully committing 100 percent to being champion. So a lot of talent gets wasted. You know I don't think Kayla Harrison was the most athletic young lady we had coming up through the ranks. She wasn't the most talented, but she was the one that had the right mind and the right heart. And she was willing to do the work to become a champion.

You look at Travis Stephens in our *dōjō*, again not the most technically superior athlete, but somebody who's willing to do the work and has the heart and mind of a champion. I think the biggest mistake people make is they see somebody who has a nice throw or flashy technique and they may look great but when push comes to shove, if that athletes not willing to do the work needed to be champion, I'd rather have another kid that's as tough as nails and mentally strong. And you know he's coach able, because I can teach the coach able kid, how to beat the flashy kid anytime.

So I think that's the biggest sin! What I see is those athletes that hang around for years and years, trying to chase a dream without fully committing themselves to what they've decided to do. Their heart and soul isn't it in every practice, so they're not truly trying to become the best they can. And yes I have that here my *dōjō* I see it. It's a sin.

Is it possible to change that person?

Yes it is. When Kayla first came to our *dōjō*, when she was 15 years old, I saw the struggle she was going through and I saw the tenacity with which she practiced and I saw how much she was willing to give as a person to win. So I made some phone calls to some people that I know and I said listen, "I need you to invest in this girl. And I need you to commit to sponsoring her to get to competitions. I promise you this will pay off in the end. Had those people not invested I couldn't have turned her into that athlete because she had nothing when she came here. She was 15 years old with no money. I gave her a job at the *dōjō* and I gave her a place to live. I give her a place with positivity, with my father and myself as role models. My dad really took a vested interest in Kayla in turning her mind around and making her strong again. You know, giving her some tough love and some lessons and some talks that snapped her out of what she was going through, and got her into a positive direction. So that's the help we were able to give her, but financially we needed help to get her to the next level of competition and to fund all of this. And as a result of what people are willing to do, they made America's first champion!

Just think about this. Kayla is Junior World champion in 2008. So Kayla proved that she could win at a junior level in 2008. Then in 2010 she shocked the whole World! Kayla won the World championships in Japan, at a time when the sport added two more people to each division. So 2010 Worlds was a much harder field than previous ones. That was monumental of course, and if you can win the World Championship you're clearly capable of winning the Olympics.

None of what I am talking about is easy. It takes a lot of effort. Just like my athletes I gave up a lot. I sacrificed a lot. I lived in Japan for six months. I've been there almost forty times in my life to train at different *dōjōs*. You're talking morning sessions of *jūdō* to evening sessions of *jūdō* and in between, weightlifting. Lots of hours of sacrificing with lots of train rides back and forth to *dōjōs*. I did that for years since I was 17 years old and I competed until I was 33 years old. I won my first medal in 1991, and I retired in 2004, so I was competing at the top level for 13 or 14 years.

Celebrating winning the 2012 Olympic gold medal in *jūdō*

I was pursuing the top of the podium and I didn't get there until 1999 when I won the World championships. Then the media talked about Jimmy Pedro to win the Olympics in 2000. So I was going into the Olympics as the number one guy in the World and all that pressure made me train too hard. I didn't have any downtime. I was just exhausted physically by the time the Olympics came around. I wanted it so bad and I was tired. I should have rested more and taken a break. And I think that's why I didn't win in Sydney. After that I had plans to retire. But as a champion, having your last match be a loss, is a real hard way to go out especially when you've got nothing at an Olympics. Just the feeling of being a loser. That's no way to end a career and that's why coming back was so sweet and the journey from 2003 until the Olympics in 2004, I enjoyed so much. This was because I had not done it for 2 straight years and I ended up being in the finals of every tournament I entered for the next two years. It was the last two years of my career and I took bronze at the Olympics so going out with a win and feeling like a champion was a lot better way to go!

I once asked a Japanese kendō master how he won a match and he said, "my spirit was bigger than my opponents." Any thoughts?
Absolutely, the energy was there for him. It's funny you say that about the Japanese because if you notice historically with the Japanese team, they are all about the gold medal. So when they get beat. They don't come back and fight through for bronze because their spirits broken so

they almost give up and don't finish the day well. The bronze medal to them is not good enough, "We lost and we don't accept defeat." Normally when you see Japanese, they don't take third place very often, unless they lose in the semi final and there's one match left. But if it's a hard road usually their spirit is broken, the dream is crushed.

Any expectations as you approached the 2012 Olympics?
We just needed Kayla to go out there and be on auto pilot to do what it is she does. I told her, "Go out there, be aggressive, be offensive, dominate every exchange, dominate every grip and don't take any needless chances that you don't need to take. The only way she can be beat you, is if you make a mistake, because if you play your solid *judō*, she can't stay in the match with you". So that was really the advice going into the final, do what you do best. Go fight and don't worry about anything else.

And then at the end it was, we've got this one, and you don't have to do anything. Just go out there, grab and stand, Don't do anything else. You've won the Olympics, so be smart! Just be smart. Shut the opponent down, control her. Don't take any chances now, the medals won. You've done the work. The only way Kayla can get beaten, is if the girl countered her. Don't commit to attacks or do anything needless.

Knowing what Kayla had been through, how did you feel?
It was an unbelievable moment! You know, you think that when you win and climb to the top of the podium for yourself, it's a great feeling because it's all about you, and you did it. But when you can go through it with someone else, together, as if both of you did it, and be an influential part, and know that you are part of that process and you helped make winning gold a reality, that's a memorable bond between two people.

When I won the World championships and Steve Cohen was the coach, it's the same. Every day, every year, on October 9th Steve emails me and he says thank you for that moment, and this is 14 or 15 years ago! He reminds me of how awesome that day was, because we share that bond. It's the same with Kayla. The Olympic final was just a memorable day that I'll never forget and it was so fulfilling because it couldn't happen to a nicer person or a more deserving person. I felt at the time when she won, I honestly felt as though it was destiny and that I wasn't supposed to win the Olympics because this young girl was going to come along in my life and I was going to get a chance to help her do it, and that was my destiny.

It feels like a story from a Hollywood movie?

It was awesome! If you think about where Kayla came from, and how low in life she was, and how she felt about herself? I would get phone calls, "Hey Kayla just flipped out!" - "What do you mean she flipped out?" - "She ran out and she jumped off the roof! Now we can't find her?" Kayla was 15 or 16 years old, and you get a call like that and it's 1:00am in the morning and the whole team is running around town trying to track her down and find her. We knew she can't call home because she has problems at home with family. Her home life stinks, so who does she go to? Where does a girl turn? She was lost and confused and felt crappy about herself.

It was definitely not normal you know. It was really my dad and myself that gave her two role models that she could follow and with two really different approaches. I think I am an affective communicator or positive communicator, and my dad's more like "tell it like it is and get your head on straight." So you need a kind of a combination of both of that. But yes, because it was such a hard road to get there, to the Olympics, it made it ever more meaningful.

When I watch the match I can see how much Kayla winning the gold medal meant to you?

You know how much I wanted her to win that day? I wanted her to win more than anything that day. She had sacrificed so much, but we had also invested so much as well. There's nobody that didn't want her to win that day more than me. She was America's sweetheart. Everybody was rooting for her, and you saw it in all the NBC interviews afterwards the television commentators. They ate that story up, because it's truly a remarkable heroic battle that she won. The demons that she had to fight in her head, along the way, made her even stronger.

> **"**
> *If we look at the practice of martial arts, the concept of budō, it is a way of perfecting oneself, of perfecting the individual and perfecting society*

18.
John Gage

KYŌSHI 7TH DAN, INT. NIHON JŪJUTSU

Chapter 18

INTRODUCTION

John Gage, *Kyōshi* 7th Dan, is one of the world's foremost martial arts masters of Japanese *jūjutsu*. He is the current head of the Nihon *jūjutsu* system and is the instructor at the US Embassy Judo Club in Tokyo. He is also a director of *Kokusai Budōin*, part of the International Martial Arts Federation.

In 1986, he moved to Japan in order to dedicate himself to the study of traditional Japanese martial arts. Like most foreigners arriving in Japan for the first time, John Gage was a little bewildered by the choices he needed to make to survive in Tokyo.

Beside his small suitcase of clothes, he had a letter of introduction to a martial arts master, Shizuya Satō Sensei, who was born in 1929. Satō Sensei joined the *Kōdōkan* shortly after the war in 1948. At this time, Japan was under allied control with many

U.S. servicemen stationed in Japan and Satō Sensei found himself teaching *jūdō* and *jūjutsu* at the various U.S. military facilities around Tokyo. In 1953 he joined a number of Japan's top martial arts masters from *kendō, jūdō* and *karate*, in establishing the *Kokusai Budōin*, of the IMAF.

So it was that 1986, John Gage joined the US Embassy *Jūdō* Club in Tokyo, under the direction of Shizuya Satō Sensei. He also studied *aikidō*, joining the *aikidō* Yōshinkan Honbu-dōjō, under the direction of the famed Gōzō Shioda Sensei (1915 – 1994).

My interview with John Gage took place at the *Jūdō* Club *dōjō* in a building within the U.S. embassy compound located in Roppongi, one of Tokyo's liveliest neighborhoods and a favorite with expats and foreigners who like to wander the many bars and restaurants in the evening. Like all embassy compounds, access was very restricted and we made sure to bring our passports. At the gate we were questioned and searched by armed guards and finally allowed to continue to the embassy *dōjō*.

John Gage Sensei, 2015

THE INTERVIEW

Can you talk about how you got interested in the martial arts?
My first interest in Japanese martial arts comes from the culture and I was interested in Asian culture since I was quite young, around 11 or 12. I discovered Asian history and later I found that Japanese culture was fascinating, and very different to Western culture. I believe that martial arts is an extension of Japanese culture too.

If we look at the practice of martial arts and I mean the concept of *budō*, it is a way of perfecting oneself, of perfecting the individual and perfecting society as a result of the individuals increasing themselves both morally and physically. The idea of this type of study is unique to Japan and to some extent Korea and China. We don't find this combination of the physical, the moral and the mental state to such an extent in the western approach to these things.

Budō is a concept of a unified study that includes the physical aspects of training, the mental aspects that come with intensive training, meaning you have to really focus on what you're doing and then there's a moral aspect to it because we learn to treat our partners with great respect. We learn to value the members of our group within the *dōjō*, and the next step is that we take this respect outside of the *dōjō* to our family and to the immediate community and then the larger community.

Can you talk about your first visit to Japan?

I had decided I wanted to come to Japan early in life, probably by the time I was 14 and from this time, it was just a matter of figuring out how to go about it, and how to make it come true. When I reached the age of 24, a friend of mine contacted me and said "look there's a teaching position that I could recommend, it is teaching English as a second language. I'd be happy to introduce you, but you have to come to Japan to do it."

I knew this was an opportunity of a lifetime. So I came to Japan. I had a small suitcase and I had a letter of introduction and that was all I had. A month after I arrived, I received an appointment for a job interview and then I started working just outside of Tokyo.

How did you meet your martial arts sensei?

I arrived in Japan in 1986 with a letter of introduction to Satō Sensei. And this letter of introduction was written by someone that Satō Sensei trained with in the U.S. Armed Services here. He was part of the occupation forces in Japan between 1946 and 1953. This man's name was Walter Todd, and I knew him in the United States and trained with him.

He gave me a letter of introduction to Satō Sensei and so I called Satō Sensei on the phone and he said come to the *dōjō* next Saturday. I arrived at Satō's *dōjō* with the letter and Satō Sensei made me watch the class. After class, we went out for lunch and at the end of lunch, Satō Sensei said "You may be my student. Come on time and train hard and I'll see you next Wednesday."

That was the beginning of a twenty plus year of what I would call internship. Sato Sensei was famous for his strictness. He was famous for

John Gage Sensei teaching at the U.S. Embassy Dōjō, Tokyo

his honesty and was famous for his integrity and he was highly respected. Satō Sensei was surprisingly feared by many senior teachers who were his colleagues and had worked with him for many years because he was so strict. Essentially in the Embassy Dōjō I worked as his assistant for many years and it was my job to ensure that when he was out of town the correct training took place. We had regular training three times a week, and I was supposed to be here to make sure the *dōjō* was prepared and start the training. I had to make sure that everyone of us was doing things properly and that I was following Satō Sensei's footsteps along the way.

And the practice itself, with Satō Sensei, is it what you expected?
That's a wonderful question! When I arrived in Tokyo, at the Embassy Dōjō the majority of people were older than me and I thought "gosh I didn't come to Tokyo to train with a bunch of forty year old middle age people." Since then I've become past forty myself and I've changed my way of thinking. But at the time, I thought this is not what I came to Tokyo for, then after some time, I came to understand Satō Sensei's method of teaching. The techniques and the practice is accessible for everyone, and is in fact valuable for people of all ages.

I also had an opportunity to train at other *dōjō*s with younger people, in fact with people of all ages at *jūdō* clubs and *aikidō* clubs and so on. So I had the opportunity to train hard with people of all ages and sizes, both here at the Embassy *Dōjō* and other places. And having that chance to train hard in *jūdō*, having that chance to train hard in *aikidō*, gave me a chance to slow down a little and work on technique. That is one thing this particular *dōjō*, and this tradition, is that we focus on the techniques and how to apply them correctly. So with this understanding of applications in place, we begin to speed up and increase the intensity.

Is there anything particular with Satō Sensei's jūjutsu?

Nihon jūjutsu is in fact, a modern martial arts that is based on Shizuya Satō Sensei's own interpretation, as he was taught or trained by senior members of the *Kōdōkan jūdō*, who themselves had a background in ancient *jūjutsu* styles. So these older *Kōdōkan* teachers, such as Mifune and Nagaoka and the teachers of that generation had in fact trained as young men in *jūjutsu* and therefore, had a background in the practical side of the techniques not found in *jūdō* because of they were too dangerous.

Shizuya Satō Sensei studied with them, and among others. He also studied with Kenji Tomiki Sensei of *aikidō*, who was in fact, Morihei Ueshiba's first 8th dan protege. And though the techniques of Morihei Ueshiba Sensei and Kenji Tomiki Sensei appear quite different, they come from the same place. *Nihon jūjutsu* then we can say, is an amalgamation of the techniques of *jūdō* which are the training methodology, the techniques of *taihojutsu*, which is restraining people, and ancient techniques from ancient *jūjutsu* as well as a modernized method of *jūjutsu* that Kenji Tomiki Sensei was teaching.

So Satō Sensei took all this and concentrated on the fundamental aspects and created a system that is accessible for people of different ages and different abilities. A system that in fact can be used and acquired in just a couple of years. It is very efficient and it is very practical. I think it is one of the best things around.

Can you talk more about your teacher, Satō Sensei?

Mifune Sensei was one of the early great *jūdō* practitioners and in fact the people know him as Mifune Jūdan (10th *dan*). He is just the most amazing practitioner you can see his videos what have you. One of his main students was Kazuo Ito Sensei.

If you look at historical photos and publications from the *Kōdōkan*, you would often see Ito Sensei with Mifune Sensei. Ito Sensei was a wonderful man. The strictest instructor you would ever meet in your life and the only instructor more strict was Mifune Sensei.

Satō Sensei's father was a *shihan* instructor at the Tokyo Metropolitan Police and he was personal friends with Mifune and Nagaoka and other most senior Japanese instructors. Satō Sensei's father died quite young after the Second World War finished, and he said to his colleagues, "please take care of my son." And being his friends of course they said they would. As it came about, Mifune Sensei said to Ito Sensei, "You have a new son. His name is Shizuya Satō. Take care of him."

So, Ito Sensei was in fact a surrogate father for Satō Sensei, and that is our direct transmission, our lineage in the *jūdō* world.

Is it possible during *jūdō* practice that a *jūjutsu* technique can be applied unintentionally?

I have seen this sometimes and I can say that I do not remember anytime that I have been guilty of this. I think it's critical in training to have the discipline to be able to differentiate between technique. To say okay I'm training with a beginner now, and I have to adjust my technique to work with that level. If a student is at intermediate level then you can push them a little harder and if they are more advanced, you have more freedom in what you can do. To have this ability to adjust your own training gives one the control after sufficient practice, to add or remove techniques as you wish.

So this idea of training in *jūdō*, and a *jūjutsu* technique slipping out, would be indicative of someone who has not trained very long I would say. I would say that *jūdō* in fact, was designed to be the safest martial art. This is why in *jūdō*, striking is removed. In the *kata*, you have strikes but in the free practice you do not use strikes. The free practice is designed so the techniques work with the joints and not against them.

All of the techniques are used in such a way that the fall is designed to be safe. All of the *newaza*, the ground techniques, are designed so that you are face to face. This is the safest way to practice. The person who is being pinned has their back on the ground and this is a position of safety. So all of the techniques within *jūdō* were selected and have been continuously improved, in order to have a safe manner of practice.

Jūjutsu on the other hand, for the most part, the techniques that were left out of *jūdō* because of the danger. These technique are for practical self defense and in fact they are techniques that some would say, are an integral part of *jūdō*. That's can be a question we can discuss another day.

66

You know there is one redeeming aspect to the Japanese methodology of teaching. Their teaching methodology is actually a guided sense of self discovery... ideally.

In the U.S. a police officer used an improper choke that killed the suspect. Should police should be better trained in martial arts?
Well I would say that the police are in a particularly difficult position in the U.S. In many communities in particular, police are faced with an unknown quantity in terms of criminals. Criminals can be armed and they can be dangerously inclined. So where to draw the line in terms of protecting the individual who is to be arrested, while also protecting themselves. This is a very difficult point.

But I have to believe that being in better physical condition and having the practical training to subdue someone with minimal harm has got to be a benefit for everyone. Let me say I've known a number of law enforcement personnel who do follow that idea, and they do follow a regimen to be in shape and in fact practice on a regular basis in how to constrain people. But my experience is they are in the minority and there are numerous reasons for that. One of them is that in the U. S. in particular, you see police sit in a car all day on patrol and it is just not good for you. It's hard to stay in shape and sit in the car all day at the same time.

Will training in Japan help you reach a higher level?
Your question, is it necessary to live in Japan to train to a high level of skill is a very interesting question. Recently I attended a seminar in Strasbourg, France and we talked a great deal about this subject during our trip going over and coming back.

I think it's fair to say that there are many individuals who are of extraordinarily proficient caliber in numerous countries outside Japan. I would say in Europe within the *kendō*, *karate* and *jūdō* communities there are numerous people who are exceptional. In Iaido in some countries there are numerous people who have many years of experience and are absolutely professional and exemplary in their practice.

I would say that there is a rare aspect of the martial arts, one that is very difficult to precisely pin down and is very difficult to obtain outside of Japan however. This is related to decorum. And there is an aspect of the Japanese sitting in *seiza*. There's an aspect of the Japanese way of moving. There's an aspect of the Japanese correctness, that you can only get a taste for when you visit Japan. This is something that is difficult to find overseas. It is perhaps something difficult to find overseas in one 's practice but it's not impossible, but it's difficult. Coming to Japan maybe the best place to find that out. Is that essential? I'm not sure it is.

Japanese instructors offer little explanation, whereas outside Japan, instructors spend time explaining technique. Do you agree?
Well you know there is one redeeming aspect to the Japanese methodology of teaching. Their teaching methodology is actually a guided sense of self discovery... ideally. So traditionally in the Japanese teaching model, less is more. In the sense that if I simply give you everything you don't have to figure it out. The Japanese concept is if you dig the information out, then you own it physically. And that idea is in fact their goal. I'm not saying it's always the most efficient way to teach, or that it always works but when it does work, it is very powerful.

> " *Shōrinji kenpō was created with the objective of country building through people building. As the founder said, it was not created as a single style among budō*

19.
Tsunehiro Arai

8TH DAN, SHORINJI KEMPO FEDERATION

Chapter 19

INTRODUCTION

A year after the release of my documentary *The Zen Mind* in 2006, I began to think about the next project. I kept going back to the documentary series produced by the BBC (British Broadcasting Corporation) in 1983 called *The way of the Warrior*. One episode featured the martial art of *Shōrinji kenpō*. I was interested because it had so many more ingredients than a regular Japanese martial art, and I think I was influenced by my work in *The Zen Mind*.

First of all *Shōrinji kenpō* was essentially a campus style university combining education, religion (Buddhism) and martial arts. It's founder, Dōshin Sō, was a former military intelligence agent who lived in China in the 1930's and 1940's. He created *Shōrinji kenpō* based on his visit to the Shaolin Temple, where Buddhism and Kung fu come together. He was fascinated like so many of us, by the 'warrior monk'. After the end of the Second World War, Dōshin Sō established *Shōrinji kenpō* in 1947, in the small fishing town of Tadotsu on the island of Shikoku. The first training *dōjō* was very small at just five and a half tatami mats in size. I visited this *dōjō* and could not imagine more than six students training at anyone time. Nevertheless, *Shōrinji kenpō* soon flourished. His teachings

offered not only self defense but emphasized a spiritual philosophy based on Buddhist scriptures and above all else, a means to foster friendships and through them, a way to develop. *Shōrinji kenpō* was an immediate hit among the people who were suffering in defeat after the end of the Second World War. Today, the *Shōrinji kenpō* headquarters is a sprawling campus on the hillside overlooking the coastal town. It houses a large educational facility with classrooms, student dormitories, library, administrative offices, a Buddhist temple and three large *dōjō*. A tall bell-tower style building is now a museum, dedicated to the founder, who is referred to as Kaiso (lit. opening progenitor; founder).

I set about contacting Shorinji Kempo, and that's when I hit a brick wall. Over the next three years I tried every avenue to talk with the World Shorinji Kempo Organization (WSKO) but with little success. In 2009 I was traveling the breadth of Japan visiting with swordsmiths for the documentary, the Art of the Japanese Sword. I had not forgotten about *Shōrinji kenpō* and I let them know I was still interested in meeting with them. The next day I was contacted by *Shōrinji kenpō*. It took me completely by surprise. Their reply was not what I expected.

They had been considering my proposal with some thought, and some years! They said under normal circumstances they would be willing to move forward with my documentary. However, the WSKO had instituted a program to re-brand *Shōrinji kenpō* and change their logo, which is no small matter for an organization with about one million members. The *Shōrinji kenpō* logo, a *manji* or *swastika*, is a well known image used by Buddhist religions that had unfortunately become stigmatized due to it's appropriation by the Nazi party. A new mark incorporating twin circles (*sōen*), would replace the *manji* on *Shōrinji kenpō* buildings, uniforms and across all their media. They thanked me for my patience and asked that I approach them in one year, when the re-branding was complete.

Due to my commitments on other films it was three years before I was able to visit the World *Shōrinji kenpō* office in Tokyo to discuss the documentary. In 2014 WSKO agreed to be episode five of my *Warriors of Budo* series with certain conditions, including final edit approval, which I had never granted anyone before. This almost become my undoing when WSKO demanded many cuts to the movie, which included my visit to the Shaolin Temple to tell the founders story in China, a segment which I was especially proud of due to my close ties with Shaolin Temple.

By the time we agreed on the final edit, and made the changes, six months were added to the production and the *Shōrinji kenpō* episode had to be moved to the last episode of the *Warriors of Budo* series. We made the deadline to our distributors by a matter of days.

Tsunehiro Arai Sensei, 2015

THE INTERVIEW

Can you please introduce yourself?
My name is Tsunehiro Arai, and I am the president of the Shorinji Kempo Association. I am qualified as 8th *dan Dai-hanshi* in *Shōrinji kenpō*.

I graduated at the Nihon University, and started *Shōrinji kenpō* in the university club. After graduation, I was employed in the *honbu dōjō*. I entered on the spring of Showa 43 (1968), right on this same time when the spring *gasshuku* was taking place. The founder was still alive then. During the *gasshuku* (training camp) I attended, waking early at 6 am, and help doing the cleaning of the *dōjō* and other preparations, and of course during *Shōrinji kenpō* practice. It is a daily repetition of this lifestyle. There is also some administrative work that has to be done. Nowadays there is the Labor Standards Act, but back in those days we worked with *shugyō* (spiritual training) in mind so we did as if we were working 365 days a year, 24 hours per day, making as if there were no holidays. That is what we aimed for.

I think that by coming to this honbu *dōjō* I have been blessed with meeting senior students, *sensei*, also the junior students and companions. Really fantastic *sensei* and companions. A great number of them, and I think this has been great for my life. Because I was blessed by living in such an environment, I believe that it is our job to make sure that those who come after us like the junior students are also able to enjoy that.

Can you talk about the founding of Shōrinji kenpō ?

At first, the founder studied various styles in China, and of course he also did Japanese *budō*. When Japan lost the war the founder returned, he combined and added the education aspect in order to create an ideal teaching. This he named *Shōrinji kenpō*, and thus it started in Japan. It was established in October of the year *Shōwa* 22 (1947), here in the town of Tadotsu in Kagawa Prefecture. I am not exactly sure, but in China the founder learned *shōrin bujutsu* (lit. Shaolin martial technique), also known as *shōrin ken* (lit. Shaolin fist). For example *taikyokuken* (lit. fist of the Great Ultimate; *tai chi chuan*) is among this *shōrin bujutsu*. They are called the fist (*ken*) of this or the fist (*ken*) of that. So it is not that he brought *shōrin ken* just as it was here to Japan, but rather he collected several *shōrin bujutu* like *giwamon ken*, etc. We know that he learned them and came back to Japan.

Then, he added the element of formal education to it. Since he first studied the Song Shan Shaolin *kenpō*, he kept that name and called his original *Shōrinji kenpō* here in Japan. That is what I have heard. He created something new. Naturally, the names of the techniques were difficult to understand in Chinese, so in order for them to be easily understood, the founder made them into Japanese as original techniques with an element of formal education. In this way he transmitted or spread them.

The founder had a background of *kendō* and *jūdō* before the war. He

> **"**
> *I asked the founder, "Sensei, what is zen?" He replied, "It is to live every instant with our best effort." It is zen in motion, so one cannot be careless about the opponent...*

himself said that in his youth he aspired to become a *jūdō* instructor, and he traveled back and forth to Kobe for that purpose. Then he went to China and learned *shōrin bujutu* in their place of origin with Chinese martial art masters.

It must have been hard to establish a new martial art in Japan?
The founder reorganized and restructured those things he had learned in martial arts according to his personal experiences and made it into a way for human beings to live. In one part, *Shōrinji kenpō* is a *budō*, in the other part, it is a form of self-defense, in other part it is a combat sport. As a combat sport and a martial art, there is the transmission of the techniques but the way of transmitting it was created with a very clear objective. Facing defeat, postwar Japan was demoralized. How to be a model of how to live as a human being under these circumstances? How to make the young continue with hope? There has to be a way to live on as human beings. The technical method of *Shōrinji kenpō* was created to serve as the vehicle through which these things were transmitted to the youth.

Therefore, the objective was country-building through people-building. I think that in those days the idea was to rebuild a devastated Japan. *Shōrinji kenpō* was created with the objective of country-building through people-building. As the founder said, it was not created as a single style among *budō* or as a mere combat sport.

The teachings are mostly born from the personal experiences of the founder. To go along with that, he combined the fighting because human beings' spirit and body are not separate. As the body is cultivated, so must the spirit. That is the way it is being done. Today, we were doing the *gasshuku* and we asked for the university students to see that however strong or skillful they become with these techniques, they must equally increase their consideration and kindness towards others.

When the founder thought about which kind of human being he would try to cultivate, he realized that it must be peaceful, brave and self-confident people. People able to see not only after their own happiness, but who can strive for the happiness of others. This is what he started. *Shōrinji kenpō* was created to raise people who can think and work towards the idea of *Nakaba wa jiko no shiawase o, nakaba wa hito no shiawase o'* (lit. "One half for my own happiness, and one half for the happiness of others". Right before his passing, the founder always told us to return to the starting point. This starting point refers to the initial objective that the *Shōrinji kenpō* that the founder created in Japan. He asked us to comprehend this and to follow that path.

How different is Shōrinji kenpō from karate?
Looking from the outside, it may seem that it is only about kicking and punching and some people might even see it as indistinguishable from *karate*. Some avoiding or reverse techniques from *aikidō* can also be seem to be the same as those in *Shōrinji kenpō*. This kind of techniques from *Shōrinji kenpō*, *aikidō* and *jūjutsu* might all seem the same. The appearance of the uniform might be slightly different, but the content appears the same. However, once one tries them oneself, one realizes the differences in execution. It is hard to explain the particularities of techniques with words instead of direct experience. When it comes to our characteristics, there is the intent to attack, the use of pressure points, the method of healing the body, among other particularities. It is not only about how to react against certain attacks, but a comprehensive martial art teaching. In our case, the method is called *chōsoku* (lit. breath tuning), which means to prepare the breathing. In the *zen* context, it is performed for long periods of time in the form of *zazen* (sitting meditation). In our case, it is *dōzen* (meditation in motion), and therefore out time in sitting meditation is short. It is often said that for *zazen* to have any effect, it requires a minimum time of 15 minutes. In our case, we do it for around 5 minutes. Of course, if someone wants to do it for longer time he is welcome to do so.

What is the founders ideas on zen?
I have myself asked the founder regarding the teachings of *zen*. I asked the founder, "Sensei, what is *zen*?" He replied, "It is to live every instant with our best effort." It is *zen* in motion, so one cannot be careless about

the opponent. One has to fully focus as to the spiritually and mentally unify with the opponent. One must practice with earnestness not think in anything else and achieve metal/spiritual unity. This is why is it called *zen* in motion. In other words, *Shōrinji kenpō* is *zen* in motion.

I think that this is exactly what the founder meant when he said that *zen* is to live at its fullest in every instant. When one tries to do this constantly, as I have for more than 40 years now, one finds that it is very difficult. When heard, it seems easy "What, is it that simple? Just have to live giving my best?". However hard I have tried to do this every moment and every instant, the portion in which I have successfully done it is in fact very small. The lifetime that I have left might not be too much, but I think of it as a homework from the founder. I thing that I have nothing but to keep on trying to live every moment and every instant giving it my best effort.

There are other things such as the way to do the *chōsoku* (lit. breath preparation) but *Shōrinji kenpō* is more focused on the moving *zen*. Also when moving we must perform *chōsoku*. So this is the one we actually focus more on. I think that various ways to do it (meditation) are valid and they will grant various results. However, the way I have been taught and that we practice is the way according to *Shōrinji kenpō*, so why not do this one?

How does the education for students work?

There are two schools, one being a normal high school and the other a vocational school. Here in the *Shōrinji kenpō* Federation, the people who teach the academic lessons and the practical lesson are the same. In the high school the curriculum is somewhat predetermined. For example, there English as a compulsory subject, so there are also teachers specialized only in lessons. However, it is mostly based on people who teach both the academic courses as well as the technical practice. That is for the school. However *Shōrinji kenpō* is conformed as a group. This group includes the Zenrin Academy, the religious Kongōzen Head Temple, the Shorinji Kempo Federation and also the World Shorinji Kempo Federation. There is also the intellectual property entity Shorinji Kempo Unity. The union of all these conforms the *Shōrinji kenpō* group.

Do you allow free sparring in Shōrinji kenpō?

In our case, *kumite* is called *randori* (free sparring). In the past, all members practiced it but now it is limited to university level competitions according to the established rules that have been compiled. This is to avoid problems

Tsunehiro Arai Sensei teaching at the *Shōrinji kenpō honbu dōjō*

regarding safety. Only those people selected to participate can do so.

In the case of children, school and high school level students, they do not do competitions. Especially regarding younger kids at school, it is better to not have them fixated with winning and losing. Instruction to them is more focused towards how to live correctly, good manners, and courtesy. This is firmly taught. They are the ones with the highest potential so they can be raised richly. There is also the problem of injury. If practiced excessively, there is the risk of sport injuries in the body, so we have them do practice while checking frequently.

So even when the same techniques are practiced, it is taught to the kids which techniques must be avoided. Also, throws are done against the floor, so kids are allowed to roll the opponent onto the floor but it is forbidden for them to throw them forcefully to the floor.

Safety is priority at all times. Additionally, there is the emotional problem. It is easy to become such that one thinks that one must win. So competition is not allowed. As one becomes able to make decisions by oneself one is made to participate more and more in competitions.

What is the requirement to be an instructor outside Japan?
In the case of overseas, the minimum requirement to become an instructor is to 3rd *dan*. In Japan the minimum is 4th *dan*. Of course, not

only having the *dan* degree necessary makes one qualify as an instructor. When creating a club or becoming director of a club, there is a Special Course for Authorization which takes place here in the *honbu* or headquarters. Similarly, when somebody wants to become an instructor abroad, that country's respective federation makes such examinations and those approved are able to obtain instructor qualifications and teach.

There are various courses that overlap. The special concentrated courses have a duration of several days. In the case of the Shorinji Kempo Federation it takes 2 days, the Kongōzen Head Temple is 3 days. Besides that there are other conditions that need to be met and courses that must be taken. Once you are an instructor there are also special courses that one must attend. If the quality of the instructors fall and the number of practitioners grow, then the overall level will decrease so there has to be a continued control over the quality of instruction.

There are predetermined times in the year where the courses are scheduled. For example, here in the headquarters it is done from one month to another month. Sometimes it is done at Tokyo. Also, the World Federation takes opportunity to have them when there is a meeting overseas. This is the system which we have implemented.

What is your opinion on competitions in martial arts?

Modern Japanese *budō*, which is formed by nine *budō*, including ourselves, have competitions with the sole exception of *aikidō*. I think that the founder conceived *Shōrinji kenpō* with the fixated objective of people building, avoiding the sense of winning and losing as much as possible. If one asks oneself what is a *budō*, it can be seen that there is this element of people building. But wherever there is this element of victory and defeat, humans tends to move towards that direction.

Recently the Sochi Winter Olympic Games took place, and what I thought is that the Japanese medalist Mao Asada, even though she could not get the medal, she showed everyone that there is more than just victory and defeat. In our case it is the same. If a medal or prize is obtained, this is something limited to very few people. However, what about those who put so much effort but did not achieve that? Their effort is certainly not a wasted one. The effort for advancing towards a goal is a victory in itself. This is the way in which *Shōrinji kenpō* sees it. This is the feeling of not giving up. The effort put into something is more of an assets that getting a medal achievement. This way of thinking is something that we strive to teach.

How do martial arts and your concept for how to live work?

Now the university students *gasshuku* (training camp) is taking place, and all the students are really eager to move their bodies, but we need to have them sit and listen to lectures, they have to take the written examination or else they cannot take the practical examination, and so on. As *Shōrinji kenpō*, we also need to see how good is their understanding about various subjects.

I would like you to remember that normally, *budō* and *bujutsu* originated from self-defense. In our case of *Shōrinji kenpō*, it was created with other objectives. That is the most important thing. Country-building through the means of people-building. In order for humankind to be able to dwell in happiness in this earth, we must cooperate with each other. We must think about others. So *Shōrinji kenpō* was created in order to raise people who are able to follow this way.

The founder did not create *Shōrinji kenpō* in order to add one more school of martial arts to the group and act as an instructor. The objective is to construct an ideal society to live in. Even if it seems like a technique to fight others, it is not so. One offers one's own body and receive the pain for the sake of the other person's development. Our opponent is doing the same for use, so it is mutual. If one is able to feel the pain and the happiness that others do, they one can sympathize and reach for mutual development. That is the way in which *Shōrinji kenpō* thinks and that I would like you to remember. No fighting, but to cultivate people who can contribute towards society. If we can contribute even one person then we have been successful.

> **"**
> *The reason for its creation is not just as a martial art, but rather to use budō to express consideration and kindness towards others*

20.
Yūki Sō

PRESIDENT, WORLD SHORINJI KEMPO ORG.

Yūki Sō, 2015

THE INTERVIEW

Interview One 2015. Shorinji Kempo Headquarters, Japan

What is your role in the organization of Shōrinji kenpō?
I am the current *Shike* (leader) of the organization created in Japan called Shorinji kempo. *Shōrinji kenpō* is composed by five related groups. Currently, it is referred to as the Shorinji Kempo Group. I work as the President of this group. Thank you in advance.

What were the founders objectives in creating Shōrinji kenpō?
Shōrinji kenpō was created in Japan in 1947, and the reason for its creation is not just as a martial art, but rather to use Budo as a strong and sturdy mean to express consideration and kindness towards others. In Japan it is called *'jihishin'* (lit. benevolent heart). The purpose is to create an environment to promote and cultivate this virtue.

Since its initial creation, many people have joined and it has been more important to enjoy doing it rather than to define who is strong and who is weak. Practice is enjoyable and done in mutual cooperation. When it is done while enjoying, one feels like getting to know the other people and work together. Therefore the social environment be-

comes a very good one. Building partners who aid and help each other is achieved not only through technical practice, but also through common interaction. This is done on a daily basis, so I believe this is why the organization has grown so fast. The World Championships and other such events take place, and often people do not only fixate on the competition but also take their families together with them. They enjoy the reunion with friends and being able to spend time in the same place. I think that this enjoyment as a group is rather unusual in a *budō*.

I am the daughter of and I was raised by Dōshin Sō, so the things which my father held when creating *Shōrinji kenpō* such as building people, treating people considerately, and also being helpful to others, are the things I was brought up by. If this was not the case, me being his daughter, then *Shōrinji kenpō* would not be more than a show. This is why I have the compromise to always do things properly in that way. It is not only my opinion, but I think it can be shown in cases when it has been required.

Can you talk about the connection to the Shaolin Temple?
Yes. In recent years, the Shaolin Temple of Mount Song and *Shaolin Kung fu* have gained a lot of popularity worldwide and this has been a cause of frequent confusion. I am often asked if *Shōrinji kenpō* is a Chinese martial art. However, they are clearly different things. When my father Dōshin Sō was in China, he went to Mount Song. There, there is a place called *Byakue-den* (White Robe Palace) inside the temple that stands even today. Inside, there is a mural painting depicting

light-skinned monks and dark-skinned monks practicing martial arts techniques in the grounds of the Shaolin Temple of Mount Song. It looks like they are having am enjoyable time.

Seen this from the eyes of my father who had trained in traditional Japanese *budō*, the image he had of martial arts was different. He had been used to an environment that is very strict and where one must do a technique or face the consequence. He was shocked and impressed to see this depiction of training looking like it was enjoyable. He then realized than improving oneself was exactly this, being able to do it and enjoy it.

This was an idea he took when he later created *Shōrinji kenpō*. At that time he still had no intentions of doing so. However, when *kaiso* (founder) left China and returned to Japan after the war, he saw that we should work together and not against each other and cultivate consideration towards others and foster self-confidence and courage. He combined his Japanese *budō* experience and the Chinese *kung fu* he had learned and the result was *Shōrinji kenpō*.

This *budō* training is not concentrated on techniques, but rather on the way of undertaking training which should be just like he saw in that mural, based on mutual cooperation and aid. In the mural, the light-skinned monks are Chinese, and the dark-skinned ones are Indian. Their countries and customs were different, yet they could undergo this training together in such manner. This is connected to living in peace. My father was very impressed by this and it became a big example for him.

The development of the Chinese martial arts, the development of the Japanese *budō*, and the development of *Shōrinji kenpō* are all different. After the diplomatic relation between Japan and China normalized, exchange between both parts has been taking place. On those occasions, it is not about martial arts exchange, but cultural and spiritual. This is not exclusive to Japan, but during war nothing but blame and hatred is produced.

This is why after a war there is a strong feeling that this must not happen again. The strong feeling of not doing war again. By no means must war be waged and people exploited. In order to do this there has to be an environment where people collaborate and help each other. It is important to educate people in order to have such a society.

Is there still a connection with China today?
Yes, for this reason, we help Chinese exchange students to come study here, and we also take Japanese school, high school and university stu-

dents to China to do international exchange. This way they can get in contact with a different culture and become friends. Also, we built a school together with the Shaolin Temple near the temple at Mount Song. The children from that school are now studying in a very good environment, and we invite them to come to Japan sometimes. They are from agricultural communities so normally they would not have a chance to go abroad.

Also, we are often told by other countries that Japan has a problem with their education, but by doing these things they can also have direct contact with other cultures and find the good things about them. We would like this to continue always, so this is why we built that school. Exchange on university level takes place with the Zhengzhou University. Zhengzhou is name of the city where Mount Song is located.

In this big university there is a library called "Dōshin Sō Library". There are 23,000 books which are mainly about Japan studies, so they are used for students learning about Japan. Our exchange between Japan and China and the Shaolin Temple of Mount Song is not centered on martial arts, but rather in human resources. Chinese martial arts and *Shaolin kung fu* is of course based on *zen* as its basic principle, just as Bodhidharma transmitted from India to China. The Great Teacher Bodhidharma did *zazen* (sitting meditation) facing a wall for nine years. By doing this the body would become damaged, so he also cultivated his body by practicing the martial arts of India. By uniting the cultivation of the body and spirit one can really grow. This is a *zen* way of thinking.

This is the same way of thinking that has been passed on to us. The technique is developed by training, and the heart is cultivated through the way in which the training takes place. This goes together with academic education and teachings. Both the body and the mind must increase in balance. I think that this is a very important point in common that we have. Lately, the Chinese martial arts have been aiming to become an Olympic discipline and this has brought a worldwide expansion and popularization. Because of this there was a period where it was often confused with *Shōrinji kenpō* but now there is a commitment between us and Shaolin Temple of Mount Song to mutually respect our differences.

It is unusual for a woman to be head of a budō organization?
It has been 35 years since I took the place of my father. This 35 years have passed very quickly, but I do think that it was good for me to take his

The Buddhist greeting of *gasshō* is a characteristic of *Shōrinji kenpō*

place. My father did not leave behind monetary assets because he returned everything to the organization. He said that instead of monetary wealth, he would leave me a role and a job to do. Now I understand this very well. *Shōrinji kenpō* is not for the diffusion of *budō*, so we who are in the center of the organization must observe society intently, and if we detect that something is needed, there are many things which we can contribute.

I think that our role is to provide our society with help when the need arises. For example, Japan is currently facing the problem of low child birth and aging population. However, around last year, the word "super" was added to describe the phenomenon, meaning that the problem of low child birth and aging population has become drastically intense. If this continues this way Japan might collapse, as this inverted pyramid cannot hold itself. The elderly want to be of service and have vitality. No matter what age they become, they want to continue contributing to society as much as possible. If the young people would see this, they would also gain the feeling and urge to work hard following this example from the elderly. If there would be more young people like this then certainly more children would be born. However, now in Japan this connection is broken.

This is why we want to provide a *Shōrinji kenpō* which the elderly can also enjoy. We want to build a community in which mothers who seek counseling and assistance with raising their children can turn to. This is the kind of *Shōrinji kenpō* that we wish to be.

Yūki Sō

Nowadays in Japan, suicide among the young has increase. There are people who are exhausted from competing and comparing themselves to others. By building an environment different from that, they can acquire the strength to live. This is *Shōrinji kenpō*. The same for children. Now communication is completely done through the Internet. Direct communication with people is difficult. I think that we can build an environment where they can communicate facing a person while holding hands, to know the warmth of people, as well as the pain, cultivating their humanity. I welcome that with a *gasshō* (palms pressed together) salute. We want to continue growing and doing this not only Japan, but the entire World.

Can you explain the greeting in Shōrinji kenpō?

Our *gasshō* (palms pressed together salute), is made at the height of the face, and we look at the partners face. This is an important characteristic. In places where Buddhism is common such as Thailand, people do it this way in a very kind manner that makes one fill with joy. When I am greeting with this salute I become happy, and in *Shōrinji kenpō* we do it this way. Sometimes people get surprised. For us, this is one of the *kamae* (guard stance), and the way of thinking behind it is that we can see the partners eyes. In Japan, we often lower our heads when greeting, but when doing this we cannot see the eyes. It does not mean that we just stare at the person, but rather we focus wholeheartedly and see their eyes. This way we can manifest respect and courtesy, and we also present ourselves. This is the initial greeting between us and a partner. At the end, we do it with a feeling of gratitude, and we do *gasshō*. Most of the people say "Thank you very much" when they do the parting *gasshō*. This are words that Japanese people say very frequently, but when this words are spoken with deep feeling they are truly wonderful. This is very important.

How did Shōrinji kenpō spread outside Japan?

The Shorinji Kempo World Federation is called World Shorinji Kempo Organization, abbreviated as WSKO. When *Shōrinji kenpō* started spreading worldwide in the latter half of the ninety-sixties, the WSKO started spreading little by little. As I mentioned before, there are no instructors who have teaching *Shōrinji kenpō* as their occupation, so we did not issue and provide instructors.

It all grew by natural spontaneity. People who had learned *Shōrinji kenpō* somewhere then went back to their countries and taught, or people on trips abroad would start *Shōrinji kenpō* in a new country. This is how our expansion overseas all started. In Japan there are many high level degree holders, naturally, because it is the country where it was founded. However, in other countries, at the beginning there was only a few people. This means that there is a limit to how much one can teach.

Given this, it is natural that one wants to collaborate with others. What was born from that was the World Federation, WSKO. I think that the way in which it came to being is different from other sports or *budō*. Now we are present in thirty six countries. At given times, it has grown to be thirty seven or thirty eight, but because or political or conflicts they have become inactive. This is very heartbreaking. So currently it is thirty six countries.

Once the number of people grow within a country then a Federation can be formed. Once this happens, it becomes a registered member of WSKO. Once every four year a World Tournament takes place. Also, there are study and training courses and seminars yearly. Because of the number of available instructors, these training courses take place regionally every two years. The World Championships originally took place exclusively in Japan, but now it also alternately takes place in other countries. Last year it took place in Osaka, Japan. The next one four years later on 2017 will mark the 70th anniversary of the establishment of *Shōrinji kenpō*. On that occasion, the host country will be the United States.

When international tournaments take place it is also a chance to hold training courses. This is another interesting phenomenon in *Shōrinji kenpō*. Normally, it would be hard to come to Japan every year, so it would be expected that many countries have the request to have events in their own countries. However, in the case of *Shōrinji kenpō*, people request for events to take place in Japan more often. This is because there is an image of Japan as the mecca. Therefore, many people want to come to the place of origin and together with Japanese culture, they want to experience the real thing. There are many people who think like this. However, this time, the people from the United States of America are giving their best preparing for the 2017 World Championships. We want to support them in that.

Recently you changed Shorinji Kempo branding or mark?
In the year 2001, a new mark was created, and in 2004 it replaced the previous one. Before this, the *Shōrinji kenpō* mark was the *manji* (swastika).

This *manji* was often mistaken for the Nazi *hakenkreuz*. However, this is the symbol of Buddhism. In principle, the teachings are present in the *manji*. Heaven and earth, yin and yang, benevolence, the balance of strength and love, and so on. This was all represented by our previous mark. Unfortunately, as we grew globally, and because its resemblance to the Nazi *hakenkreuz*, it was legally banned in many countries. For this reason it could not be registered as our mark. We have the commitment to be active worldwide, so we wanted to have a mark that would be common for all places. This is our reason.

Now our mark has this shape, the background shield is the same as before, with four sides. The new *sōen* (twin circles) mark is created by rotating the *manji* infinitely. This way is becomes a circle. The twin-circle mark is the union of two of this. It would not be good to create a new mark without any meaning behind it, so giving its due importance to the *manji* mark and making it express infinite movement, the circles were created. This is why we chose the twin-circles mark.

How does martial arts and helping others work together?

As I mentioned before, *Shōrinji kenpō* is not about defining who is weaker and who is stronger, or about defeating an opponent. It is about becoming a person who is helpful to others. That is our original way of thinking. However, in order to be helpful to others, we must have enough strength ourselves. If one does not have wisdom, knowledge, and love, then one cannot do it. Therefore, first of all, '*jiko kakuritsu*' (self-establishment) is required. This means undergoing training to become stronger oneself. When one becomes able to do something like *Shōrinji kenpō* one becomes very happy, and we gain self-confidence. As self-confidence grows, courage also emerges. If we have courage, it will also be transmitted to others around us. This is the first step to becoming helpful.

When this happens people around us become happy, and this in turns makes us gain even more self-confidence. It is about repeating this cycle time after time. This is personal confirmation. Applying the strength acquired from personal confirmation for the sake of others is called '*jita kyōraku*' (mutual happiness between oneself and others). It means to collaborate in order to live happily. The basis for this cycle is the family.

When a child is born, the parents are very happy. This happiness must be transmitted to the child. In Japan, it is hard to transmit this feeling through speech. It is not well communicated so as a result the re-

> **" The fundamental point of the Shōrinji kenpō teachings is 'Nakaba wa jiko no shiawase o, nakaba wa hito no shiawase o' which means "Half for your own happiness and half for other people's happiness"**

lation between parents and children has become very thin. We think that this has become a big problem. Specially but no exclusively for Japan, if we are able to express thankfulness and tell the children what they provide to us, then they will also become able to express themselves like that.

In Japan there is a saying "raise your children while looking at the back of your parents" (means supporting your parents). This is the proper way. In order for adults to be shown this consideration, it is they who must change first. As a result the children will also change. It is not a matter of which is more important, strength or love. No matter how much love one feels or wants to manifest, if one has no strength then it is not possible to do it. Strength must be cultivated.

On the other hand, no matter how strong one may be, if there is no love then it becomes mere violence. In that case love must be cultivated. Both are important. It is not enough to give importance to our families, we must also be able to show our example. One must also see others not as opponents of enemies in battle, but rather as companions and family. It is family, so when someone needs us, we want to go right to them and help. When we are in need, there are people who come to aid us. Our way of thinking is creating and expanding an environment where this occurs.

So one must improve themselves in order to help others?
In other countries besides Japan, and of course also within Japan, there are many religions. There are the teachings of *Shōrinji kenpō* and also those of *Kongōzen*. In general terms, people form all over the world are learning the teachings of *Shōrinji kenpō*. The very fundamental point of the *Shōrinji kenpō* teachings is *'Nakaba wa jiko no shiawase o, nakaba wa hito no shiawase o'* which means "Half for your own happiness and half for other people's happiness."

When said in Japanese it is a easy to understand this teaching. How-

Yūki Sō awarding rank diplomas at the 2017 Shōrinji Kenpō World Takai in California. Photo: Jon Braeley

ever, it is often misunderstood in other languages. Half is our own matters, and half is other people's matters. Many people understand this as not thinking only about ourselves, but instead thinking about ourselves half of the time and about others the other half. However, in some countries where individuality is first, thinking about oneself is a given. With that understanding, in those cases it would not be necessary to say that one ought to think about oneself first. It would be sufficient to say that we should think about others.

However, the *Shōrinji kenpō* teaching that states "Half for your own happiness" does not mean this. It means that in order to care about others and society, one must first care and give importance to ourselves. Otherwise, one cannot do that for others. What does it mean to take care of oneself? Is means gaining self-confidence, courage, and potential to collaborate. It is cultivating this strength. "Half for your own happiness" means improving oneself.

We use ourselves for the sake of others, and when we become reliable to others and become a reason for other's happiness, then this becomes our own happiness too. And again, this pushes us to improve further, and so on. Anywhere you go, this teaching causes a deep impact. Also, in any place it is a virtue to consider others instead of only talking and thinking about oneself only. Without this way of thinking it would be impossible to have peace in society. Prioritizing the self, prioritizing the feeling of selfish victory, this will certainly not lead to peace. Even in the twenty-first century human kind continues to repeat the same mistakes. It think that it is about time for this to change. If we cannot really accept and respect our differences then peace will not be achieved.

We would like to promulgate this way of thinking starting with the ones closer to us like our friends and family. I think that both Japanese and people from other countries can sympathize with this. Now I said the ones closer to us, but in *Shōrinji kenpō* daily practice takes place in a *dōjō* and there are monthly events when volunteer activities are done. This is a usual practice for us. This way, we can actually test the body and spirit we have cultivated during practice contributing to society.

According to the feedback we receive we can acquire self-confidence and verify our progress. This is not only in Japan, it takes place in other countries as well. It happens often that because the techniques are so appealing some people focus too much on that aspect. We have this activities in order to avoid this.

Interview Two 2017. Shorinji Kempo World Takai, California U.S.

What is your message on this 70th anniversary year?
Let me say first that *Shōrinji kenpō* is not the organization to make the martial arts popular but develop the human resources through the martial arts practice. The true strength of the people is compassion with their kindness. *Kaiso* held this as the true strength value. I think it was very exceptional case that a lady inherited a founder's duty in this martial arts world. Since I was born, I was fostered by *Kaiso* in how we can create World peace and be richer in our daily life. I do believe that I am holding *Kaiso's* spirit as a part of my mind and body. Therefore, it is my mission and my duty, to pass his desire directly to other people, since I am his daughter.

How do you think Kaiso would react seeing this worldwide event to mark the anniversary?
I bet he would be very surprised at seeing today's event. It is 37 years since *Kaiso* passed away. It is 70th years anniversary this year which I found I have been in charge of this organization longer than *Kaiso*. At the early stage of my father, he was not so aggressive to expand *Shōrinji kenpō* overseas. It is because we could teach the martial technique from one to another by using *kata*. However, the teachings are not easy to be

understood directly without any modification since each country has its own different culture, religion, customs and language. *Kaiso* allowed the practice of *Shōrinji kenpō* to whoever had his or her passion proactively but he was not so aggressive to send the instructors and expand *Shōrinji kenpō* to overseas at all.

Even so, *Shōrinji kenpō* has become popular in more than forty different countries and *Kaiso* would have been very surprised at seeing what we have today on this World Taikai on this anniversary year.

In the United States martial art competitions are popular. Do you allow members to compete?

We, at *Shōrinji kenpō*, do not compare nor compete with others. I think it is our value to make you be able to do something you were not capable of doing before. It is quite important that you believe your own capabilities. When the people were born, everyone has a lot of capabilities. But it would be difficult that you find them by yourself nor someone often admire them.

Shōrinji kenpō has the education system not to compare nor compete with others and we support to make you do something you could not do with helping each other. Then, you may find your own capabilities which you were not aware of and you can have some confidence about yourself. This will be a big power to live for anyone in each country. There is one more thing. Because of non-competition, you can build a good relationship with others. I find at this event that there are many happy *kenshi* who could see each other again. It is my first time to see at a World Taikai that one of our Japanese *kenshi* (fighter) was crying and a foreign *kenshi* approached to hug and comfort her. I am very proud of this. I think it is one of *Shōrinji kenpō*'s best characteristics.

> **"**
> *From the start, the idea was to teach both philosophy and techniques as a way to develop people and foster friendships*

21.
Yoshitaka Suzuki

9TH DAN, WORLD SHORINJI KEMPO ORG.

Yoshitaka Suzuki, 2017

THE INTERVIEW

You are one of Kaiso's first students. How do feel on this 70th anniversary of Shōrinji kenpō?

Yes, this year is the 70th anniversary of the founding of *Shōrinji kenpō*. I was one of his students who worked for *Kaiso*. The main reason Dōshin Sō or Kaiso had for starting *Shōrinji kenpō*, what we call his intention, which to put it simply, was to raise better human beings. *Kaiso* always stressed people's character and the aim of his advice was peace. Really, he wanted to increase by even one those who would work toward making a more peaceful world. This requires benevolence, love, courage, and a sense of justice. He hoped to increase by even one those who embrace these principles and make the world better than it is now. However, this can't be done alone by oneself.

When *Kaiso* was young he did various sorts of work in China, and he learned that the belief to improve the world, when solely held by an individual, will come to nothing. The efforts of the many create the world we live in. Without pooled effort human society will not improve. This belief was strong. In any case, improving individuals aside, there's the forming of friendships aspect.

Improving individuals, fostering friendships, this is the way to improve things and make an ideal world. These were the core thoughts. For 33 years, from its founding in 1947 until his death in 1980, *Kaiso* untiringly promoted this vision.

When Kaiso founded Shōrinji kenpō, how different was it?

Although based on Chinese martial arts, the techniques in *Shōrinji kenpō* were completely new, completely different. From the start, the idea was to teach both philosophy and techniques as a way to develop people and foster friendships. Even so, the thought was not to immediately recruit practitioners. As I mentioned earlier, he started by preparing the 'field'. At the center of this 'field', the philosophy and techniques were of course there, but a supporting system was needed. What Dōshin Sō came up with was a curriculum. An example is the way of advancing to the techniques of a higher *kyū* or *dan* grading. Because you can do this, you can now do that. If you can't do this, you won't be able to do that. When you get so you can do this technique, you can go on to the next technique.

So Kaiso created a detailed training syllabus for Shōrinji kenpō?

Yes. For *kenshi* (lit. fistsmen; practitioners), naming a technique, we can use *kagite* (lit. hand hook) as an example. If one can't do *kagite*, one can't do *kotenuki* (lit. avoiding/removing the forearm) well. Knowing how to do *kagite*, one can do *kotenuki*. If one can do *kotenuki*, then one can move from *kotenuki* to *gyakugote* (lit. reverse forearm). In order to do *gyakugote* one must be able to do *kotenuki*. Once one can expertly do *gyakugote*, and

The original dōjō built by the founder is on the far left

only then, can one do high-level techniques such as the variant *ryūnage* (lit. dragon throw) followed by *ryūgatame* (lit. dragon immobilization). He created the curriculum and the textbook that lays out the order in which to progress.

In addition he stressed *kumite shutai* (lit. paired practice as core), working together in pairs, and wanting one's partner to get stronger as much as oneself. By practicing techniques on each other, both will get stronger and more skilled. All sorts of things were considered over the year in coming up with this system. Starting with no disciples he prepared and prepared, and created the field. With the field set he built the bridge to welcome people.

Do you remember the first dōjō?

Yes I do. At the very beginning, practice was conducted in an extremely small five and a half *tatami* mat *dōjō*. From the start, connecting people and expanding circles of friendship was the intention in improving individuals. He prepared that small five and a half *tatami* mat *dōjō* as a '*juku*' (cram school) to greet everyone, including his new students.

Why is the slogan of the 70th anniversary year, 'Be the Bridge'?

The message for this year's 70th anniversary is "Be the Bridge." This means one should become the one who builds the "bridge" to connect to other individuals and groups. In 1947 when *Kaiso* began *Shōrinji kenpō* in a tiny *dōjō* it wasn't to build those bridges at the start. Before building

Today the *Shōrinji kenpō headquarters is a large campus*

a bridge, he created what he called a "field." The kind of field that makes one think, "I'd like to go there." So this was the groundwork in preparation to building bridges.

Meaning, first, came the teachings and then a path to raise people to be strong, kind, and intelligent. To do that he organized his thinking as a body of teachings. Also, to have courage. He also organized the teachings and re-imagined the techniques that he had learned in China to match the situation in Japanese.

With a bridge and the feeling it might lead to places one would want to go, one would attempt to cross. Unfortunately, there are valleys and large rivers, and it's not possible to just do that. And so, to cross to the other side some work has to be done. I believe the slogan "Be the Bridge" refers to this.

Once the preparatory work was completed, Kaiso went about building bridges. First with the people around him. Then others began to cross the bridge thinking things like, "They're up to something interesting" and "I'd like to see what's there." Those that crossed and found things interesting, felt a bit stronger than before, somehow different than before. Those thinking this way, little by little and individually, built bridges. And those people built other bridges.

As to bridges, there's not just one. Bridges have an end point and have obstacles to overcome. They also can be crossed in both directions. In any case, this building of bridges brought people together. In America now, for instance, people speak of bonding to refer to strong human

He prepared that small five and a half tatami mat dōjō as a 'juku' (cram school) to greet everyone, including his new students...

ties. In Japan we use the word '*kizuna* (bonding between people).' While these deep ties, *kizuna* or bonding, are extremely solid, there's a tendency to exclude those outside one's circle. In contrast, for example as several young American sociologists note, there are bridges without bonding relationships that sideline others. That is, building solid two- way bridges leads others to build bridges. That's the way relationships multiply. In Japanese this is described with the word '*en*' (Pratītyasamutpāda; dependent, also a 'predestined connection').

This concept is perhaps difficult to grasp for people unfamiliar with it, but it's a central idea in Buddhism. *Kaiso* utilized this '*en*' principle. He expanded the circle while building strong interpersonal connections. That's how he began. After that 33 years passed after *Kaiso* passed away. And, since *Kaiso's* death and the installation of General Secretary Yūki Sō, a further 37 years have gone by.

The path laid out by *Kaiso* and still followed today has existed for a total of 70 years. After 70 years of *Shōrinji kenpō* now is a good time to build new bridges. Through *Shōrinji kenpō* you can live more fully as you work to help others do the same. Half for oneself, half for the happiness of others. To grow the ranks of people with this purpose in mind, the message of the 70th anniversary became, "Be the Bridge."

And build bridges also. Quite a few bridges have been built already. Not only within Japan, *Shōrinji kenpō* has spread to around 40 countries. It's because bridges have been built among people that it has expanded as it has. It is necessary to once more review the foundation of these bridges. Have they deteriorated? Are they broken? Through this inspection we can make it so others join us. Secretary General Yūki Sō believes this. And this year, by constructing many new bridges, by increasing the number of life-enhancing fields, even by one, and assuring the current fields are truly attractive, it may be possible to improve more lives through *Shōrinji kenpō*, with the techniques that embody it, being an interesting way to be become stronger, kinder, and wiser. To bring in new people,the current fields should be reviewed to insure they are as they should be.

With this passion, it should be possible to build new bridges and make the current fields, our *dōjō*, even more attractive. And, by strengthening the bridges we build, greatly increase the number of new participants and allow us to grow. So this is the message behind "Be the Bridge" from Yūki Sō for our 70th anniversary.

Yoshitaka Suzuki

> *Since the Kaiso era we do not have changes in our technique themselves. However, there are some changes in how we teach...*

22.
Kazuhiro Kawashima

8TH DAN, WORLD SHORINJI KEMPO ORG.

Chapter 22
INTRODUCTION

Any anxiety that I harbored over whether the Shorinji Kempo organization liked my first *Shōrinji kenpō* documentary, disappeared two years later, when I received an invitation to document their 70th anniversary year in 2017. I was surprised considering the legal jockeying we went through to get final edit approval on the first movie.

Hiroshi Onaka, the instructor of the Northern California *Shōrinji kenpō* school contacted me. He speaks excellent English and explained the WSKO plans for their 70th anniversary World Taikai, to be held in San Mateo, about 30 minutes from San Francisco. I did not hesitate to say I would attend. I love San Francisco!

I agreed to film the week long *taikai* and travel a few months later to the headquarters in Japan, where celebrations would also be held. The *taikai* in California would bring instructors and students together from every corner of the World and promised to be a great opportunity to film study sessions and seminars. Fortunately I would have friends in San Mateo at the same time who could help me.

On the first day of the World Taikai I paid my respects to Yūki Sō, shortly after her opening speech and thanked her for the invitation to

Beating the *taiko* (drum) at the 2017 *Shōrinji kenpō World Takai*

be with *Shōrinji kenpō* again. At the end of her speech she said, "Let's have a fun *taikai*!" I was about to learn that she meant every word and to discover this was far more than a martial art event.

On the first day, we found a wonderful old English pub just minutes from the event, that became the *taikai* happy hour. Each evening we would be joined by instructors and students for a pint of '*Old Speckled Hen*' beer and talk about home, work and family or friends. Mid week all attendees and instructors attended a raucous barbecue that would have put a Miami Beach spring break party to shame. Throughout the week, I was made to feel like a close family member and I roamed around making new friends, almost forgetting I was there to film a documentary and record interviews. I was building new bridges.

Kazuhiro Kawashima Sensei, 2017

THE INTERVIEW

Can you describe your role at this World Taikai?
I am Kazuhiro Kawashima and I am responsible as the secretary of general at World Shorinji Kempo Organization and the chairman of Shorinji Kempo Federation for Shikoku region in Japan.

Can you describe the technique you were teaching today?
Today at the study session one, I was in charge for *gōhō* (strong/hard

Kazuhiro Kawashima

method) techniques for 6th *dan* and above. Since they are instructors who are all 6th *dan* and above, I taught the basic *gōhō* forms and its applications to instructors.

In *Shōrinji kenpō*, there are sole forms which is called *'tandoku enbu'* (solo martial demonstration) and this is one of basic forms. We also practice these forms in a pair and I taught how we can apply the changes from the basic forms.

Has the technique changed from when Kaiso was teaching?

Since the *Kaiso* era we do not have any changes in our technique themselves. However, there are some changes in how we teach. In the *Kaiso* era, rather than explaining in words, they just showed the technique and demonstrated what to do. Today we focus on teaching the principles and why a techniques can work. So to answer the question, I can say that nothing is changed in our techniques but except how to teach.

Can you explain the basic concepts of Shōrinji kenpō technique?

Shōrinji kenpō techniques are *'gōjū ittai'* (lit. unity of hardness and softness). In our techniques, there are both *gōhō* (strong/hard method) and *jūhō* (soft method). For *gōhō*, there is the five elements of *atemi* (striking the body). Location of *kyūsho* (vital points), *maai* (distance), *kakudo* (angle), *sokudo* (speed) and *kyojit su* (lit. emptiness and fullness; attack where openings appear). These are the elements of five *gōhō*.

In the case of *jūhō*, as I mentioned earlier there are some principles. I categorized the *jūhō* principles into nine; for instance, the 'S' shape,

Kazuhiro Kawashima Sensei at the 2017 *Shōrinji kenpō World Takai*

reversed and *tori* grappling. In the case of *tandoku enbu* (paired practice), before we make *enbu*, we need to practice through different processes such as the basic forms of *Shōrinji kenpō* like *hōkei* (lit. method forms; techniques, *kata*).

Then we move on to *un'yōhō* (lit. effective application method; confirmation of technique application), which is where we take the technique we have learned and practice with your partner. This teaches you '*maai*' or correct distance. Then it becomes *enbu*. Especially, the beginning of basics such as a stance and foot work are very important. If these basics are not solid, a form will be collapsing even if you could make some *enbu*. As I talked about earlier, it is important to deliver a technique accurately. A technique that includes *kyūsho* (vital points), must be applied correctly. The same with *maai*, in paired practice. When I teach, I make sure that we apply our techniques right.

What is your attitude to tournaments?

When we are young, we have a tendency to care about competition such as winning and losing. When I was young, I had such a motivation. In Japan, currently we have *taikai* for both high schools and colleges. I make sure that we should not end up with victory as the our achievement. I can understand they want to get a medal and an award when they are young but in the case of *Shōrinji kenpō*, that is not the goal. This is the point what I teach the young Japanese practitioners.

Zazen (sitting meditation) before practice, 2017 *Shōrinji kenpō World Taikai*
Photo: Jon Braeley

Does this apply to foreign students?

This is same in the overseas. For the overseas, the biggest concern for *Kaiso* was whether or not they could understand the essence of *Shōrinji kenpō*. That is the spirit not just only the techniques. The overseas instructors would follow this teaching. The purpose of *Shōrinji kenpō* is to foster the people who understand '*kenzen ichinyo*' (lit. oneness of fist and meditation; body and mind as one) and '*riki ai funi*' (lit. strength and love are not two; strength and love stand together). Then, I would make sure of teaching them not to be concerned with winning or losing in competition.

How does your Shōrinji kenpō change as you get older?

When you are young, it is necessary that you train hard. After getting older, you start losing the physical strength and endurance. But *Shōrinji kenpō* is a martial art that is a way for you to enjoy practicing a long time throughout your life. Same as in the overseas, I tell the foreign instructors that this is an important point when we teach.

I started *Shōrinji kenpō* when I was 16 years old; that is 47 years ago. You can easily find out my age. When I was 25, I had a chance to practice *Shōrinji kenpō* under the founder, Kaiso since I wanted. I could not imagine at all that I would teach *Shōrinji kenpō* like this not only in Japan but also in the overseas. Through practicing *Shōrinji kenpō*, I became to believe the possibility and never give up until the end. This belief supports myself in my life. I still remember that *Kaiso* used to told me not to give up until the end.

What is your goal at this World Taikai?

This 70th anniversary theme is "Be The Bridge" and this is an appealing theme. I would like to pass *Shōrinji kenpō* teachings onto the next generation not only in Japan but also in the overseas. The 70th anniversary World Taikai in California is a good way to meet foreign practitioners.

> **Kendō fights are not the matter of winning or losing, it is the matter of learning and living with the samurai spirit....**

23.
Jun Takeuchi

8TH DAN INTERNATIONAL KENDO FEDERATION

Chapter 23

INTRODUCTION

In 2003 I visited the offices of the Japan Kendo Federation, which is within walking distance (if you like to walk, that is), of the *Nippon Budōkan* in Tokyo. My purpose was to interview Jun Takeuchi who is responsible for the Kendo Federation's international division. The underlying theme of my interviews that year were not to discuss martial art technique or training methods or competition. I was looking for a common thread to unite all the martial arts by looking at their origins and how they changed over the centuries or decades to where we are now. As the popular phrase suggests, "If you want to see into the future, then you should look back into the past."

A few days after the interview, I met with Jun Takeuchi and his associate from the JKF, Ari Kurose, at the All Japan Kendo Championships at the *Budōkan*. I was excited to be filming the championships and before entering the arena, where the quarter finals were already underway, my two hosts wanted to present me with a *shinai (lit. bamboo saber; slit bamboo sword)*. So the three of us walked around the perimeter of the *Budōkan* looking at the *bōgu* (protective gear; kendō armor) on offer from the suppliers who had set up stalls. I was itching to start filming but of course, I could not refuse this kind offer. Eventually a *shinai* was selected

Jon Braeley with Jun Takeuchi and Ari Kurose at the 2003 All Japan Kendo Championships

and I thanked them both for the very gracious gift. As we walked away toward one of the entrances into the arena, Jun Takeuchi examined the *shinai* that I was holding, and declared that the *tsuba* (hand guard) was just not good enough. He held up the *shinai* to show the basic black plastic guard above the handle, "We must replace the *tsuba*!"

So back again we walked to the stalls, searching for a *tsuba* supplier. Now *tsuba* come in a wide assortment of colors and materials, and it seemed my hosts, Jun Takeuchi and Ari Kurose, did not take this lightly, carefully searching among a variety of guards. As my frustration increased, a new *tsuba* was finally selected, made with a hard resin and patterned in gold and brown, and was fitted to my *shinai*. I thanked them both for their kindness and the care they had given to my gift. After more bows, I turned and quickly made my way into the arena, just in time to start filming the semi-final matches.

Jun Takeuchi Sensei, 2003

THE INTERVIEW

Can you talk about the concept and beginning of kendō?
The English interpretation of *kendō* can be written as "The Way of the Sword". The Way of the Sword is the philosophy of *kendō* that Japanese *samurai* had learned from the ancient war using swords. And this philosophy of *kendō* has been the back bone of *kendō* practice ever since.

Because ancient *kendō* uses real swords, it was a deadly and horrific fight. It was the matter of one's life or death. The players were taking chances of one's life or death in *kendō*, either he dies for his weakness and mistake or his indefatigable spirit successfully carries him over the deadly fight.

The Japanese *samurai*'s wish was that if he has to die, his death must be beautiful to anyone's eyes. The *samurai* must have courage to die beautiful. If he should stay alive, live a proud life as *samurai* and he must leave behind nothing to be ashamed of. He always has to be prepared for death that could come anytime and unexpectedly. And, that is what we mean in *kendō* philosophy when we say, "The Way of the Sword".

In order to be prepared to end one's life, everything around the *samurai* - his daily life, his house and his clothing must be clean, well organized and well taken care of. In this way he can end his life without disgrace. This is also *kendō* philosophy.

And kendō emerged from this?

The swords that were developed in ancient Japan were replaced with the bamboo *shinai* to practice *kendō*, so no one has to die in a *kendō* fight. Thus, the *kendō* player must fight as if he is using a real sword and he must have the same *samurai* spirit. And that is the way of practice in *kendō* today. This has not changed.

There are four ways of an attack in *kendō*, that is, to score points. These are *men*, *kote*, *dō* and *tsuki*. When you have been hit by these attacks you will lose points but because of the bamboo *shinai*, there is no

Discussing sword technique (*kenjutsu*) at the Kendo
Federation offices. 2003

blood shed. There is no serious injury. The *kendō* is considered as one of
the sports these days and because of *shinai*, you do not die and can fight
repeatedly. But, the player should carry with them, and always remember the *samurai* spirit and practice *kendō* as if he is *samurai*.

Kendō matches are not only a matter of winning or losing, it is also
the matter of learning and living with the *samurai* spirit. *Kendō* is not
just a sport or a martial art, the basic philosophy of k*endō* is to be a good
human being.

Do you have advice for non-Japanese who start kendō practice?
I hope that the globalization of *kendō* is not only that of practicing *kendō*
techniques but learning about the *samurai* spirit. I want the world to
understand the *kendō* spirit.

In order to learn *samurai* life and their spirit, it is also important to
know the Japanese ancient history and let the world to know. There are
many Japanese history books written in the past. And, I think that we
should market old and newly written Japanese history books to the world.
There are also many Japanese history books that were translated into English by non-Japanese such as Americans and British. But I think we
should write books in English that need no translation so they can read
the original published in the wording of the writer.

A long time ago, there was a Japanese writer whose name is Nitobe
Inazō, who published a book in English, about *bushidō*, the English title
is "Soldier in Japan". He is Japanese, but he didn't publish in Japanese,

but in English instead.

My future target and effort is to introduce *kendō* all over the world, not only technique of *kendō* but the spirit.

How does this philosophy apply in a kendō competition?

In general, even using *shinai* in a fight, the player has fear of being hit. But he has to over come this feeling, and have the courage to fight without hesitation. If he was using a real sword, he can get killed, but he must not feel fear. Concentrate and clear your mind. You cannot fight thinking something else of your life. In order to reach this stage of the mind, you need long and hard practice. Through long and hard practice you can fight naturally with a clear mind.

That technique is called "*mu*" in *zen* Buddhism. Your mind is focused in fight and has no fear; you have no other thoughts and your mind is blank and clear. This is '*mu*', and, you will find that you can act very naturally. You learn '*mu*' from long extensive practices. There is no easy answer to learn '*mu*'. Learning the *kendō* spirit is a very long road and it was said that there is no end. In English we would say, "The training of *kendō* never ends."

And would this apply at school level?

It would be too difficult to teach small children the philosophy of *kendō*. Therefore, we teach small children how to hold the *shinai* and let the children enjoy a game of *kendō*. Praise the child if he won, encourage him if he lost, and let the children be interested in *kendō*. This is for elementary children.

For the children in Junior High, they are still too young, so we teach the basics of *kendō* techniques and also teach the fun of practicing *kendō*. In the meantime, we discuss about *samurai*, Japanese history and *samurai* spirit. For the older children in Senior High school, the practice is a little harder. And for the collage students, it gets even harder. We encourage reading Japanese history and teach to respect their opponents and their parents. Be considerate and kind to the opponent when you win. Think of the time you have lost and you were miserable. In this way, your spirit will be strong and make you respect other people.

What has kendō given you in your everyday life?

Many things. When you practice *kendō*, you learn to live a well regulated life. The practice starts very early morning each day and you have to practice after work or school again. You practice with various people; instructors, seniors and the young. All the players practice hard and sweat together for the same goals.

By practicing *kendō*, you will become healthier and improve your posture. When you have straight posture, the inside of your body is balanced and the stomach and lungs become stronger and healthier. From *kendō* practice you can learn to respect, be polite to seniors and become a proud citizen in your social life and in society.

> " *Kendō is a way of life as opposed to the techniques of death....*

24.
Yoshihiko Inoue

8TH DAN KENDŌ

Chapter 24

INTRODUCTION

Yoshihiko Inoue, *hanshi* 8th *dan*, is a legend among *kendō* practitioners around the World. His knowledge of *kendō* and of *budō* in general is vast. Inoue Sensei is one of those grand masters in *kendō* in the old traditional style. His quote on the practice of *kendō*, is often repeated, "*Kendō* is a way of life as opposed to the techniques of death."

Inoue Sensei's books on *kendō kata* are essential reading for all *kendō* enthusiasts. He was the author of '*Kendo Kata: Essence and Application*' among other titles. His teaching of the three forms of the *Nihon kendō kata*', are taught today in schools throughout Japan.

I was fortunate to meet with Inoue Sensei at the annual Kendo World Keiko-Kai that took place in the summer of 2012. Hosted by Kendo World Magazine and Alex Bennett, 7th *dan kendō*. This event features many of the top 8th *dan kendō* masters in Japan today. This was an opportunity to feature them in the *kendō* episode of the *Warriors of Budo* series. Kendo World Magazine is based in Tokyo and funded by the writers who willingly give their time to spread *kendō* around the World. How I wish similar publications existed for *karate* and other martial arts. It is unfortunate that politics and rivalry among the many schools and federations make this impossible. Kendo World truly does cross borders.

Yoshihiko Inoue teaching at the annual Kendo World Keiko-Kai, 2012

At the annual Kendo World Keiko-kai I was able to film a remarkable demonstration of the *Nihon kendō kata* by two female *kenshi*, (lit. swordsmen, swordwomen; *kendō* practitioner), and I am still in awe of how they avoided being cut by their swords.

Inoue Sensei was eighty seven years old at the time of our visit and though he showed great vigor during the Kendo World Keiko-kai, we kept our interview as short as possible. Sadly Inoue Sensei passed away a year later. He lived a long life in the practice of *kendō*, and able to give his wisdom on Japanese *budō* to so many.

Yoshihiko Inoue Sensei, 2012

THE INTERVIEW

Inoue Sensei can you talk a little about the history of kendō?

Kendō has undergone many changes. The *kendō* from the Heian period, the *kendō* from the Muromachi period, the *kendō* of the Kamakura period the *kendō* from the Edo period, the *kendō* from the Meiji period onwards. And then, from the 20th year of the Shōwa period (1945) onwards, the *kendō* after the defeat in the war. They are all different.

In Japan, from the Heian to the Muromachi period, during the age of the warring states, the *kendō* of those times had the purpose of defeating an opponent. The killing of an opponent using a *katana*. This was *kenjutsu*, the technique of the sword.

During the Edo period, a moral aspect was added to it, and thus the former *kenjutsu* became *kendō*. Around the beginning of the Meiji era, what once was called *kenjutsu* became what is called *kendō*, it transformed into a 'way.' It changed once again in the Taishō period, when it became more of a teaching tool.

In the Shōwa period, once again it became something used for war, meaning that its purpose was that of killing the opponent. And then later, after the defeat in the Second World War, in the year Shōwa 25th (1950) Japan declared to the world its abandonment of war. Therefore, there also is the *kendō* post declaration to the renunciation of war.

And why did these changes come about?

The main objective of *kendō* became the development of the human character. The development of the human character means that through the disciplined practice and the right mental attitude, one can make a contribution towards peace and prosperity for all humanity across the world, thus reflecting our humanity. This is what it means to develop the human character in *kendō*. Therefore, it became something that can contribute towards peace and prosperity in the world.

We just saw a beautiful demonstration of the three forms of Nihon Kendo Kata, can you comment on this kata?

First I shall tell you what the *kendō kata* (forms) are. They are the ideal appearance of the human being. It is not only that of Japanese people,

The Nihon Kendo Kata demonstration at Kendo World Keiko-Kai in the Nippon Budōkan, 2012. Photo: Jon Braeley

but for all of mankind. We must all carry on a correct way of living.

The first *kata*, called '*ipponme*', (lit. first one), represents the ability to enforce what we believe is correct, to expresses correctness. Then, the second *kata*, '*nihonme*', shows that the ability to enforce must not be used in every situation, but rather by the human heart, meaning to show mercy.

The first *kata* represents the human skill. The technique. The second *kata* represents the human heart, in other words, compassion and love. A person who lacks these cannot be called a human being. That is why in the second *kata* the opponent is not cut down to kill him. The third *kata* represents courage, which is yearned for by people all around the World. We all want courage, to be a human being who possesses courage. The *kata* which expresses this courage and bravery is the third *kata*, '*sanbonme*'. This is to have the courage to let one's opponent live.

Thus, the *kendō kata* is an expression of the human heart and spirit. These movements express the human heart. This is what *kendō kata* is. Likewise, from the fourth *kata* and onwards each of the kata progress as a determination of spirituality.

What are your thoughts on kendō as a sport?
Unfortunately, there are places outside of Japan, in foreign countries, where *kendō* is understood merely as striking each other with bamboo

> **66**
>
> *During the age of the warring states, the kendō
> of those times had the purpose of defeating an
> opponent. The killing of an opponent using a
> katana...*

shinai. Nowadays, the Japanese people also have this understanding. Originally, the objective of *kendō* was a matter of life or death with the *katana*. The exchanging of blows with the *shinai* is a sport! It is not *budō*!

There is this difference. And this is not a difference between Japan and the other countries, since the excessive sportification of *kendō* is common for all today. *Kendō* is the mutual improvement and development of the human nature.

This is the cultivation of *kendō*, the practice of how to embrace humanity. In the west, Christianity states that mankind was created by god in close resemblance to himself, his image. The human being according to the Japanese people is not unlike every other creature or plant upon the earth, they are all the same. The human being and the grass that grows nearby or the spider that roams around are all gods.

In this sense, that is why if one can come to comprehend this through *kendō*, everyday life becomes resembling that of the gods. This is the result of the training of *kendō*. If this knowledge is acquired then life and society are so enjoyable, without mutual hatred. This is *kendō*.

On the question of *kendō* being a sport, if one competes, regardless of who they are, one wants to win. This is simply human nature. One wants to win, but in human beings, including one's opponent, there exists a god. If one comprehends this, then it is not a matter of doing whatever it takes in order to win. One's conduct will unconsciously not allow us to achieve the highest objective of *kendō*.

So this is what I mean by the present day excessive sportification, where too much care is put into the final result and all that matters is winning. I believe that this must be reformed.

> **"**
> *Kendō is profound. The 64-65*
> *year old me still doesn't get it.*
> *In kendō, there are people who*
> *are 75, 80, 85, 90, and even*
> *over 90 years old and they are*
> *doing kendō*

25.
Hiroshi Ozawa
8TH DAN KENDŌ, KŌBUKAN DŌJŌ

Chapter 25
INTRODUCTION

Hiroshi Ozawa Sensei, *kendō kyōshi* 8th *dan*, is one of Japan's leading *kendō* masters, and is known around the World for his groundbreaking book, *Kendo, The Definitive Guide*. It is one of the most popular *kendō* books in the English language. Hiroshi Ozawa Sensei comes from a long line of very highly accomplished swordmasters, his grandfather being Aijirō Ozawa (1864-1950), a politician and *kendō hanshi* (lit. model respected person; highest rank). Aijirō Ozawa built the first 'family *dōjō*, the Eishingijuku ('Progress and fulfillment' private school) *Kōbukan* (Hall of Encouragement of military valor) *dōjō* in Saitama, a suburb of Tokyo in 1891. The family *dōjō* today is in Nakano Ward, and is usually referred to simply as the *Kōbukan*.

I was interested in Ozawa sensei because he is a highly regarded *kendō* master that believes that the study of modern *kendō* should include classical swordsmanship, or *koryū*. This is the sword techniques of the *samurai* or *kenjutsu*. I had agreed with Ozawa Sensei to make two visits to his *dōjō*, the *Kōbukan*. The first visit for the *koryū* class where the practice would be *Mizoguchi-ha Ittō-ryū* school of swordsmanship and then a second visit to the *Kōbukan*, where Ozawa sensei will teach *kendō*.

When I visited the *Kōbukan* to film the *koryū* class, one of Ozawa Sen-

Ozawa Sensei and Trevor Chapman (right) in the *Kōbukan*

sei's favorite students, Trevor Chapman was visiting from Nottingham in the United Kingdom, which happens to be near where I was born. Trevor met Ozawa Sensei in 1990 and immediately set about becoming one of his regular students. His first visit to the *Kōbukan* was four years later and Trevor has visited every since year. I interviewed Trevor during a break in the *koryū* class and asked him how he juggles his family life with traveling to Japan, he said "My wife Sharon is very supportive. She understands how much *kendō* means to me." He added, "*Budō* has given me a lot of insight in how to challenge things in my own life and how to continue going even if you are not successful the first time. There is an old saying that *kendō* makes this possible, "fall down seven times… get up eight times.""

Trevor was in Tokyo to take the important 6th *dan* examination at his fourteenth attempt. This is not usual in *kendō*, where passing most tests at your first attempt is very rare. During our conversation he told me that with the high cost of Tokyo hotels, Ozawa Sensei was kind enough to let him sleep in the *Kōbukan* each time he visits. He said, "Oh it's fine to sleep in the *Kōbukan*. I wake up early at 6am and start cleaning the floor. Afterward I get to practice by myself."

Sadly, shortly after our meeting, Trevor contracted cancer and passed away two years later in 2017. I feel honored to have met Trevor Chapman and film his practice with his close friend Ozawa Sensei.

My interview with Hiroshi Ozawa began after his class in the *Kōbukan* and finished upstairs in his family home above the *dōjō*.

Hiroshi Ozawa Sensei, 2014

THE INTERVIEW

Can you tell us about Mizoguchi-ha Ittō-ryū and modern kendō?
The *Mizoguchi-ha* school of *Ittō-ryū* was founded at the beginning of the Edo period. That old practice of the *Mizoguchi-ha* school of *Ittō-ryū* and modern *kendō* do not seem to have many points in common. That is to say, in modern *kendō* there are things from *koryū kata*, (ancient martial forms) *kata* from the *Mizoguchi-ha Ittō-ryū*, which are used to show us how to manage the body This is the single most important thing.

Then, besides the management of the body, there also is the '*seme*' (intention of attack). In every technique, from the first to the fifth, and also in the *kodachi* (short blade) forms, one advances three steps with the intention of an attack. One approaches the opponent with the intention to attack, revealing the technique beforehand. The opponent responds to this, and in turn, by responding or counter-attack victory is achieved. This is the characteristic of the *Mizoguchi-ha Ittō-ryū*. In other words, the way to manage or handle the body and the intention of attack are very useful in modern *kendō*.

Can you talk about your father and grandfather's kendō?
My family, my father and grandfather, do not practice *Mizoguchi-ha*. My grandfather practiced *Ono-ha Ittō-ryū*, and so did my father. The relationship of my family to *Mizoguchi-ha Ittō-ryū* came through my older

sister's husband, who was an 8th *dan sensei* named Kōzō Andō.

Sensei went to Aizu (the western-most region of Fukushima Prefecture) when he was on his 30's, and after seeing the *kata* he had the resolution to learn them. Thus, he was taught by Suzumu Sensei, a *hanshi* 9th *dan sensei* from Aizu. Upon his return to Tokyo, and so as to not forget what he learned, he invited me to practice with him. This was about 40 years ago. Therefore, my family connection with the *Mizoguchi-ha Ittō-ryū*, was through my brother-in-law, Kōzō Andō Sensei.

How does the training differ between kendō and koryū?

Modern *kendō* practitioners are using the *shinai* very straight. *Men*, (cutting strike to the head), *kote-men* (cutting strikes to the wrist and head), *kote-dō* (cutting strikes to the wrist and torso). It is always in a straight line. The *koryū kata*, use footwork and the way to handle the body. What to do against an attack from the opponent? What to do against the technique from the opponent? If one pressures the opponent, how will he or she respond?

Here, in the case of the *Mizoguchi-ha Ittō-ryū* one strikes, responds, counters the response, and again responds back.

For people who practice modern *kendō*, including the Japanese practitioners, I say if you ever have the chance, I recommend you practice *koryū kata*. I would dare say that you must do so. It helps modern *shinai kendō* greatly. For this reason I think that you should give it a try.

One more thing; There also is the *Nihon kendō kata*. If you practice only this *kata*, that also works too. Every time you go to practice, even if only for 10 or 15 minutes, even if only the *kendō kata*, that is good enough. I think that if you do this every practice, without a doubt your *kendō* using a *shinai* will be transformed.

Can you talk about the format for your kendō classes?

The practice of my *kendō* class is not separated, meaning that training is training, competition is competition, and examinations are examinations. *Kendō* practice like the one we just did today is such that training, competition, and examinations are all done within a single practice class.

Regarding the content of the practice, I think that you will tell by seeing the video footage you filmed, that it consists of doing *rei* (formal bowing), advancing three steps, perform *sonkyo* (formal crouching), raising up, and then exerting attacking pressure mutually. Then, continue

Ozawa Sensei teaching *Kendō* in the *Kōbukan*

to exert attacking pressure and strike the *men* (lit. head/face; area in the headgear that is considered as valid striking target in *kendō*). This is one of the patterns or methods of practice.

One more thing. It is not that one arbitrarily goes for an attack. As the opponent approaches to attack our *men*, we continue to exert attacking pressure and do a *debana* (preemptive strike) to their *men*. Strike a *debana men*. Strike a *debana kote* (lit. forearm; area in the protective gauntlet that is considered a valid striking target in *kendō*). Or else, one can parry and use *ōji waza* (counterstrike technique). Additionally, one could block the attack and strike the *dō* (lit. trunk, torso; area in the protective body guard that is considered a valid striking target in *kendō*). *Kaeshi dō*, or deflect the opponent's *shinai* upward and counter striking the *men* (*suriage men*). This type of practice, where the opponent attacks our *men* and we use the opportunity to perform preemptive strikes, counter attacks, or other techniques which are effective responses against an aggression initiated by the opponent.

The important thing is not only the striking in itself, but also the *zanshin* (lit. remaining mind; alertness/awareness) after a strike or thrust. It is the preparation against retaliation from the opponent, this is what is called *zanshin*. We do this when practicing. We strive to continue in this state in every moment.

One more thing. For example, the opponent comes attacking our *men* and we do a preemptive strike to the *kote* in response to that. What follows is the opponent coming towards us in a collision course. In order to make our *kote* strike valid we must be able to throw the opponent's body out of balance with our strike. The opponent comes against our *men* and we strike their *kote*, and then we must do *taisabaki* (lit. body handling work). Move the body to the right, move the body to the left. Do this without going out of balance ourselves. It is this kind of practice.

That is about it for what we aim for in a basic practice session. From there, we have sparring practice *jigeiko* (free sparring practice), which is actual sparring done with a partner. This is an extension of what follows basic practice - sparring practice. This is practice also for the sake of competition and for grading examinations. This is practice for competition and this practice can help you to set all of the technique up at once.

The winner of the 2014 All Japan Kendo Championships, Yūya Takenouchi was only twenty one years old. Why do you think he was able to beat experienced competitors?

Yes, I was there, not for all of the championships but I went to the All Japan Championships. My impressions? Well that I cannot try to beat the young people in their game! (Laughs). That was my impression. However, I was thinking about how to move in the case people like that would come charging against me. I was thinking about that while watching. Physical strength, technique, heart/spirit. There is the concept of '*Shin gi tai*' (lit. spirit, technique and body).

Regarding the spirit, they are still quite young, so they leave that for later. Spirit, technique, and physical strength. I cannot meet with physical strength or technique anymore. As a matter of course, the person who won is only 20 years old, right? Maybe 21 years old? If a 21 year old goes against a 64 year old, I cannot meet against his physical strength. In that case, what can I do against him? If he comes attacking against me, how should I move in response to him? I was watching while thinking about this.

I think that I would not be able to strike him. The reason for this is that his reactions are fast, dodging and approaching are also fast. The footwork must also be very fast. I think I would not be able to strike him. But I also think that he would not be able to strike me either!

If I attempt to strike him, he will strike me first. But if I keep my *kamae* (guard stance) and wait for his attack I think I can achieve a parry and counter strike to his *do*. Maybe I can also strike with a preemptive

Hiroshi Ozawa

21 year old Yūya Takenouchi, winning ippon strike in the final, 2014
All Japan Kendo Championship final. Photo: Jon Braeley

attack. However, I think that a parry is more plausible because there might not be enough time to do a preemptive attack, because his reactions are so fast. I was observing while thinking this.

Is age a factor in kendō and how does this change your practice?
One of the most difficult things, and one which I look towards achieving, is becoming able to practice the same way regardless with who I practice with, be it school kids, high school kids, university students, 6th *dan*, 7th *dan*, or 8th *dan* masters. *Kendō* is profound. It is very profound. The 64-65 year old me still doesn't get it. In *kendō*, there are people who are 75, 80, 85, 90, and even over 90 years old and they are doing *kendō*. In comparison to that, one could say that I am in the younger side. I wonder if I can continue *kendō* up to that point.

What can I do in order to continue *kendō* until that point? Naturally, one should practice against young people like him, who is very young.

Sport reflexes, sport ability, physical strength. These things all decrease with age. Against this, what can one do? One is bound to lose in terms of physical strength. I practice every day while thinking about this. I am practicing every day. This is what I consider training to be.

Are you still active in competitions?
Yes. I participate in competitions two or three times per year. However, I will say a few things. Well, to the 64-65 year old me, training is not done aiming to participate in competition. It is instead to pursue the ideal of *kendō*, the theory of *kendō*, one could say the ultimate or essential point of *kendō*. The *gokui* (essential point). I continue to train to achieve this.

You are known for the practice and teaching of classical sword technique (koryū) at your dōjō, how has this affected your kendō?
This is a good question. Japanese people do not often ask this question. I mean Japanese *kendō* practitioners. *Koryū* is the origin, the roots of *kendō*. How to explain this? When doing *koryū* practice, one does *taisabaki* (body management), and techniques like this with the *bokutō* (lit. wood saber; also *bokken*, wood sword) or *katana*, in case of demonstrations. These things are invariably included within the *kendō* practiced nowadays, included in its techniques. The spiritual part is also included within it. I have trained in *koryū kata* for around 42 years, and in fact, especially lately, I have come to notice that while doing sparring practice I find myself doing *koryū* techniques. This makes me feel that those 42 years where not in vain!

About *koryū*? What we just did, the *kendō* practice, I think it is easy to notice if you see it. It is all straight forward. *Men* strike and *kote* strike are very straight. *Koryū* is much more about *taisabaki*, circular body motions. If this is understood, one's *kendō* increases in rank. That is why I would like everyone in the *dōjō* to listen to what I am about to say. *Men* is straight, right? *Kote* is also straight. *Dō* is done like this... tan, tan! Circular motions. This becomes an ingrained habit. Once this permeates our body, when doing *kendō*, during sparring practice, this emerges. It is quite entertaining!

This is the kind of content that I wish to tell to everyone. Please explain this to all the people training in their *dōjō*. To the *kendō* practitioners around the World. However the *dōjō's* that are doing this kind of basic practice, those including *koryū*, might not be that many.

> **"**
> *The origin of kendō is using a katana to kill people. This is the beginning of kendō. It is kendo's roots. Therefore, the starting point is that kendō without a katana cannot be!*

26.
Uki Terukuni
8TH DAN, ICHIKENKAI KENDŌ, HAGA DŌJŌ

Chapter 26
INTRODUCTION

During my research into the current state of schools of *kendō* in Japan, I was drawn to some historical photos and archival footage of pre-war *kendō*. One sword master that I kept referring to was Jun'ichi Haga, who trained in the classical style of *Shindō munen-ryū*.

Jun'ichi Haga maintained the tradition of classical swordsmanship before and during the Second World War periods. In the pre-war period, a more energetic and free-style *kendō* was not unusual, where foot sweeps and *jūdō* style techniques using throws, were used to unbalance one's opponent. Our cover photo on the previous page shows Uki Terukuni Sensei sweeping the opponents feet from underneath him!

Let's not forget that if a *samurai* lost his sword in battle, he would continue his fight regardless, using *jūjutsu* or other empty-hand methods to stay alive. Jun'ichi Haga was a proponent of this more realistic attitude to *kendō* practice that today would be prohibited in competition rules.

The *Ichikenkai* (lit. one-sword association) *Haga Dōjō* was established in the *Shōwa* period, in the 1930's. In the decades since, this *dōjō* has maintained the pre-war traditions of *kendō*, with disregard for conforming to a more standardized curriculum of *kendō*, or what is termed modern *kendō*. The post-war standardization of *kendō* did however help to spread *kendō* outside Japan, where competitions thrived.

Jun'ichi Haga passed away in 1966 and the training hall was moved to the *Nihon Budōkan's* smaller second *dōjō*. A revival in the pre-war free-style *kendō* has slowly taken root in this new *Ichikenkai Haga Dōjō*, overseen by it's president, Uki Terukuni, who was tasked to preserve the tradition of the *kendō* founded by Jun'ichi Haga. Our interview takes place in this same Haga *dōjō* at the *Budōkan* in Tokyo

Uki Terukuni Sensei, 2014

THE INTERVIEW

Can you please introduce yourself?
I am the head instructor of the *Ichikenkai Haga Dōjō*. I serve as the director, my name is Uki Terukuni.

Can you tell us how the Ichikenkai Haga Dōjō came about?
This *dōjō* began when Jun'ichi Haga Sensei gathered a group of young people to practice *kendō* and *iaidō* at the National Gymnasium in Kanda, Itsusubashi. From around the first half of the 30s decade of the *Shōwa* period (around 1950), Jun'ichi Haga Sensei became the center of gravity of the *dōjō* and started teaching *kendō*.

After the Tokyo Olympics in the year *Shōwa* 39 (1964), the National Gymnasium was closed, and practice started to be done here instead, in the second small *dōjō* in the *Nihon Budōkan*. It continues to be so until the present day.

And what about your own involvement, how did that happen?
I came to Tokyo from the distant Gunma Prefecture on the year when I entered University in *Shōwa* 37 (1962). Since April of that year I was instructed by Haga Sensei. I have continued to practice until the present day.

Talking in terms of age, it has been more than 50 years since I first enrolled in the *dōjō*. During this time, I also was part of the University *Kendō* Club, but at the same time I also received instruction from Haga Sensei. And so, I continue to practice until the present day.

Do you know about the pre-war training of Haga Sensei?
I cannot say much about the days of old because I was not there myself, but from what I have heard when he was being instructed by Haga Sensei in his fifties, Nakayama Sensei made him undertake very hard and strict practice. Details about his young age such as the actual relationship with Nakayama Sensei and so on, I only know from the writings which Haga Sensei left behind or what I heard from him while he was still alive. I have not seen those things by myself.

You practice iaidō in the Haga dōjō. Can you talk about this?
This is a very complex matter, but my opinion is that the origin of *kendō* is using a *katana* to kill people. This is the beginning of *kendō*. It is *kendō's* roots. Therefore, the starting point is that *kendō* without a *katana* cannot be! *Kendō* did not begin with the bamboo *shinai*.

For this reason, it is basic training in this *dōjō* that we practice both *iaidō* and *kendō*. The way we undergo practice here is by learning both disciplines using a *katana*, and applying this to *kendō*.

The most important thing in *kendō* is the *kizeme* (intention of attack with the spirit). Communicating the feeling of "Strike, strike, strike!" towards the opponent while pressuring for an attack. The intention of attack with the spirit, the way to handle the spirit, I think that this is the most important thing in *kendō*. I think that this can be understood by actually seeing *kendō*, but the form of entering into attack, these things - *kendō* is the exchange of feelings, so in this exchange of feelings one must express them completely and attack.

How does the kendō you practice compare to competition kendō?
Well this is not only limited to *kendō*, but in all martial art competitions there are rules to follow. Therefore, not only for *kendō* but for all compe-

titions alike, they consistently change along with changes in the rules. As for myself, I do not make any detailed rules. When wielding a *katana* and fighting, the feeling is not like a competition in which one abides to the rules that have been determined before. This is why we do *yokomen'uchi* (strikes to the sides of the head), and also *tsuki* (lit. thrust; area in the throat guard attached to the headgear that is considered as valid striking target in *kendō*). In the case of thrusts, it is broadly accepted, but as for the side-head strike, the way of moving the body to execute it is a very useful technique, so we endorse it.

If techniques are not acquired at a young age, it becomes impossible to remember them in the old age. This is why one must practice side-head strike while young. Regarding foot techniques, in the case when the opponent's body is loose or unbalanced, one pushes sharply and swipes the feet to bring him down. It is not a matter of bringing the opponent to the ground without reason, but as a didactic tool. I think that feet-sweeping is a necessary technique for this purpose.

In the case where our *shinai* has been taken or has fallen out of our hands, the measure we take is to grapple. It does not mean that I endorse grappling, but as a basic knowledge for a *kendō* practitioner, we must know that once we lose our *shinai* there is nothing left but to grapple. Grappling is included as the minimum preparation and readiness as a *budō* practitioner.

And I see practice in classical swordsmanship (koryū) at this dōjō?
Originally, *kendō* began as an activity which involved the use of a *katana* (single bladed sabre), as a combat method which employed the *katana*. For this reason, proficiency with the *katana* is a plus for *kendō* practice.

I believe that the way to swing the *shinai* and the way to swing the *katana* are exactly the same. Following this, '*te no uchi*' (lit. inside of the hand; way to grip the sword; also *tenouchi*), the way of gripping the *shinai* and the way of gripping the *katana* are also the same.

Kendō and *iaidō* are both practiced at the same time in our *dōjō*, so improvements in *iaidō* will be reflected as improvements in *kendō* as well, because they are correlated. It is inconceivable that one becomes skilled in *iaidō*, yet remains unskilled in *kendō*. Here, we improve in *iai* and improve in *kendō*, becoming better at both simultaneously.

What are the schools of swordsmanship or iaidō that you practice?
In this *dōjō* we do *Ōmori-ryū*, *Hasega-wa eishin-ryū*, and also *Oku-iai*

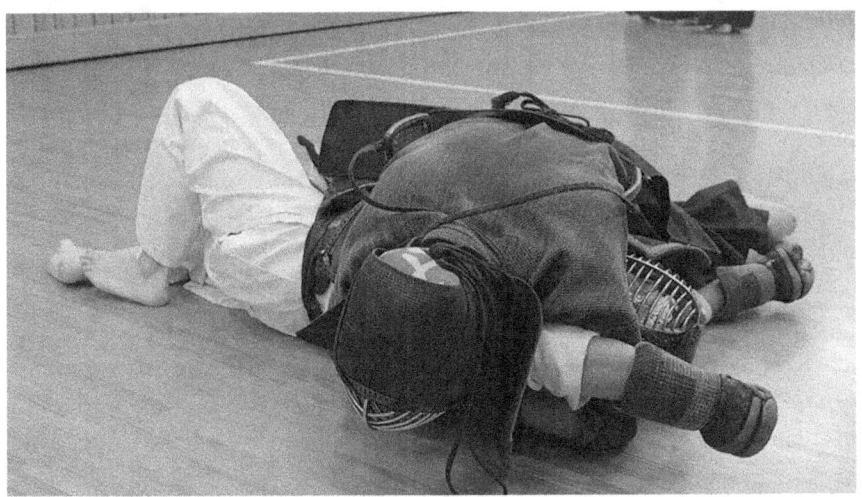

Sweeping your opponent and grappling them to the floor if one loses their *shinai* is rooted in pre-war *kendō*. Photo: Jon Braeley

from *Toyama-ryū*. At the time when I started *iaidō*, the *iaidō*-practicing population was small, and there were no blunt swords such as the ones commonly used nowadays. From the beginning, one used real sharpened blades. The *iaidō* population was really small. I started *iaidō* when I was 18 years old, and I used a *shinken* (lit. live sword; sharpened blade) ever since the beginning. It is not a coincidence that the term used to describe a live-blade is the same term used in modern Japanese to describe becoming serious about something; one must wield a *katana* with a serious feeling in the heart. For this reason, everyone in this *dōjō*, starting from the beginners, use live-bladed (*shinken*) *katana*.

Nowadays, the words *kobudō* (old-style *budō*) and *kobujutsu* (old-style martial arts) are used, but as for myself, I feel that there are no such things as *kobudō* or *kobujutsu*. It applies to everything that is the interval from ancient times to modern day when transitions and changes occur. However, I think that if the *iaidō* and *kendō* from the actual period are practiced without forgetting its origin and essential spirit, then there is no need for such words as "old".

How has kendō practice changed over the years?

As I talked about this before, with the change of times the rules of a competition gradually changed. For this reason... the shape of the practice of *kendō* has changed along with changes in the way of thinking of the *kendō* organization. This has been happening, and I think that it will continue to happen in the future as well. However, as for myself, I use the *katana* as in the past, meaning to cut down people. In fact, I have never cut down a person. Nonetheless, I practice with the indispensable feeling and readiness to do so if necessary. In *kendō* we say that it is more important to win over oneself than to win over an opponent. This is an old teaching or saying regarding victory. The most important thing is not winning over another person, but to conquer oneself.

In competitions, there are winners and losers, but in the path of dedicated training that is *kendō*, there is only the self evaluation of oneself. In *kendō*. I think that the most important thing is the formation and pursuit of the maximization of the potential which we possess when we are born. This means to follow our own feelings on a path of dedicated training.

We often hear about limits and retirement in doing competitions. However, in this *dōjō* there are people who are over 80 years old, and are still giving practice their best effort, without self-imposing limits, testing themselves as to how far they can go. With consideration about how they can, as human beings, live so that the can contribute to society, how to enjoy living, how to live fully 365 days a year. This is how we undergo our practice of *kendō* and *iaidō*.

> **"**
> *Kendō is not something I can just turn on when I am in the dōjō. I have to live kendō every day. That was the realization that I came to when I passed 7th dan*

27.
Alexander Bennett
KYŌSHI 7TH DAN KENDŌ

Chapter 27

INTRODUCTION

Alexander Bennett, *kyōshi* 7th *dan kendō*, was born in New Zealand and arrived in Japan in 1987 as a 17 year old high school exchange student. During this visit, he saw *kendō* for the first time, and though he never intended to take up a martial art, he enrolled for the *kendō* class.

In the thirty years since then, Alex Bennett has made Japan his home and *kendō* his life. His resume is impressive, holding two Ph.D's in Budo studies and attaining 7th *dan kyōshi* in *kendō*, 5th *dan* in *iaidō*, *naginata*, *jūkendō* and *tankendō*. He is a professor at Kansai University, where he teaches Japanese culture, history and *kendō*. He also serves as the vice president of the International Naginata Federation and is a member of the international committee of the All Japan Kendo Federation.

Alexander Bennett is a co-founder of the Kendo World Magazine, and author of several martial arts books in English and Japanese, his more recent being '*Kendo, Culture of the Sword*' and '*Japan, The Ultimate Samurai Guide*' (Tuttle Publishing). He recently published a new translation of the '*Hagakure*', (lit. Hidden by leaves), a classic text based on the observations of Yamamoto Tsunetomo and an insight into *samurai* culture. I know what you are thinking - does he find any time to sleep?

Alex has been a great supporter of what I was doing with Empty Mind Films and our paths have crossed frequently in Japan. He was always willing to lend his advice and help to open doors where needed. His knowledge and understanding of *budō*, in both its history and where it is today, is unparalleled, both inside and outside Japan. When I completed The *Warriors of Budo,* a seven episode series on Japanese martial arts, I sent Alex my script and he kindly agreed to record the narration.

The following interview took place in 2014 in Alexander Bennett's office at Kansai University, Osaka.

Alexander Bennett Sensei, 2014

THE INTERVIEW

Can you talk about your work with the Kendo Federation?

Well I have been living in Japan now for over 20 years. About 23 years, and throughout that time I have been practicing *kendō* and *naginata* and also *iaidō*. In this time, I found myself in an interesting position in Japan where organizations like the *Nippon Budōkan* and the All Japan Kendo Federation and the Naginata Federation and so forth really want to try and disseminate the various aspects of the arts that they represent to the international community. However, they often don't have the necessary skills, be they linguistic, or whatever, to efficiently or effectively achieve these goals.

So in the last five or ten years or so, I've been called upon by the *Budōkan* and also the various Federations to help them with translation and interpretation. Often times, this is generally helping them with finding information about the state of a specific art and a specific country. Really just helping them with international activities, especially with regards to *kendō* because that's really the main martial art or *budō* art that I practice.

When it comes to interpretation or translation it pays to have a fairly extensive knowledge of the actual technical aspects of that *budō* and not only that, but the history involved and how it became what it is today, the social and cultural context involved. So when you are trying to interpret for a seminar or translate some information for a book it really does help to have that specialist knowledge as a practitioner.

Because of this experience as a practitioner and as a researcher of the Martial arts, the *Budōkan* and the All Japan Kendo Federation, and the International Federation come to rely on me for many aspects of their international propagation, or their plans for spreading the arts worldwide. I don't think I am the first person to do this, but I have been in this position longer than anybody else has up until now.

You recently published a second PhD thesis on budō?

The first PhD thesis on *budō* I did was at Kyoto University and it was researched and written in Japanese. It was an attempt to try and give the nebulous term '*bushidō*' some kind of definition. The word *bushidō* gets bandied about quite often without any real understanding of what it means. The differences that you would encounter in different periods. It just seems to be a generic term for the *samurai* way. Whatever that is, whenever it was and wherever it was. So for my first thesis, I actually applied the anthropological definition of a religion that was created by Clifford Geertz, to try and explain more in tangible terms what *bushidō* could have been.

Following on from that about ten years later, which was 2012, I completed another PhD at the University of Canterbury in New Zealand which was in English even though I resided in Japan, I did my research there. And that theme was not about *bushidō*, but about the historical development of *budō* culture specifically *kendō*, or the 'Way of the Sword' from medieval times through to the present day. I looked at how *kendō* evolved and the various political or cultural forces that really fashioned *kendō* into it's current sort of form. Particularly in modern times we see the utilization of *budō* culture, particularly *kendō* as a way of fostering a kind of 'Japanese-ness'. A sense of Japanese identity particularly in the modern period. After the Meiji Restoration, the class distinctions of the *samurai* and the commoners gradually disappeared but various aspects or vestiges of *samurai* culture were sort of reinvented if you like, to represent a sort of Japanese uniqueness in the world.

It became one of the cultural legacies of the *samurai* that the Japanese utilize to try and differentiate themselves from other countries are other cultures in the world. There's an immense amount of pride in Japan for *samurai* culture. Interestingly a lot of it was sort of like, well I use the word 'reinvented.' A lot of tradition is reinvented anywhere in the world to suit certain political or nationalistic objectives and *kendō* and other martial arts were very much used as tools to this end.

So a lot of the research that I did, particularly in the modern era, really looked at some of the darker nooks and crannies of *budō* culture. This is especially if you look at the 1930s and 1940s where it was a part of the militaristic regime as a way of fostering nationalistic sentiment and the idea of self sacrifice for the greater good of Japan, and it's leaders. Then as a result of that in the post war period, and the occupation, the martial arts were actually banned for a certain period. Because they were considered by the occupation forces as being potentially dangerous and running counter to the new democratic ideals which they were trying to promote in Japan to re-create a modem society that fits in line with the rest of the world.

Because the martial arts were banned for a while, it was a period of introspection and again reinvention of the martial arts into a different kind of form where they do not promote so much the various spiritual aspects or the Japanese aspects, but instead try to promote the martial arts as modern sports where competition was the central focus rather than education. So it was on the basis of this, that the martial arts, and I talk about *kendō* mainly, was able to be reinstated in Japanese society and eventually in the Japanese education system. Be it as a sport but gradually the dissatisfaction with this kind of competitive mentality over the potential that *budō* or *kendō* has, as a way of educating the self. As a means to self perfection.

This is cause for a lot of contradiction in the way that *kendō* was promoted and my thesis really looked at the process in which these contradictions were reconciled and how *kendō* and *budō* really now have come, once again, considered to be representative of what it is to be

Alex Bennett at the annual Kendo World Keiko-Kai, 2012   Photo: Jon Braeley

Japanese. Even if many Japanese have not done martial arts before, it is still considered to be a really important cultural legacy unique to Japan and therefore something that must be treasured and something that can be presented to the rest of the world as a kind of cultural contribution to World heritage. Of course this has many other political motivations as well, in a sense that it can be representative of Japanese soft power. It can be considered something that the Japanese have created, they specialize in, and it's a beautiful cultural legacy that represents Japan but it is something that people from any country or culture can utilize in their own lives as away to make themselves better human beings.

Whether you agree with this or not, is really not the point of my thesis. It was really about trying to clarify the various cultural and political motivations that have fashioned *budō* into what it is today and also how it is being spread internationally.

This is what you mean by globalization of budō?
Regarding the globalization of *budō*… well that's a loaded term because globalization to many people in the martial arts world, also represents a watering down of the Japanese essence of the martial arts. But if you talk about the international dissemination of the martial arts rather than the globalization, it really started back in the 1880s or 1890s with Jigōrō Kanō, who is the founder of *jūdō*. He was also an educator who went overseas numerous times to investigate other education systems and so

forth, in Europe and the United States. He also went in his capacity later on, as a leader of the Japanese Olympic Committee.

Jigōrō Kanō always used the opportunities to be overseas to demonstrate the techniques and the principles of *jūdō* and he was very proactive in promoting branches of *Kōdōkan jūdō* outside Japan. Recruiting people who were perhaps involved in another form of *jūjutsu* and bringing them into the *Kōdōkan* family.

So in a way he's a bit like an evangelist for his education principles and ideals through the culture of *jūdō*. He was very much influenced by Western education ideals, and individuals such as Pierre de Coubertin, the father of the modern Olympics. So his outlook was, on the one side, extremely Japanese, but it was also very international, and as a result from the 1880s to 18090's I guess, you would start seeing a growing number of people practicing *jūdō* in various places throughout the world and in certain areas of the United States and in Europe like the United Kingdom and Germany, and later on, places like France.

So this is really where it started and *jūdō* was popular because it had very clear practical benefits. A small person could defeat a larger person not through physical strength, but by using the physical principals of soft overcoming hard and strength actually being used against the person who was trying to apply it. And so this was of course quite fascinating and there were demonstrations throughout Europe and the United States where little Japanese *jūdō* practitioners or *jūjutsu* practitioners were pitted against huge muscular champion wrestlers who were local heroes if you like. Often they were soundly defeated by these diminutive Japanese *jūdōka*. This of course would only add to the mystique and the appeal of *jūdō*.

This happened quite early, around the turn of the 20th century and it really snowballed from there. However, with other Japanese martial arts, the benefits were not as obvious, especially the physical benefits. I am talking about martial arts such as *kendō* and perhaps *kyūdō* or *naginata*. *Kendō* had an early start in the West particularly with Japanese immigrants to the United States or South America but not so much in Europe.

The Japanese immigrants participated in the martial arts, such as *kendō*, *sumō* and *jūdō* not so much as a sport or for practical reasons of self-defense, but really as a way of maintaining links with their Japanese heritage. And so, especially in *nikkei* (lit. Japanese descent) communities, those people with Japanese heritage, the martial arts became established quite early on but it was not really for the broader population. The other

Alex Bennett surrounded by 8th *dan kendō sensei*

immigrants did not really see the relevance especially in something like *kendō* but this changed in the post war period.

Really I think most of the international dissemination of *budō* has been a post war phenomenon. Especially from the 1960s… 1970s… 1980s, you see considerable interest generated. Again, compared to Japan interestingly, the most popular martial art internationally would be *karate*. And this really started from the 1960s and 1970s and for similar reasons to the popularity of *jūdō*, in terms of it's practical application. It is perceived as something useful. As something you can learn to defend yourself and then if you stick with it, you can glean various spiritual benefits or educational benefits as well. So *karate* captured peoples imagination quite early and quite rapidly and I guess this was aided in part by people who have absolutely nothing to do with *karate* like Bruce Lee for example.

The people drawn to martial arts had a '*Kung fu-karate*' what's the difference mentality! Obviously there's a lot of difference but they wouldn't see that to start with. So *karate* took off at a rate that had never really been seen before. In fact today, it's far more popular outside of Japan than it is inside of Japan than it was back then.

And what about martial arts within Japan?
In Japan, *kendō* has always really been the number one martial art in terms of the practicing population. There are a number of reasons but one of

the main reasons is really that it can be directly linked to *samurai* culture. Even though the *samurai* only made up something like 5% or 6% of the entire population when they actually existed as a distinct status or class. Japanese today still have a very favorable image of the *samurai* as being heroic, noble, manly and chivalrous and so on. As someone ideal. The ideal and the reality, I would suggest are very different, but still, that image is enduring and *kendō* really fits into that.

But this did not happen so much in the West apart from the *nikkei* communities which were doing it because of the their cultural links or their Japanese heritage. Westerners really don't see the relevance except that, it's maybe exotic. I think *kendō* sort of started to gain a following in countries which were quite early, like America and the United Kingdom and it was really through, I would suggest, movies like Star Wars (laughs), with the light sabre which kind of made people take notice of *kendō*. They would say it was something that's really spiritual and this has the potential to develop your inner self. Again it is the attraction to *samurai* culture which really took off in the West in the 1980's. Japan's incredible economic success at this time and which again was linked to the culture of the *samurai* and *samurai* strategy and *samurai* martial arts. So *kendō* gained a bit of a following because of that and really people were attracted to the exoticness of it all. Regardless, I am more aware of *kendō* now as a competitive sporting activity that has other benefits as well if you continue it. You can really start using it as a framework for your life. It provides ideas and concepts and philosophy that can be practical in the course of your daily life and not just inside the *dōjō*. So there is that attraction to it that people are becoming more aware of now.

The international dissemination of martial arts in general, except say for *jūdō* which has been an Olympic sport since 1964, and has more affiliates in the international Federations than most sports around the world could ever hope to achieve. So this is the Olympic aspect of *jūdō* which makes it very popular. *Karate* has the practical aspect which makes it also very popular.

There are various *kobudō* traditional martial arts outside Japan, which quite frankly are of dubious lineage a lot of the time, but they have a kind of exoticness that is attractive to a lot of people interested in martial arts. *Kendō* has that exotic aspect. But generally speaking most other martial arts, apart from *jūdō* and *karate*, are not nearly as wide spread outside Japan. Really that's not through lack of trying. The representative bodies for the various martial arts in Japan really consider it important, or almost prestigious to have an International Federation. This is seen as a sign off success if you like. As a validation.

However there is also a certain amount of weariness attached to that as well because if you make an international body, or an International Federation then that means that Japan becomes one member among the many. Which means that Japan could possibly lose its leadership role and the way in which that particular martial art is propagated overseas. Which would mean that particular *budō* could lose it's Japanese essence. So in one sense that kind of globalization is desirable but it's also fraught with danger. An often quoted case in point is *jūdō*.

The Judo Federation was the first Japanese *budō* to actually create an international Federation. In fact it was created in Europe and not in Japan. For many years of course, Japan took a leading role in the way in which *jūdō* was popularized. But in recent years that is not the case and at the moment to my knowledge, there is not even a Japanese officer in the international Judo Federation. It is run entirely by non-Japanese.

This is a point of great concern to Japanese and other *budō* arts, because they see *jūdō* has having really veered from the path of *budō*. It has become an international sport rather than adhering to the traditional educational ideals of the founder, Jigōrō Kanō. It has become an activity in which people try to win at all costs us and as a result of that, there's a loss of respect for the traditions. There is a loss of respect for your training partners and your opponents who are seen as obstacles to your ultimate success in tournaments. This is certainly not the case with all *jūdōka*. I know many *jūdō* practitioners who really follow the path of *jūdō* as a way of self perfection. A way in which they can develop themselves physically and mentally and psychologically and spiritually. But the perception in Japan is that this not always the case and so when you're dealing with, for an example the Kendo Federation which I am involved with or the Naginata Federation, there is very much an underlying sort of motivation in which control of this form of traditional Japanese culture must be maintained in Japan so that it can be conveyed in it's correct form, that is, it's Japanese form to generations in the future.

So on the one hand it's considered to be a great contribution to the world heritage and on the other hand it's best left in Japanese hands so that it is promoted correctly. In the early days of the creation of these international federations this is probably desirable because all of the resources and all of the knowledge, or at least the majority of it, is based in Japan. The great teachers and all of the books and teachings and stuff are based in Japan. There is only a handful of people who would have such knowledge outside of Japan, depending on the *budō*. So in this case the guidance from Japan is absolutely necessary.

However, some martial arts are getting to the stage now, where they have a huge following of very knowledgeable, very skilled, very understanding non-Japanese practitioners. Trying to work out where they fit into the grand scheme of things is in a way, like throwing a cat among the pigeons in the *budō* world in Japan. While there are a lot of very open minded, understanding people in Japan, there are also some people who just do not get that actually non-Japanese people can excel and understand these *budō* arts. Not just as a sport and not just as traditional Japanese culture but something that really does offer the individual, regardless of where they come from, incredible value in their life. It has universal values that sort of transcend ideas of traditional Japanese culture. It really goes to the heart of what it is to be human and a lot of people around the world not just in Japan really understand that, which is why it's such an incredible phenomenon.

I think that the export of *budō* is generally speaking, Japan's most successful cultural export by far. Because of that, it is a double edged sword because often the Japanese governing bodies don't want to relinquish their authority. So it is with the globalization of *budō*, and that term in itself is almost a bad word in Japan.

The term international dissemination of *budō* is used, the implication being that it's the Japanese that are disseminating it. That is really in some circles the preferred sort of method of promoting *budō* overseas. But having said that, in order to do that requires a real concerted effort and financial commitment which the Japanese government has been very generous with up until now. For example, through organizations like the *Budōkan* which is funded to do this. However, what's really missing is teaching resources, which I think are deficient and proforma most of the time.

There is a dearth of reliable information that people outside Japan can really get their teeth into to help them understand further, the ways of *budō*. The philosophy behind it. Up until now the international dissemination looks good on paper. You have *sensei* from Japan going overseas with recognized delegations sent by their Federation and so forth. But it's really not as concerted as you would think or the way it's portrayed over here in Japan.

I think the greatest contributor to the international dissemination of *budō* is not the various Federations who oversee the *budō* in Japan. Its really at the grassroots level where you have exchange students coming to Japan or Japanese exchange students going overseas where they have a common interest in *kendō* or *jūdō* and get involved in the local community.

This leads us to your publication, Kendo World Magazine?

Yes. The creation of Kendo World Magazine in 2001 was precisely because of the dearth of information, or reliable information on *kendō* in the international community. People were hungry and they would hold onto every word that a visiting Japanese person who did *kendō*, maybe even at a low level, would say in the *dōjō*. It was like "everybody wants this information. They want to know the deepest secrets. They want to know the *budō* spirit, the *kendō* spirit. They want to know about *bushidō*... what it is?

Because there are so many misconceptions and the greatest misconception perhaps, with regards to *kendō*, is that what we're doing is exactly the same as what the *samurai* were doing 300 years ago. Well it's not! There has been a long and fascinating process, an evolutionary process that has been influenced by all sorts of cultural, political and social factors that has made *kendō* what it is today.

There is very little information in English about any of this. About how *kendō* evolved? What is the underlying philosophy or spirit of *kendō*? What is it's cultural relevance? How can it be useful or relevant to people who live outside of Japan? People who are not Japanese and don't have that Japanese connection in terms of their heritage... their DNA. What is it that *kendō* has to offer and how should you approach your training in *kendō*? Is it a sport? Is it *budō*? What's the difference?

And so you know, there are a lot of people not just in *kendō*, but I am speaking from a *kendō* perspective, that wanted this knowledge that was not available. The International Kendo Federation was created in 1970 and since then it has been based in Japan. The World championships are held every three years. I have been involved in the World Championships since 1991 and every tournament you see, has this huge growth, not only in the numbers but also the technical ability of the people coming through. It used to be Japan up here (high) and the rest of the World down here (low) but its gradually coming up to the extent that the Japanese are actually taking the World Championships in *kendō* very seriously now. So my point is, there is this growth in *kendō* but it hasn't been matched by the creation of reliable information about what *kendō* really is. So there are a lot of gaps in people's knowledge. They are doing this traditional Japanese *budō* art, but their real understanding of where it's come from, and therefore where it could be heading is quite flawed in many cases.

So with all this in mind we created Kendo World Magazine in 2001 and our motivation really, was that we lived in Japan, myself and my New Zealand friend who did *kendō*, with a network of foreigners in Japan who had access to all this information to great *sensei* and to literature and they could understand it and they could read it.

The International Federation and the All Japan Federation, they were doing their bit but it was certainly not enough. They were sending teachers overseas to seminars and showing students how to strike '*men*'… Well you know that's fine and it's very important, but you know, people wanted more, they need more to make sense of it all. So we launched the magazine, and I don't know if this was our responsibility, and maybe it was a little bit arrogant to do so.

Did you face difficulties starting Kendo World Magazine?
Well yes. First, you have always got the problem of translation or interpretation. The information is as good as it is translated. It could be the most sublime wisdom in the world but if it's not translated well or conveyed correctly then it means nothing. So we sort of collated all this information and I must say that the All Japan Kendo Federation was very supportive of us in doing this. They provided resources for us and gave us introductions to people so we were able to do interviews. We were also able to translate articles from the already established Japanese magazines.

We started to draw upon our own personal contacts to start assembling and providing correct useful meaningful information about various aspects of *kendō* culture, including the history of *kendō* culture, the philosophy, the techniques and also the competitive aspects as well. We could write about the various issues that *kendō* faces in Japan and in the international community. Since then of course the Internet has really taken over, and in many respects there is a lot of information available about *kendō* now, but we have continued to publish Kendo World Magazine because people know that what they are getting in Kendo World is reliable, useful and interesting information. It was also a way for us to bring the various regions that practice *kendō* like the South Americans, North Americans, the Europeans, the Koreans and other Asian countries, New Zealand, Australia and the Japanese together.

This is in terms of keeping track of what's happening everywhere in the *kendō* community and not just Japan centric at all. And fortunately people have supported us throughout the years, even though they have much more access now via the Internet, they always turned to Kendo World as an important source of reliable information. And that was something that the International Federation probably should have been doing but they were quite happy to let us do that, because they trust us, and for this we are very grateful. It was because of my activities through Kendo World that the All Japan Kendo Federation called on me to help with various aspects of their international operation and I'm actually now a member of the international committee in the All Japan Kendo Federation. This is because of what we've done with Kendo World Magazine, which they consider an asset as well.

I should make it clear though, that we're not a mouthpiece for Japanese *kendō*. We are not a tool to be utilized by them but they trust us because they know that the people who are involved in *kendō* World love *kendō* to bits, and we are so passionate and enthusiastic about the knowledge that we have access to while we are over here in Japan that we want to share that. So they understand that what we're doing is not trying to take away their authority or anything like that. If anything we're trying to help in the in quest to let people around the world understand what *kendō* really is.

Kendō grades are notoriously difficult to pass at higher levels. Can you talk about your experience?
So in *kendō*, the grades go up to 8th *dan*. *Dan* is for technical proficiency. And then they have another set of titles called *shōgō* (lit. designation/ti-

tle), which are *renshi* (lit. tempered respected person), *kyōshi* (lit. teaching respected person), and *hanshi* (lit. model respected person). They are sort of teacher qualifications if you like, or certifications saying that you are a master, or grandmaster or whatever. So it's slightly different to *dan*. And I passed my 7th *dan* examination. So it's seven out of eight on my first attempt a few years ago. Which, really, for an amateur *kendō* practitioner, is the highest you can realistically hope to go, that is, 7th *dan*. 8th *dan* is like a different realm altogether. People who become 8th *dan* are often almost deified, you know. They are treated like Gods almost, because 8th *dan* is just such an incredibly difficult examination. You have to have held your 7th *dan*, for ten years. You have to be 46 years or older to be able to even sit the 8th *dan* examination and the pass rate is less than one percent. So you've got a lot of really skilled, strong 7th *dan*, going for 8th *dan*, and they will never pass the examination.

So I passed my 7th *dan* examination when I was 39, which is relatively young, and I passed it on my first attempt. I will be able to sit for my 8th *dan* when I am 49. Well it's mandatory that you do ten years of what they call '*shugyō*' (ascetic or disciplined practice), or hard training and study before you can be eligible to sit for the 8th *dan* exam. I probably will not pass it. And so for me to pass the 7th *dan* grading for the first time, when it is generally accepted that most people's *kendō* career in terms of your grade pretty much stops there.

For me it was, well a great surprise. I had expected, really, that I'd probably be sitting the examination for five or six, or maybe even ten times before I passed it. But I did pass it on the first attempt. And, you know, my first reaction was, how did I do that? What did I do right?

A few days later, I actually bumped into one of the examiners. There's a panel of examiners, and they just look at your *kendō*, and they will go no, or yes! And obviously you have to get a majority of yes votes. And you don't know what they're looking or whether you performed well in their eyes or not. But when I saw this examiner a few days later, just out of the blue, I said to him, "Was my grading really that good?" And he said, "Yes. We watched your *kendō* and we felt at ease. That you had mastered your art in terms of your technical ability. Your mental approach. The way in which you are able to convey or use your key to overpower your opponent to create openings, which you were able to capitalize on without thinking about it. So it was very natural."

And that was the feedback that I got. Normally you wouldn't get

Alex Bennett taking the 7th *dan kendō* examination

feedback but I just happened to bump into this examiner, who was obviously a well known 8th *dan sensei* in his own right. And so when I passed the 7th *dan* examination, initially I was a little bit perplexed. But then having heard what the examiner told me, then well, I thought I should be a lot more confident in what I am doing. Also I was also very humbled because I realized that I only have ten years to really take my *kendō* up to a much higher level in terms of my understanding. In terms of my technical ability and my presence in front of my opponent. And in perfecting my art even further. I've created a sort of Alex Bennett *kendō*, which has got me my 7th *dan*, but it has to go to an even higher, to a much more profound level, if I ever have a chance of ever passing the 8th *dan*.

Now I must stress that the whole point of *kendō* is not to pass grades at all. It's not that, "I'm putting everything into passing my 8th *dan* so I can retire as a *kendō* God." That's not the case at all. But what the grades do is they provide benchmarks or milestones. They provide you with, and I hesitate to use the word tangible because sometimes they're not so tangible, but you know, clear cut indicators of where you are and where you should be heading.

So for me now with 8th *dan* a few years away, I'm sort of thinking all the time… "What is it about my *kendō* that needs to be fixed? What is it about my *kendō* that is me? What is it about my *kendō* that is my art that I should be pursuing?" So having that in the back of my mind keeps me honest. And it keeps me in a sense, motivated. It keeps me humble as well. And also, it really drives home the fact that if I want to achieve that higher level, my *kendō* is not something that I can just turn on when I turn up to the *dōjō* or go into the examination. I have to live *kendō* every day. I have to breathe it twenty four seven. It has to be a total part of me. My *kendō* has to be me and I have to be my *kendō*. And that was the realization that I came to when I passed 7th *dan* examination.

Evidently I already sort of had that but I didn't realize it and it drove home to me that this is how *kendō* has affected me. It has become part of my DNA. It is everything that I do in my life now. My work relations is profoundly affected by what I have learned consciously or unconsciously through my years of rigorous *kendō* training. And another important aspect of that, is that there is no perfection of your art. If I was to pass the 8th *dan* examination, that does not mean that I have perfected my art at all. 8th *dan* teachers tell me that all the time! It just means that you have achieved a very high level but if you look over there, there are much more higher mountains that need to be climbed.

So *kendō* has really become a part of the way I interact with people and the way I deal with problems. It also in many ways, is a barometer of my life. It's like… well, everybody fails at things. They have certain episodes in their life that they're not proud of. And *kendō* is something that to me now… I will think to myself, "well you know, as a *kendō* person who is trying to perfect the art of *kendō*, is this the way I should have reacted? Is this what you would expect of somebody who is trying to perfect the way?" *Kendō* sort of polices my morality. In *kendō*, you can be the Japan champion, or you can be the World champion. But you can go into the *dōjō* and you can get your backside spanked by some person who nobody even knows.

I'm young'ish and still physically very strong and fast. In many ways I'm sort of at the peak of my physical powers. Which is a little bit odd if you look at it from the typical Western sporting perspective, with most people in their twenties or thirties at their peak, but for *kendō* this age is really peaking physically. But gradually, as my physical powers or strength decreases, I have to compensate for it with stronger psychology. A stronger spirit. And I will always come up against people who are in their eighties or in their nineties, who I cannot touch, in spite of me being in my prime, if you like. And why is this? It is because their mental stance, their mental *kamae* if you like, is so formidable. It is so strong that

> **❝**
> *So for me, 7th dan was a goal that I have*
> *achieved. 8th dan is a goal that I'm going for.*
> *But the reality is, there really is no end to it. It is*
> *an endless spiritual journey...*

they can see all of these holes, not only in my *kamae*, because the holes that come in your *kamae* or your stance, are actually an extension of the holes in your mind. They are the weaknesses in your spirit. The hesitation, the surprise, the doubt, the fear. And they pick these off!

So you're always learning. You might be the champion, but there's always somebody who's just going to completely take you to pieces. Because you, as a human being are never perfect. But through *kendō*, and through training and through these experiences, you learn to identify what your weaknesses are. And if you want to fix them, you have to be quite humble.

You have to be quite ready to accept your weaknesses. You have to be ready to accept the remonstrance that the lessons that you're taught by anybody and everybody in the *dōjō*. Which is actually a hard thing to do! Especially when you get higher up in the grades because you are afforded a respect, because of your grade. And there are expectations that go with that respect. And you sometimes fall into the trap that you have to act like a 7th *dan* or an 8th *dan*. But if it's just bravado on the surface, then it's not real and coming to grips with that, with me at the moment, in trying to really get to the essence of what my art is, requires that kind of understanding. That kind of humility.

This really connects with the whole idea that *kendō* is a way for developing the spirit and the human character. Just because you do *kendō* or just because you do *budō* does not mean that you're going to become a wonderful human being or a person that demonstrates a high sense of morality or self perfection. That is not the case at all.

However, *kendō* does provide the framework for the philosophy which you can choose to live or not live. And I now see in *kendō* something that... well I say this because it's such an integral part of my very being, that my constant struggle is to be honest with myself and maintain that humility and continue trying to develop myself, warts and all, and accept that there is no end to it. But it's so fulfilling at the same time.

What you can get that, you know, the physical aspect and also the, and I use the word spiritual a lot, and I sort of hesitate because I realize it is such a loaded word, but it's almost a spiritual liberation that comes with it. It's addictive, but *kendō* is also really a guide that has guided me even further into the deepest reaches of my soul, of my existence that I don't think I ever would have thought of before. So for me, 7th *dan* was a goal that I have achieved. 8th *dan* is a goal that I'm going for. But the reality is, there really is no end to it. It is an endless spiritual journey.

You said aspects that got you your 7th dan test were hidden. Now your objective is to reproduce them again?
Well, they are hidden because you don't think about it. It is not something that you can pretend. It is exactly a demonstration of your inner strengths and weaknesses. But, you know, the fact that I was able to pass the 7th *dan* was to demonstrate my inner strength that I didn't even know about. (Laughs). But that's what they're looking for. And that's why the grading, sometimes it's like… "why did that person pass and this person didn't? I mean, he was able to hit his opponent hundreds of times, in the short time that was available, but this person didn't do anything." But you see, it is not even whether you are successful at striking your opponent. It is your presence. And how your body and mind are completely in sync. And that is something that, unless you've been doing it yourself for many years, many decades, you cannot identify. It's not something that you can just explain in black and white.

And so the fact that I was able to pass that grade, was an indication to me that I have actually developed something. It is it actually affected me in such a profound way that I wasn't really aware of. If I was aware of that, and I tried to feign it, I would have failed the examination. So it really has to be natural. And I think that sort of shows just how martial arts can be extremely positive in your development as a human being but potentially very dangerous as well. This is something that all people who practice the martial arts, especially instructors must be acutely aware of. The potential is there to just completely transform your outlook. The way you deal with people. Your morality in many ways. It's quite frightening. You know, for me, it's a beautiful thing, but it could also be quite scary, I think.

You know, if you want to get good, you have to confront things about yourself that you probably do not really want to. And so I say for me *kendō* is now, to use another loaded term, it's sort of like my own personal "thought police" (laughs). It really dictates the way in which I portray myself in front of other people and ultimately to myself as well. Fortunately my "thought police" keep me honest. I think!

Can you discuss your translation of the Hagakure?

Yes I can. The *Hagakure* is, I would say, probably the most infamous book written about *bushidō*. It was written in the early 18th century. The first two chapters in the *Hagakure* were sort of dictations

by Jōchō Yamamoto (buddhist name) or otherwise known as Tsunetomo Yamamoto, who was sort of a retired *samurai* from the Nabeshima domain, which is down in Kyushu. And when I say retired *samurai*, I mean his overlord died and he wanted to also follow his Lord in death by committing *seppuku* (lit. cut abdomen; ritual suicide by disembowelment), as a form of ultimate loyalty. That's really what it is - you follow your Lord in death. But this actual practice, known as *junshi* (lit. following into death), of committing suicide when your Lord dies, was outlawed by the domain a few decades before, because every time a Lord died, everybody else would kill themselves. Obviously, this is not good for the running of the domain. And also the *bakufu* (lit. tent government; also 'shogunate'), the military government, also decreed that *junshi* was to be outlawed.

So Jōchō Yamamoto couldn't commit suicide. And it is a show of his loyalty that instead of committing suicide, he became a monk. He retired from worldly affairs and sat in his hermitage, contemplating his time and service of his Lord. He also contemplated the way in which young *samurai* of the day have really forgotten what it is to be a true *samurai*. They had forgotten what the way of the warrior - *bushidō* (lit. way of the respected military person) was. And so he was a little bit frustrated, a bit of a curmudgeon, perhaps. And one of his juniors, if you like, from the Nabeshima domain, came in and recorded his gripes and his various anecdotes. These really shed some light and provide a window on the kind of frustrations that *samurai* had during the Tokugawa period, which was a time of peace.

Now you can remember that *samurai* were primed for war, they'd had centuries developing a subculture that was based on military exploits and honor through your strength of arms, or through your dedication to the point of death, If required. Now over time, wars became a thing of the past. But the *samurai* still occupy the top echelon of Japanese society. So you have a group of professional warriors who don't have any way of demonstrating their valor. Their worth as warriors. So there was a lot of frustration and this peace thing was a bit of a problem in the sense that, obviously, the way the warrior lived their life, the expectations were still there, but the reality was not. And so the *Hagakure*, in many ways, shows modern readers a lot about the lifestyle, the expectations, the trials, the tribulations, the frustrations, the dilemma, of being a warrior during peace. And my translation of the *Hagakure*, although I'd studied various aspects of *bushidō*, of *samurai* culture, for many years, is the main point of my research.

What I found through translating the *Hagakure* was that in order to translate it properly, you really have to read between the lines a lot of the time. You have to understand what is not stated, to really get what is stated. And even Japanese scholars or Western scholars you know, if they're ever going to quote from the Hagakure, it's usually proforma. The standard quote is the 'way of the warrior is found in death' or 'I have found that the way of the warrior is to die.' There are various interpretations, as the nuances are slightly different but that's the standard quote. Which is, when you think about 'the way of the warrior is found in death or is to die,' is quite harsh. It's indicative of a very harsh world that seems to really belittle the whole concept of life. It's as if something happens and what the warrior then needs to do is just rush in there and just throw caution to the wind and die. This is the way you would literally translate it.

By translating the *Hagakure* and actually really trying to get inside the text rather than just translating what was written on the pages - to really try and get inside that mindset, requires an extensive understanding of the cultural and social context of the times. I mean if you try and read it based on a modern sort of moral outlook it's quite repugnant. So getting rid of all those preconceived ideas and the kind of stereotypical shallow understanding of *samurai* culture and really trying to feel what he's trying to say, and to do it completely is impossible. But you do need

Alexander Bennett

to have this very open mind and try to get inside the mind of what Jōchō Yamamoto was saying.

I discovered many things that I had completely overlooked in my research up until now. And I guess the most important thing is the book itself. That when I say it's infamous is actually that it was infamous because of this hard-line approach. A hard-line approach to death and the fact that it seems very disorganized and just a mishmash of all sorts of bad tempered observations about the discrepancies of the political system at the time and the way in which young *samurai* just didn't get it anymore.

But if you look at the *Hagakure*, it's actually very well ordered and there seems to be a very distinct method in this madness. Actually what I took away from this translation was a new found respect for Jōchō Yamamoto and that if you contextualize what he's saying, the contradictions that seem to appear in the text are because each time he mentions some anecdote or talked about something, he was actually talking about it with a certain group of people in mind. Maybe with a different rank of *samurai* where the expectations are different.

But I think the most profound thing that I got out of it was that actually 'the way of the warrior being in death' was an affirmation of life. What he was really sort of saying was, you have one life to live and you don't want to waste that so you should approach everything you do, as if it's your last. Without worrying about the consequences or worrying about whether your finances were going to suffer because of it. Or worrying about whether you have made some terrible transgression which will result in your ultimate punishment, which by the way, was usually death. If you think about life like that all of the time, then you'll never reach your true potential.

You have to feel that everything that you do is the most significant thing in your life, and I think that was really the underlying theme in the book. Which I really felt by reading between the lines. Unfortunately many of the passages in the *Hagakure* are misunderstood or they are utilized in ways which take it completely out of context. The *Hagakure* was a text that was relatively widely read in the Second World War for obvious reasons. If you look at it on face value it's saying 'a true warrior sacrifices his life for the greater good.' That interpretation is possible of course but I think in a way, I sort of got to know Jōchō Yamamoto. I wouldn't say he's a friend (laughs) but I could sort of see where he was coming from and if you add all the bits together i think he was a very sentimental man, who really treasured his time on this earth when death was such a matter of fact thing at that time. I mean public execution and *seppuku* or death by disease. Whatever it was just part and parcel of everyday life, in a way that you know we moderns would be absolutely abhorred or disgusted by it.

Obviously their ideas about death and dying in life are obviously very different to ours. Our standpoint is very different. But again I think as human beings there is a humanistic essence that transcends cultures and places and time, and he touched upon this in the Hagakure.

I think it is incredibly relevant at least to me, in understanding what my life is all about and how important it is that i make the most of that it. It sounds very sentimental when I say that but I really felt it. He had some great lessons through his direct contact with death which was as I said before, was part and parcel of life at the time. It's something that I have never had contact with except the odd funeral with, maybe a friend or family or a sensei or something like that. So it's not really a reality to me in my current state, but it is to Jōchō Yamamoto, and he was able to convey so many messages about the profundity of it all that would never have occurred to me.

So for me, it was personally a fantastic journey into the mind of what I would say is not a special man by any stretch of the imagination. He's just a typical 'Joe Tanaka' *samurai* in his twilight years, reflecting on the meaning of it all from his experience and that experience is something that I think is still applicable.

> **"**
> *None of our members in the 600-year long history of our tradition have been cut down in challenge matches. Nor have any of them cut others down*

28.
Rizuke Ōtake
TENSHINSHŌ-DEN KATORI SHINTŌ-RYŪ

Chapter 28
INTRODUCTION

Tenshinshō-den Katori Shintō-ryū needs no introduction to the many devotees of classical Japanese martial arts and schools of swordsmanship. Founded in the mid Muromachi period of the fifteenth century, by Ien-ao Iizasa Chōisai, a swordmaster of some reputation, *Katori Shintō-ryū* was established in modern day Chiba close to the Katori Shrine where Chōisai Sensei was in retreat. The Deity of Katori *Jingū* (Grand Shrine) is said to have passed on through divine transmission (*Tenshinshō-den*) the teachings (kata) of *Katori Shintō-ryū*.

This tradition has been passed on through the centuries, and the classical *bujutsu* is still practiced today, under the leadership of Risuke Ōtake Shihan (since retired and passed to his son, Nobutoshi Ōtake). In 1960, *Katori Shintō-ryū* was awarded the status of Intangible Cultural Asset by Chiba Prefecture. It is the first martial art in Japan to be designated as a cultural asset. Risuke Ōtake Shihan was designated as the school's guardian.

Katori Shintō-ryū has an extensive curriculum, with class practice mainly in *kenjutsu* (swordsmanship), with other martial arts, such as *iaijut-su* (sword drawing), *bōjutsu* (staff), *naginatajutsu* (halberd), *sōjut su* (spear)

Risuke Ōtake, Jon Braeley and Paul Martin outside the *Shinbukan Dōjō*

and *jūjutsu* (unarmed combat). Add to this studies in strategy of warfare and you get a sense of being transported back to the age of the *samurai*.

Studying at *Katori Shintō-ryū* is taken very seriously with prospective students undergoing a thorough interview that ends with *keppan* (lit. blood seal) the signing in blood, of an oath of allegiance to the school. Risuke Ōtake Sensei oversees this ritual in order to preserve the secrecy and integrity of the school's teachings.

You cannot simply walk into *Shinbukan* (Hall of divine military valor) *Dōjō* of Risuke Ōtake Sensei, located in the countryside near Narita City in Chiba. You must be invited with an appointment. For this I am indebted to a practitioner of long-standing at *Katori Shintō-ryū*, Phil Relnick Sensei, who spent forty years in Japan, training in a number of classical Japanese martial arts. Today Relnick Sensei is teaching *Shintō Musō-ryū jōjutsu* and *Katori Shintō-ryū* at his *Shin tōkan Dōjō* back home in Washington state in America.

I met with Phil Relnick in downtown Tokyo at his hotel in late October of 2009. His wife was taking part in a demonstration of *ikebana* (lit. living flowers; Japanese flower arrangements) at a large department store. Like me, Phil Relnick has a passion for *rāmen*, a noodle soup that is so much more than it's name suggests. When I am filming in the cold winter months in Japan, our film crew likes to start the day with a steaming hot bowl of *rāmen*. Phil was excited to tell me that nearby the hotel was a famous *rāmen* restaurant and even though it was only 11am we headed out to beat the expected lunchtime queue that always appears for good *rāmen*.

Unfortunately, the line was already two blocks long and by our estimate, not all of these would-be diners would reach the door before the *rāmen* ran out. However some enterprising chefs had set up *rāmen* shops nearby, knowing they would be serving those who cannot wait in line, which included Phil Relnick and myself! Once seated and with the *rāmen* ordered, the call was made to Risuke Ōtake Sensei at the *Shinbukan Dōjō*.

For the visit to *Katori Shintō-ryū*, I would be taking Paul Martin, who was my guide for the documentary, *Art of the Japanese Sword*, which I had been shooting that year with many of Japan's top swordsmiths. Paul, who apprenticed at the British Museum, is a leading expert in the Japanese sword, and holds a license to appraise historical *samurai* swords, which is very rare for non-Japanese. This turned out to be a very good move. During the interview, Ōtake Sensei produced a magnificent Japanese sword that had been in his family for many generations and drawing the *katana* out of its scabbard, handed it to Paul for his inspection. That was not the only highlight of the interview. Ōtake Sensei had planned a surprise. We would be filming the rare induction of a new student, who would be signing an oath of allegiance in blood, to *Katori Shintō-ryū*. Truly a memorable visit.

Risuke Ōtake Sensei, 2009

THE INTERVIEW

Can you talk about the history of Katori Shintō-ryū?
To briefly explain the history of *Katori Shintō-ryū*, the founder of our tradition, Master Ienao Chōisai, was born 620 years ago in the Iizasa district in Tako town, Shimosa in 1387. He served the warlord Naomasa Ashikaga. The domain in which he lived was known as Chida manor in those days. He participated in numerous battles and was renowned for having never been defeated, but at around 60 years of age, was witness to the downfall of the Chiba family under whom he had served. At this point Master Ienao Chōisai realized that people, households and nations are sometimes powerless to change situations regardless of the efforts they may expend.

He thus bequeathed land and money to those who had served him and released them from his service. He himself then underwent 1,000

days and nights of ascetic martial arts practice within the Katori Shrine, and devised the *Katori Shintō-ryū*.

Since our art is transmitted directly from the deities of the Katori Shine, we refer to it as *Tenshinshō-den* (direct and authentic transmission from the deities) *Katori Shintō-ryū*. Following this, a wide variety of martial artists joined our tradition as students, including the swordsmen Nobutsuna Kamiizumi, who went on to teach the Yagyū; Tsukahara Tosanokami of Kashima, the father of Bokuden Tsukahara; as well as Ippasai Morooka and Masanobu Matsumoto. While these men learned *Katori Shintō-ryū*, they later went on take on students in their own newly-devised martial arts traditions under different names.

So for 600 years, *Katori Shintō-ryū*, has been considered the fountainhead of Japanese martial arts. However, the founder of our tradition, Master Ienao Chōisai, realized that aspiring martial artists thought that they could become famous by winning in a challenge against the renowned tradition of *Shintō-ryū*. When such martial artists came to challenge the master, he used a teaching that is still transmitted today, known as '*kumazasa no oshie*' (lit. teaching of the bamboo grass). The master would sit atop the *kumazasa* (bamboo grass) and invite the visitor to join him, with the understanding that if the visitor was also able to sit down, the master would accept the challenge.

Such martial artists realized the *kumazasa* would be crushed if they were able to sit down. While the founder of our tradition would be seated atop the *kumazasa*, visitors realized they would be unable to attempt such a feat, and would withdraw their challenge. This teaching is still passed on today as '*kumazasa no taiza*' (standoff sitting atop bamboo grass), suggesting that winning by engaging in combat (such challenge matches) is not true victory.

So the challenge would not take place?

True victory is won by achieving one's goals without conflict. For this reason, none of our members in the 600-year long history of our tradition have been cut down in challenge matches. Nor have any of them cut others down. This is one distinguishing aspect of our special tradition.

To be clear, the martial arts we diligently practice today are highly efficient arts of killing others. Our founder taught that one must not engage in conflict or strike others down, and that winning without conflict is true victory.

Samurai of Katori Shintō-ryū did not participate in combat?

I once went on an overseas trip to deliver a lecture, and was fielding questions from the audience. Someone put their hand up and asked "Do you really need to learn things people shouldn't do?"

However, winning without conflict is difficult unless one is strong both mentally, spiritually and technically. I thus explained that it is fine for one to become stronger through one's study of the tradition, as long as one did not use what one had learned.

Our tradition taught that martial arts were not for use in conflict, but rather for achieving peace in the Warring States period. So *samurai* did not enroll in *Katori Shintō-ryū* during the Warring States period. While several of the swordsmen who studied with our founder were *samurai*, the actual warlords were unable to join – they had a duty to engage in conflict (civil war). Since they were involved in the waging of war, they were unable to enroll.

It was not until the age of peace, the Edo period, that large numbers of *samurai* enrolled in our tradition. *Samurai* from many of the respective domains came to study, such as *kenjutsu* instructors from various domains in Kyushu.

Famous students from our tradition include students of Master Moritsuna, the 4th generation grandmaster, albeit in the Warring States period, like Shigeharu "Hanbei" Takenaka, a famous strategist who served under the warlord Hideyoshi Toyotomi. These sorts of *samurai* did enroll in our tradition. In his case, he did not come to *Katori Shintō-ryū* to study – there are no records of him here – instead, we presume that when the 4th generation grandmaster, Master Moritsuna traveled to various domains, he visited *Minonokuni* (Mino Province, present day Gifu Prefecture) to engage in ascetic practice and taught him there.

Shigeharu Takenaka was strongly influenced by this study, and had a disdain for war, begrudgingly engaging in warfare, and capturing castles without engaging in conflict. He passed away at the young age of 36 of tuberculosis. It is my view that had Takenaka lived to an advanced age, Tokugawa would have not have usurped power from Toyotomi. He was born in the 1544, and passed away at the age of 36.

The vast majority of *samurai* students, such as Kojūrō Katakura of the Date family - a name inherited by several generations- not the Kojūrō Katakura of the distant War-ring States period, but a descendant several generations later named Kojūrō Katakura Muranori, who joined our tradition and received *menkyo kaiden* (lit. license with complete transmission; initiation and license into the tradition). He was the lord of Shiroishi Castle – present day Shiroishi near Sendai – and a hereditary retainer in Sendai to Masamune Date. Aside from these men, the majority of *samurai* joining *Katori Shintō-ryū* did so after the heralding in of the age of peace. You see, Japan was ruled by the warrior class from the Kofun period in the 3rd century to the 6th century, where powerful regional families fought each other, establishing the nation of Japan through ongoing victory and defeat in war.

Much of Japanese culture is thus influenced by the culture of the warrior class. The martial arts are a part of the warrior class culture that has supported Japan's warrior class and history to date, and it is my desire this be passed on through the generations. At the same time, *Katori Shintō-ryū* transmits lethal knowledge, so we must ensure it is not used irresponsibly or to violent ends in life. Martial artists thus must possess humility and selflessly serve others – what I consider the true *bushidō*.

Bushidō that is devoid of this spirit of humility is nothing more than violence. So in *Shintō-ryū*, applicants are required to take a blood oath, with part of the oath being that one will do no harm or inconvenience others, although this is implicit rather than explicit today. Applicants therefore make a blood oath before the deities and pledge to not inconvenience others before commencing study. Many martial artists in the Warring States period had a penchant for dueling and engaged in

Risuke Ōtake drawing blood from the student to sign the oath

shinken shōbu (lit. victory or defeat with live swords; challenge matches with real swords) or fought each other with *bokutō* (wooden sabre). There are stories that some of them defeated scores, as many as sixty opponents without being defeated. These men were murderers, and thus have no descendants today.

So Katori Shintō-ryū flourished even during this time of conflict?
Yes. This is why our founder master Iizasa in Katori lived to the age of 102. Taking average life spans into consideration today, one would have to live to around 200 years or age to replicate this achievement. Not even a single student claiming to study *Shintō-ryū* in the 600 year history of our school has laid down there life wastefully engaging in challenges.

The only related person that did so was Masanobu Matsumoto of Kashima, who, although I do not know if this is fact or legend, is said to have gone on to become the founder of *Kashima Shin-ryū*, or to have founded *Jikishinkage-ryū*. Matsumoto must be the only individual in our lineage to have been killed in combat, and was killed in the Kashima Insurrection.

No other students in this, the art said to be the oldest of Japan's martial arts traditions, has been killed wastefully. This makes our martial art an almost miraculous form of ascetic practice.

Our master, Ienao Iizasa Chōisai, had a preference for peace. He purposefully lived this way, despite being the leading martial artist of his time, and prayed for the righteous prosperity of his descendants, as well as for peace and good harvests throughout the land.

> **"**
> *Katori Shintō-ryū transmits lethal knowledge.*
> *We must ensure it is not used irresponsibly or to*
> *violent ends. Martial artists must possess humil-*
> *ity and selflessly serve others. What I consider*
> *the true bushidō. Bushidō devoid of this spirit of*
> *humility is nothing more than violence...*

While people may find the fact the leading martial artist of his time prayed for peace and proclaimed that people should not engage in conflict contradictory, I consider this to be the true way in which martial arts should be engaged.

So Katori Shintō-ryū is passed on through the generations in times of peace?

It is like this yes. For example, today our government is encouraging the creation of swords by swordsmiths. Yet swords are by their nature weapons. Japanese swords were first created some 1200 years ago, with swords before this time brought from China by swordsmiths.

Metallurgy was thus introduced to Japan by swordsmiths from the continent. Japanese swordsmiths learned this weapon-forging technology from them. Curved swords were first produced 1200 years ago, and have been used in conflict until the era of peace. The Japanese government today respectfully designates some of these fine swords from long ago as National Treasures or Important Cultural Assets.

Japanese swords are some of the finest blades in the world – international cultural assets. The government today permits their creation as works of art. They are Tangible Cultural Assets. I consider that few swords as fine are produced during times of war. Such times are gestation periods for fine swords, with such fine swords then reappearing in times of peace.

It has been this repetition of war and peace that 60 years after the war, allows swordsmiths to produce swords approaching the quality of the Kamakura period, which pleases me to no end.

I would like to see Japanese swords preserved for many hundreds of years to come, not as weapons, but rather as works of art the warrior

class respected. I would also like to preserve *Shintō-ryū*, the techniques of using such swords, as a form of warrior class culture, for eternity. I consider the preservation of Japanese swords and the martial arts we study one and the same, in terms of preservation as cultural assets. Both Japanese swords and the combative technology to use them are forms of warrior class culture, and it is my intention to work for the rest of my life to ensure they are correctly preserved.

Can you talk about the swords in your study?

Yes I can, first let me explain about Japanese swords. Curved swords are said to have first been created circa 987-989AD. However, before them, Tōta Fujiwara who shot Taira no Masakado through the head with a bow and arrow during the Tengyō Insurrection wore a *kenuki-gata tachi* (lit. tweezer-shaped large curved sword) that still exists to this day. *Kenuki-gata tachi* have distinct curvature close to their *tsuba* (sword-guard), as well as in their blades. Curved swords were thus in existence before circa 987-989AD, around 1200 years ago.

For my Japanese sword, this is a blade by Magoroku Kanemoto with a two character signature. It has a *hi* (blade groove) carved into them near their *shinogi* (ridge-line), called a *bōhi*. A *hi* groove makes a sword lighter, since it eliminates a substantial amount of steel, and it also prevents the sword clinging when cutting, since it allows air in, and ensures the sword passes through effortlessly. In addition, a *bōhi* is 'H' shaped similar to the rails on a railroad, and ensures the structure does not bend left or right under stress, so they are often carved into swords.

Engravings first appeared on swords in the late-Heian Period, with 95% of them derived from *mikkyō* (esoteric Buddhism). *Shingonshū Mikkyō* (lit. Mantra sect of Esoteric Buddhism) was spread to Japan by Saint Kūkai, who received 3 years of difficult ascetic training in Chang'an in China under the tutelage of 8th generation Saint Huikuo. *Mikkyō* places a large emphasis on magical arts, and places the greatest reverence on *Dainichi nyorai* (lit. ultimate suchness of the great sun; skt. *Mahāvairocana Tathāgata*), as well as a large number of Buddhist deities including bodhi sattva, rāja and deva.

Samurai mikkyō devotees therefore engraved *mikkyō* deities onto their swords. 95% of the engravings on blades are *mikkyō* derived. The remaining 5% were engraved from the *Shintō* period (Edo period), and include auspicious designs unrelated to *mikkyō* such as carp swimming up waterfalls, cherry-blossoms, as well as pine, bamboo and plum, that comprise less than 5% of engravings. The remainder is all *mikkyō*-derived.

People often talk about the sword and *zen* (profound meditation; from chn. '*chánnà*' and skt. *dhyāna*); "movement in stillness" and encourage the practice of *shikantaza* (single-minded seated *zen* meditation), and say *samurai* emphasized that the '*kenzen ichinyo*' (lit. oneness of sword and *zen*). It has a good ring to it, and some warlords certainly learned *zen*. The Yagyū family had a Zen Buddhist temple in their home village and followed *Zenshū* (lit. *Zen* (Meditation) sect of Buddhism), but in the majority of cases, warlords from the Heian to Kamakura periods were followers of *mikkyō*.

Mikkyō contains a wide variety of methods such as '*kuji no hō*' (lit. method of the nine signs) and '*jūji no hō*' (lit. method of the ten signs). *Fudō Myōō* (lit. Immovable Wisdom King; skt. *Acalanātha Vidyārāja*) is one of the 'wisdom kings' of *mikkyō*. The expression seed syllable '*hāmmām*' (in Japanese, pronounced as '*kānmān*') from the mantra '*Namah samanta vajrānām hām* (in Japanese, '*Nōmaku sanmanda bazaradan kan*') and even the single syllable '*hām* represents *Fudō Myōō*.

The famous '*Bizen Osafune Kagemitsu no tachi*' (long sabre made by Kagemitsu of the *Bizen Osafune* school of swordsmiths) is said to have been used by the famous warlord Masashige Kusunoki in the Kamakura period was shortened and may have already been like this when Masashige Kusunoki used it. A part of a dragon remains on its *nakago* (tang) despite the sword having been shortened. It is known as '*koryū Kagemitsu*'

Katori Shintō-ryū is Japan's oldest surviving martial art school, founded in 1447

(lit. Kagemitsu's small dragon) and is now a National Treasure. The warlord Masashige Kusunoki was active in the Nan bokuchō period, and is known historically as an outstanding Nan bokuchō period strategist and warlord.

The engraving of a seed syllable on the rear of his blade says 'kānmān', representing '*Nōmaku sanmanda bazaradan kan*'– *Fudō Myōō*'s mantra – with the other side depicting a *Kurikara* (abbreviation of skt. *Kulikah rāja*; a dragon God King), entwined around the sword. This is another representation of *Fudō Myōō*. This sword tells us he was a *Fudō Myōō* devotee.

Engravings therefore clearly tells us that warlords were followers of *Shingonshū Mikkyō*, and not *Zenshū* Buddhism. *Katori Shintō-ryū* also has the '*kuji no in*' (lit. nine signs seal)– *rin, pyō, tō, sha, kai, jin, retsu, zai, zen* – each accompanied by *mudra* (hand signs) that is used when engaging in challenging activities. These nine signs are made, and sealed with a tenth character (*jūji no hō*), with the *mantra* '*Abira un ken sowa ka*' (from skt. '*A vi ra hūm kham svāhā*'; mantra of *Mahāvairocana* alluding to the union of the five elements). This is actually *mikkyō*.

The vast majority of Japan's culture came from China, including the *kanji* (Chinese-originated ideographic characters) in our written language. Most of our culture has traveled this way to us east of China. The Buddhism and martial arts used by the likes of Zhang Liang and Huang Shigong have also been transmitted to us in Japan. These things have been conveyed East to us from the continent. The Pacific Ocean lays to the East of us, so this culture stopped here in Japan, and took on forms suited to us, such as with Buddhism and the martial arts.

This has all been improved upon by the Japanese to suit us. From this perspective, considering that *samurai* even had spears and some castles also have *jūji no hō* engraved on them, it is clear the majority followed *Mikkyō*, not *zen*. This is clear on examination of Japanese swords.

Shintō-ryū also transmits a vast esoteric curriculum, such as *kuji no in and jūji no hō*. This includes *ninjutsu* (espionage art), *chikujōjutsu* (field fortification art), *inyōgaku* (yin-yang cosmology and divination) and *gunbaihō* (troop deployment methods) – academic studies that are still practiced today. The magical arts of *mikkyō* are also practiced in their fullest sense. I therefore assume there is no other tradition like ours, in terms of its academic curriculum.

Our founder also studied the majority of the academic fields of his time, including Shintoism, Buddhism and Confucianism. This knowledge has been preserved through the generations. Even the house in which our founder was born some 600 something years ago is still in existence today in the town of Tako.

The 20th generation descendants of the founder Ienao Iizasa Chōisai, is an unbroken lineage and alive in Katori. Also the family's *dōjō*, the oldest such *dōjō* amongst Japanese classical martial arts traditions, built around 350 years ago, is designated a cultural asset by Katori city. It is the oldest *dōjō* amongst Japanese classical martial arts traditions. I therefore consider it extremely fortunate that I have been able to devote myself to this tradition.

> **"**
> *The naginata that we do nowadays is 'modern naginata'. However, this naginata inherited its techniques from old style koryū naginata*

29.
Wataru Suzuki
RENSHI 6TH DAN NAGINATA

Chapter 29
INTRODUCTION

The *naginata* is an interesting weapon in Japanese martial arts. In it's military usage it was similar to the European glaive or pole-arm. Both consist of a wooden pole with a single edged curved blade at the end. It was essentially a battlefield weapon and unlike the *katana*, was not meant to be carried around at all times.

The *naginata* was used effectively in a number of battles between various clans in the medieval period, where it was used to dismount horseman. When wielded by a foot soldier, the long reach of the *naginata* could clear a section of the battlefield to allow mounted *samurai* to ride through. It was not however, the long-range weapon heavily favored by the *samurai* who preferred a *yari* (long spear) which is lighter and could be thrust at the enemy while on horseback.

The *naginata* rose to prominence when it was featured in the classic "The Tale of the Heike", which is an account the Genpei War fought between the Taira clan and the Minamoto clan. Later, in the more peaceful Edo period, the *naginata* went from the battlefield to being a weapon that could be used to defend the home, giving rise to the popular notion that wives of noble status and *samurai* class would stay at home practic-

A female *Naginata* expert faces a *kenjutsu* master. Photo: Jon Braeley

ing *naginatajutsu* (*naginata* applied techniques). There is some merit to this, and it was not unheard of that a *naginata* was used as a dowry of a women of nobility.

Today, with the steel blade replaced with wood, the *naginata* has taken it's place alongside other traditional martial arts (*koryū bujutsu*), and practiced in the *dōjō*. For sparring and competitions *kendō* style *bōgu* (protective equipment) is worn.

Naginata is a popular choice for girls in school looking to include a martial art in their curriculum. I was not surprised then, in my search for a *naginata* instructor for the *Warriors of Budo series* to be recommended to Wataru Suzuki. He is a *naginata* instructor, teaching a girls class at a high school in the suburbs of Tokyo.

Wataru Suzuki Sensei, 2015

THE INTERVIEW

Can you please introduce yourself?

My name is Wataru Suzuki. I am a physical education instructor at the Saitama Sakae High school. I have the title of *renshi* in *naginata*.

Can you tell us how you came to study naginata?

I started practicing in my second year of junior school. This was really because I was following my mother, who had also started practicing

naginata at that time. Before I realized it, I was fully absorbed into training in *naginata*. Back when I started in the second year of junior school I thought it was strange that there were only girls practicing. I did not notice there were no other boys my age. I became aware that it is seen as a *budō* for women only after I was really into it so there was not turning back. Regardless of *naginata* being for boys or girl or whatever, I have continued to walk this path teaching *naginata* until today.

Did you practice any other martial arts beside naginata?
I began with *naginata*, but afterwards I also started doing *kendō*. While practicing both simultaneously, I noticed that *kendō* techniques are instantaneous. On the other hand, because the *naginata* is so long, there are techniques involving changing the grip and I found this very appealing. Also, instead of defining the outcome in a single blow, *naginata* techniques are more fluent and involve seizing the opponent. I particularly find it very interesting. That is the reason I prefer to practice *naginata*.

And there is a Naginata Federation I believe?
Yes. The previous generation of instructors from the All Japan Naginata Federation practiced *koryū* such as *Tendō-ryū* and *Shinkage-ryū*. They were able to think above that and together they discussed about and determined the ways in which they could transmit their knowledge of *naginata* on to the new generation. I believe it was around the 1950s when the Federation was first established.

High school *Naginata* students practice *kata*

The *naginata* that we do nowadays is 'modern *naginata*'. However, this *naginata* inherited its techniques and many basic elements like *'te no uchi'* (lit. inside of the hand; subtle way to grip the weapon; also *tenouchi*) from old style *koryū naginata*.

You mentioned Tendō-ryū. Do you practice koryū of naginata?

When my technique was not mature enough or should I say not completely acquired, I had a chance to observe *Tendō-ryū.*. Among the techniques I saw, there was one called *yaechigai* (lit. layered difference; a cut where the posterior end of the *naginata* switches from the front left side to the back right side). I thought that it could be used while using the *bōgu* (protective equipment). I tried it during practice and even during a competition and was able to execute it successfully. I think it was just a lucky strike, but I could do it with *'Ki-ken-tai icchi'* (lit. agreement of spirit, sword and body as one) and good body movement so the judges in the competition raised their flags in approval. From that time onwards I have tried it many more times but most of the times it does not become a valid strike. I am still working hard on it.

What are your thoughts on International naginata competitions?

During the 5th *naginata* World Championships which took place in Japan and also the 4th World Championship, I had the impression that the male category overseas had increased its strength considerably. If we

The shin as a *Naginata* target has its roots in slashing at mounted *samurai*

in Japan do not train harder we might be defeated from the top positions of overseas competitors. We are organizing intensive training course and so on. It is a traditional Japanese *budō* so I feel that we have the basic responsibility to display techniques that can serve as role-models for other practitioners, especially those abroad.

It is not enough just to win, we must adhere to *Ki-ken-tai icchi* and the other principles to which *naginata* techniques are subject to. We are preparing a good *naginata* which the world can take as example. It is still not official, but I think that I will be appointed to prepare the male Japanese team to display such *naginata*. I am training hard in order to do that.

Do you strike the same targets as kendō?

Not all of them, no. In *kendō* the *sune* (shin) is not a target but in *naginata* the shin is a valid target. The *naginata* as a weapon was used to mow down horses and men, and cavalry soldiers. It was used for killing and wounding with a characteristic slashing attack in a descending arc. For this reason attacks in the lower part of the body like the shins are a characteristic of *naginata* even today. This is why the *suneate* (shin guard) is a valid target.

I understand you fought with naginata against kendō?

That is right, I have been allowed to do it several times (fight against *kendō* using *naginata*). It is a long object with a long-distance reach so for a *kendōka* who is not used to *naginata*, it is easy to get hit in the sune (shins). When fighting between *Naginata* and *kendō*, one really feels like one is fighting in a battlefield from the old days. I usually attempt to win by doing thrusts to the throat and strikes to the head of the *kendō* player. We all have our preferences when fighting, and I try to win with attacks other than the sune (shins).

If the distance is shortened to the one normally used in *kendō*, we can expect to be attacked very quickly. It is important to have the mental preparation to avoid shortening the distance and to maintain a good distance for the *naginata*. I have the chance to practice with many *kendō* instructors often. Although they are doing *kendō* they also attack my shins and shorten the distance to one adequate for *kendō*. It is a very good chance to learn, and by practicing against *kendō* there are many things that can also be used to improve my *naginata* techniques.

I have also had experience with practitioners of *Nitō-ryū* (lit. two blades style). I believe it was *Niten'i chi-ryū* (lit. 'two heavens as one' style). The *Nitō-ryū* fighter is not only good at technique but also the management of distance and the way of handling the two swords. Whenever that person comes to practice it is quite intense even if there is no contest of winning or losing. Unlike normal *kendō*, the *Niten'i chi-ryū* style fighter will pressure for the attack from above. Fighting against *Nitō-ryū* is always a great chance for study.

What are the rules for naginata in competition?
The regulations of the All Japan Naginata Federation stipulate that the weapon is to have a length between two meters and ten centimeters and two meters and twenty-five centimeters. Any length that falls within this range is acceptable. It is not permissible to use a *naginata* longer than two meters and twenty-five centimeters. Junior school students and small children use ones adapted and shortened to their heights.

For practice a *bōgu* (protective equipment) is worn just like in *kendō* when doing sparring. Otherwise there are some risks such as bamboo pieces sticking into to face and so on. The *ishizuki* (lit. stone thruster; butt end of a spear-like weapon) can be used to thrust at the opponent, but when doing combat wearing protective equipment it is prohibited. However, it does have protective leather covering just in case as it would surely hurt if it strikes the shins and so on. For safety, both the front and back ends of the *naginata* have protective caps.

Wataru Suzuki

> 66
>
> *Being the only girl at this jūkendō keiko, I am among high ranking remarkable instructors who can teach me a great deal. Therefore I am very happy to be the only girl!*

30.
Yayoi Nakanowatari
RENSHI 5TH DAN TANKENDŌ

Chapter 30
INTRODUCTION

There are two Japanese martial arts that share their roots in the military with the introduction of firearms in Japan. The first is *jūkendō* (the way of the bayonet) and the second is *tankendō* (the way of the short sword). *Jūkendō* is the martial art of the bayonet, where a long wooden rifle or *mokujū* is used to thrust the bayonet. *Tankendō* is an offshoot of *jūkendō*, where the bayonet, in this case a short bamboo *shinai*, is hand-held like a short sword.

In *jūkendō*, the aim is very simple. There are three main target areas for the thrusting strike of the bayonet, being the heart, throat and lower left side of the opponent. In preparation, the attacker will try to parry the opponent's *mokujū* (wood rifle and bayonet), to open up the target for the strike. In *tankendō*, the targets are the same as *kendō*, with the addition of a thrust to the torso and a close quarter thrust to the torso when both opponents are locked in a struggle.

The idea that the *samurai* owned and used firearms as early as the 16th century, is often met with surprise. The feudal lord Nobunaga Oda was one of the first military commanders to recognize the potential of firearms in battle and equipped his soldiers with matchlock guns around the mid-16th century. His one advantage being firearms could be learned by anyone, such

Hanshi Masaharu Kuwahara started *jūkendō in 1939 in the military and the police*

as a low-ranking foot soldier, in a short period of time.

The two and a half centuries that followed, known as the Edo period, ushered in a time of peace under the Tokugawa shogunate, and guns were relegated to being used for hunting. The arrival of the U.S. Navy with Commodore Perry in 1854, forced the opening up of Japan to the outside, and so began a new age of firearms. Indeed, the more sophisticated firearms, composed of heavy guns, rifles and pistols, leveled the playing field when enemies met in a conflict, and signaled the end of the *samurai* warrior class.

Japan looked toward Europe and the United States to arm its military. The French bolt-action Chassepot rifle, had a long blade, or bayonet attached to the barrel and the ruling shogunate imported 40,000 Chassepot rifles in 1867. The following year was the start of the Meiji period and the French military missions to Japan had enormous influence in the rise of *jūkendō* or bayonet technique.

I was fortunate to have Baptiste Tavernier as part of our documentary team in Japan, who is a leading researcher in *jūkendō*. We visited with Baptiste to a seminar by the All Japan Jūkendō Federation, led by Masaharu Kuwahara, *hanshi* 9th *dan*, who has been practicing *jūkendō* for an astonishing seventy five years. He has spent his entire life in the service of Japan, both in the military and in the police force. We talked to Masaharu Kuwahara Sensei for a short time, conscious of his age, still teaching at 89 years of age. He told us, "I started learning *jūkendō*

Yayoi Nakanowatari

when I was fifteen years old and continued after high school. During the Second World War, I was in the Pacific conflict in a nursing unit but I still continued my *jūkendō* practice. After the ending of the war, I joined the police force in 1950 and in 1954 *jūkendō* became part of our training. Back them it was called *'jūkendō kakutō'* (lit. regulated combat in *jūkendō*). So after the war we practiced *'jūkendō kakutō* as *budō* and battle technique were eliminated with more focus on spiritual training. This is how it became *jūkendō.*" At the end of the interview I asked Masaharu Kuwahara sensei how he was able to train with so much strength at his age, and he replied, "I discovered that once you are past eighty five, you must thrust the bayonet with your spirit." This interview is featured in Episode Six of *Warriors of Budo.*

During my visit to the Jūkendō Federation training camp, I met a delightful female practitioner, Yayoi Nakanowatari, who was the only female among the attendees. She studies both *jūkendō* and *tankendō* but told me she prefers *tankendō*, with it's shorter range and combative technique that make victory easier and faster to determine. She also added, "Being the only girl at this *jūkendō keiko* (practice), I am among high ranking remarkable instructors who can teach me a great deal. Therefore I am very happy to be the only girl!"

We arranged to see Yayoi Nakanowatari at the All Japan Tankendō Championships which take place annually at the *Nippon Budōkan*. We also speak to Keisuke Etō, of the All Japan Jūkendō Federation. That interview follows

Yayoi Nakanowatari Sensei, 2015

THE INTERVIEW

Can you please introduce yourself?
I am Yayoi Nakanowatari from *Honma Dōjō* in Kanagawa Prefecture.

We are at the All Japan Tankendō Championships in the Nippon Budōkan. Can you tell me what is happening right now?
From here onwards, the team's matches will take place. It is a three-member league, and I will fight third, acting as *taishō* (lit. military general; team captain who fights last). When it comes down to my match, I will do my very best to not be defeated and be able to win.

Have you studied swordsmanship or iaidō?

I have never used a real live blade! Normally, we use this *shinai* made of bamboo for practice and matches. A live blade was used sometime in the past, but now the practice of *tankendō* continues as a *budō* for the development of the human character using bamboo.

Are kendō practitioners at the Tankendō Championships?

I have seen some, but not many came today. Generally speaking there are many *tankendō* practitioners who also practice *kendō*. The reason for this is that the *kamae* (guard stance) is right-foot forward both in *kendō* and *tankendō* alike so many people practice both *budō*. For people who have been practicing *jūkendō* where the left foot is forward, starting *tankendō* where the right foot is forward can be difficult. However, both *jūkendō* and *tankendō* have similar tactics to *kendō* and other *budō*.

Tankendō is a *budō* which anybody can begin practicing. The implements are also relatively lower cost. Most of all, results can be obtained within very short matches. Also, it is a *budō* where the matches are defined instantly based on tactics. I have loved *tankendō* since I was a small girl and I have continued practicing all the way. It is a competition which people can participate regardless their age. If you find it interesting, I would like you continue your practice, or to give it a try at beginning to practice.

How did you achieve your success in competition?

I am often told that I have *kanroku* (dignified presence). Actually, one

Yayoi Nakanowatari (right) in the final of the 13th All Japan
Tankendo Championships. Photo: Jon Braeley

should move in a more active and youthful manner but in my case I have
no physical strength so if I move too much I would be defeated on the
grounds of physical strength. Against this, I have a combat style where
I carefully probe my opponent and when I detect their approach I respond with a counter attack, so that I can firmly define the match to my
advantage. That is all.

What is your next match in this Japan Championships?

We are now doing three-person matches. I am the *taishō*, the team captain who fights last, with the responsibility to take the result of the match
according to the performance of the *senpō* (lit. advancing spearpoint; first
combatant) and *chūken* (lit. middle firmness; middle combatant). My
feeling right now is by no means allowing myself to lose if it happens
that the final result of the match depends on me as *taishō*.

Unless it is a match where the final result has already been decided
and it is just a formality match, if the final victory or defeat depends on
me I will do my best not to lose. I will do my best to win by getting *ippon*.

Yayoi Nakanowatari is now joined by Keisuke Etō from the All Japan Jūkendō Federation.

My name is Keisuke Etō from the All Japan Jūkendō Federation. I work
for the organization which is organizing this tournament, the All Japan
Tankendō Championships.

Keisuke Etō of the Jūkendō Federation faces Yayoi
Nakanowatari at the annual Jūkendō seminar

Due to the date of this tournament coinciding with a *kendō* tournament, this year we have around twenty less participants compared to last year. However, the content has been very good, with great technique being displayed and very exciting matches.

Can you talk about the valid target areas in tankendō?
Techniques which become a valid *ippon* are strikes to the *dō* (torso), the *nodo* (throat), the *men* (head), and the *kote* (wrist). *Men* and *kote* are strikes, while *dō* and *nodo* are thrusts. These can become *ippon*.

There are also techniques which involve grasping the opponents right hand which is holding the short blade and thrusting. This *seitai-waza* (restraining technique) consists of restraining the opponent's hand holding the weapon and thrusting. These are characteristic of *tankendō*.

And can you tell us what would constitute a penalty?
Regarding *hansoku* (lit. against rules) which is foul play penalty, first there is a penalty for exiting the delimited area for the match. There is another penalty for dropping the *shinai*. Also, if one tries to purposely make the opponent drop his *shinai* by striking it and so on, then it is the one who does this who get gets a penalty. Striking on a place where there is no protective gear is also a penalty as it is considered a dangerous action. These are the main penalties for foul play.

In Tankendo the opponent can be grasped while the short
bamboo blade is thrust. Photo: Jon Braeley

What is the relationship of tankendō and jūkendō?

Tankendō is one of two disciplines together with *jūkendō* which are under the All Japan Jūkendō Federation. They both work like two wheels on a cart, and both are promoted. There are *tankendō* practitioners who only do *tankendō*, and then there are some practitioners who do both *tankendō* and *jūkendō*. From all the registered practitioners in the Federation, about 60% of them practice *tankendō*.

Referees in a competition such as this national level tournament are required to have a level of *kyoshi* 7th *dan* in both *tankendō* and *jūkendō*. If they do not, they cannot serve as referees for the All Japan Tournament. The Jūkendō Federation is hard at work setting its efforts in promoting *tankendō* overseas. We would like to continue to increase the number of foreign *tankendō* practitioners outside Japan.

What would you need to do to spread tankendō abroad?

These are my own words, but regarding the internationalization of the Tankendō Federation, I think that this is something that needs to be done from now on. It has still not been debated about whether or not we should be creating an independent International Tankendō Federation. However, a lot depends on the degree of propagation that *jūkendō* has. If *jūkendō* also becomes more popular then the chances of *tankendō* being able to become an independent international federation will Increase. As for as the Jūkendō Federation, we would like to see an increase of both together. We still have not reached the point where we discuss in much detail. There is a possibility, however, that because *tankendō* has more practitioners abroad then it will become an independent international organization before *jūkendō*.

How many members does the Federation have?
Currently, there are 40,000 registered members of the Jūkendō Federation. This number is updated every year, so it varies from year to year because of, for example, people who forgot to register for a given year and so on. However, it is safe to say that about 40,000 practitioners are registered in the Jūkendō Federation. About 70 to 80% of the members are part of the self defense forces, the military and so forth. However, lately there has been an increase in junior school and high school level practitioners.

In *tankendō*, there has been a significant rise in female practitioners like housewives and university students. In some regions like in Tohoku, there are many university students who now practice regularly. We would like to continue increasing the number of practitioners of *tankendō* who are not members of the military.

> *The original way of thinking about budō dates from back before the Edo period. About the latter half of the 16th century*

31.
Takashi Uozumi
PROFESSOR OF BUDŌ STUDIES

Chapter 31
INTRODUCTION

The following interview took place at the office and library of professor Takashi Uozumi at the International Budo University where he served as Professor and Director of the *Budō* and Sports Research Institute. Shortly after this interview with professor Takashi Uozumi he moved to the Open University of Japan in 2015.

Professor Uozumi completed a doctoral course in ethics at Tokyo University and his field of research is Japanese thought, existential thought and physical culture. He is regarded as Japan's foremost expert on the history of *budō* and an authority on Miyamoto Musashi, the 16th century swordsman.

Professor Uozumi has published many papers and books on *budō* including: "*Miyamoto Musashi - Nihonjin no Michi*" (Miyamoto Musashi, the Japanese Way), "*Teihon Gorin no Sho*" (The Book of Five Rings), *Yumi no Michi - Eugen Herrigel to Shi Awa Kenzō*". (The Way of Archery - Eugen Herrigel and his Master *Kenzō Awa*), and "*Bashō ni okeru Shi to Jitsuzon*" (Bashō – His Life and Poems).

My first interview with professor Uozumi was in 2013 for the movie, *One Shot. One Life* on *kyūdō* (Japanese archery). The second interview which is the one published here, took place a year later. My close friend,

Baptiste Tavernier, who is a graduate of the International Budo University assisted in this interview and Juan Diego Fonseca undertook the translation. Cuts and editing are kept to a minimum, so parts may be repeated, like a natural conversation.

    This was an astonishing interview and unlike any that I had recorded in the past. Professor Uozumi did not require any questions or prompts or even a break during our recording which lasted almost six hours! The only time we paused was to replace camera batteries and make lens adjustments to allow for the falling light as we approached early evening! As I pressed record on the camera, and about to ask the first question, professor Uozumi said, "Why don't I begin in the year 1600?"

Professor Takashi Uozumi, 2014

THE INTERVIEW

Regarding the history of budō, there are various ways of thinking about this. In general terms, we have '*gendai budō*' (lit. present age *budō*; modern *budō*), that is to say *budō* which was created post-Meiji period. The original way of thinking about Budo, dates from way back before the Edo period, about the latter half of the 16th century.

    Within *budō*, besides 'modern *budō*' there is also '*kobudō*' (lit. ancient *budō*; traditional *budō*). Should I talk about those *ryūha* (lit. style and denomination; schools of martial arts)? Nowadays there are about 88 *ryūha*, but back in the day there were many more. The oldest remaining ones date from the latter half of the 16th century. At the time there were old *bujutsu* (military techniques) such as *kenjutsu* (sword techniques), *jūjutsu*, *sōjutsu* (spear techniques), *kyūjutsu* (bow techniques), *bajutsu* (horseback riding techniques), and so on. Each of these old *bujutsu* had its own particular *ryūha* with its techniques and their own way of teaching them. There was also the theoretical. The "theoretical writings" and transmission scrolls that served as a curriculum when educating, which were very much completed by that age. These type of things came into being in the Japanese society, around the 17th century and afterwards.

In this period we have for example, the Battle of Sekigahara where the Tokugawa Shogunate took hegemony of the country in the year 1600. Afterwards, in the year 1615, there was the Siege of Osaka, and after this, there was a period of peace that lasted for 250 years. Therefore after the year of 1600 there was a big turn around. After this date, we have the Edo Shogunate that began in 1603. In the Edo Shogunate period, the various feudal domains were established.

During this Edo Shogunate, the whole country was unified, however there were still some *daimyō* (lit. large nominal (rice field); landowners; feudal lords), about twenty to twenty five *daimyō*, who remained from the Warring States Period. From that point of view, the ways of doing things in the Warring States period was frozen, and it was in this shape, that Japan became integrated into a single country. At that time, during the Warring States, the political, economic and military affairs of the various territories, together with the *daimyō* and their own unique peculiarities, remained intact.

Nonetheless, Japan was overall unified under this *bakufu* (lit. tent government; military government; also 'shogunate'). The shogunate monitored the smaller feudal lords. Around the year 1600, the Tokugawa Shogunate system was very much in its completed form. At this time, the other *daimyō* were categorized as lower rank retainers, and their military implements like artillery and firearms, these kinds of weapons were heavily restricted.

The other military matters such as troop training were also restricted and limited by the shogunate. At the same time, the *bushi* (*samurai*) of old, thought of the vitality for battles or war as a thing to be developed. Thus, the techniques of *bujutsu* continued to be developed and taught among the *bushi*. The Edo period continued for 250 years and during this time, the *bushi* were at the highest level of the social structure known as '*shi-nō-kō-shō*' (lit. samurai-farmer-craftsman-merchant). The *bushi* lived all gathered together in a sec- tor called '*jōka-machi*' (lit. town below the castle; castle town), which means that they gathered around the castle and established their residences close by.

At these castle towns, the *bushi* who gathered there, worked in official positions, which composed of the organization of military affairs. At the same time they concentrated on their own training of *bujutsu*, as their private activity. This held true for both the shogunate, same as the older days, and the different *ryūha*, each one being different depending on their social status. So the *ryūha* were different according to the social status. The *bushi* had various *ryūha*, each one with their own way of teaching, and each of the *ryūha* had their own characteristic development, meaning they were developed in particular ways.

Within this, we had should I say, '*ōgi*' (lit. inner technique; secret teachings, quintessence). The core teachings of *bujutsu* were abundantly written in what is called '*denshō*' (lit. transmitted texts; transmission scrolls). Among these text, the one which is most certainly confirmed is from around the year 1650. In other words, the first half of the 17th century. In this age, victory was determined by engaging in battle, by going to war. However, a period of peace followed and the *bujutsu* of old was converted into a *bujutsu* for times of peace

Someone who symbolizes this very clearly is a '*heihō*' (lit. army principles; art of war) instructor for the *shōgun* (lit. general, commander; de facto ruling military dictator), who was also the *kenjutsu* instructor for the *shōgun*, called Munenori Yagyū. The two art of war instructors for the *shōgun* were Munenori Yagyū of the *Shinkage-ryū*, and the other one being Tadaaki Ono of the *Ittō-ryū*. From these two, it was Munenori Yagyū who wrote the '*Heihō kaden sho*' (Hereditary Book on the Art of War), otherwise known as "*The Life Giving Sword*", translated by William Scott Wilson. What is clearly stated in this text is that in the age of warring states, in the age when battles took place, the *katana* existed as a life-taking sword. However, as things were pacified by the Shogunate, the *katana* had to become a life-giving sword.

The instructor Munenori Yagyū is one who introduced some Zen Buddhism ideology in *kenjutsu*. Munenori Yagyū's *zen* instructor was the *Zenshū* priest Sōhō Takuan. He was also the Zen Buddhism instructor of the *shōgun* Iemitsu. Munenori Yagyū was often by the side of the *shō-gun* Iemitsu, and he introduced Zen Buddhism teachings into *kenjutsu*. Of course, *kenjutsu* involves putting one's life on the line as it is a very dangerous activity. There is fear involved, as well as the will to win over an opponent, also there is the urge to show off what one has acquired through training.

When these things are transcended, it is called *mushin* (lit. no-mind; state of mind characterized by the absence of illusory conceptions and thoughts; empty mind). It is to overcome desire. As a matter of fact, *mushin* was an essential component in *kenjutsu*. This is often expressed as 'kenzen icchi' (lit. sword and *zen* as one), which implies that the ultimate point of the sword and the ultimate point of *zen* are one and the same, which is *mushin*. These are the kinds of things and thinking that existed during this age. Munenori Yagyū included this idea and theory into the "Hereditary Book on the Art of War" written on the year 1632.

He wrote this while keeping in mind his role as the designated *ken-jutsu* instructor of the *shōgun*. As part of his teaching *kenjutsu* to the *shō-gun*, he also taught him about how to interact with people in everyday life, as an important addition. As the *shōgun* he had to keep peace among the *daimyō* and over the whole country, and the ways in which battles could be avoided were also part of the *heihō* (lit. army principles; warfare tactics, 'art of war'). The general term 'art of war' includes a broad scope of things. There was the 'dai no heihō' (greater *heihō*), about how to win, and there was 'shō no heihō' (smaller *heihō*) which included *kenjutsu*. When the *shō no heihō* was confirmed and added into the *dai no heihō* it became the 'taishō heihō' (lit. large and small *heihō*; holistic approach to art of war).

At the same time was Musashi Miyamoto. He was 9 years younger than Munenori Yagyū and yet since he was 13 years old Musashi Miy-amoto had actual combat experience, especially in a battle in *Kyūshū*, in which he participated. Therefore, he had actual battle experience, and when he became 21 years old, which is after the Battle of Sekigahara, he moved to the capital and there he fought against famous warriors. Afterwards, he continued to fight and win against warriors from all over the country, aiming to be recognized as the very best warrior under the sky. He fought over 60 times, and won every time. He had all this experience which during his twenties. This is during a time when the Edo Shogunate system was still not established. During this time there were many *daimyō*, around 87 of them, who were not taken in by the shogunate which generated a large number of *rōnin* (wandering masterless *samurai*). It is said that these *rōnin*, who were people who no longer had a household to serve in employment as they had been abolished, were more than 500,000 in total.

Among these *rōnin*, many of them were eager to show their skills and went on '*musha shugyō*' (warrior's training pilgrimage) where they would face others in real combat to show off their abilities. This was an age when this occurred very often. It was in these times that Musashi went through more than 60 fights or duels, losing not even once. However, right after the end of the battle known as the Siege of Osaka, Musashi became a *kenjutsu* instructor exclusively for *daimyō*. He was given the role to teach feudal retainers.

The teaching was not only *kenjutsu*, but he also had to teach broader theoretical matters. Once he reached his thirties, he decided that he would train to seek deeper ways, as it is written in the "Book of Five Rings". In his fifties, he wrote that he had come to understand about the way of self-accomplishment. During this period he was in the town of Himeji. There is a large castle in Himeji, and there was a 'hereditary *daimyō*' (descendant of a *daimyō* who supported Ieyasu before the Battle of Sekigahara) living in that castle town. He was an important *daimyō* for the Tokugawa Shogunate. Musashi Miyamoto was teaching the *daimyō* and feudal lords at Himeji as their guest.

At this time, Musashi's adopted son was in fact taken in to serve as an official in the household of this hereditary *daimyō*. So, during this time Musashi was teaching *kenjutsu* to the *daimyō*, and through *kenjutsu* teaching, he added even more things. Afterwards in his last years Musashi went to Kumamoto where he also taught *kenjutsu* to the *daimyō*. It is here that he wrote the *Book of Five Rings* after realizing that he would pass away before long. He took this resolution to write the *Book of Five Rings* around the age of sixty. At that time, the average age of death was around fifty years old. While looking back over his own life, he decided to leave behind a writing of his teachings, like many *bushi* of that era did.

While reviewing his *kenjutsu*, Musashi also viewed it as '*taishō heihō*' (holistic approach to art of war) just as Munenori Yagyū did. So the art of war had to be developed holistically and Musashi also approached the art of war in similar way.

At that time, social class division was based on the '*shi-nō-kō-shō*' (samurai-farmer-craftsman-merchant) system and in order to fit into the

Takashi Uozumi

Book of Five Rings written by Musashi Miyamoto (Professor Uozumi copy)

samurai class one had to practice *kenjutsu*. Musashi introduced his first hand combat experience and the overview of his life-time pursuit in the *Book of Five Rings*. In the book Musashi said that the highest symbol of a *bushi* (*samurai*) is to carry a *katana* (sword), and as such, one must know how to fight using a *katana*. That way of fighting was said to be learned by confronting 1,000 people and even confronting 10,000 people.

Not only the way of fighting, but also the way of living as a *samurai* had to be learned. Things such as this are also included into the study and cultivation of *kenjutsu*. In everyday life too, one should constantly have the intention to win, even in the way of behaving one should have the intention to win, even in the way of looking at things one should have the intention to win. Of course, this also included winning in *kenjutsu* as well.

This means to win at governing over the people, to win at governing the country. Including this into the larger art of war, in order to excel at it, people had to develop it. When doing this, one needs to take a grasp of oneself, to constantly reflect upon oneself. At this time one took the idea of '*kū*' (lit. emptiness; void of immutable intrinsic nature, from skt. *shunyata*). One had to continue to train in this way, as a matter of fact, it is not only in *kenjutsu* but many more things which are connected. Once it was accepted that one trained this way and with other connected matters, one became able to win naturally, without even having to think about it. This was a result of the constant and repeated reflection done over those matters. This is what is meant by *ku*.

The Munenori Yagyū we were talking about before wrote the *Hereditary Book on the Art of War* in 1632, while Musashi wrote the *Book of Five Rings* in 1645. These two books are known as legendary works on *ryūha kenjutsu* and *budō* in general in the early modern period. *Kenjutsu* not only as a technique or method to obtain victory, but also as what it meant to be a *bushi* and how to forge oneself and gain the disposition to live as one. When seen from this point of view of development, it is just as these people said, it is a '*michi*' (lit. path, way; teaching, method; alternate Japanese reading of '*dō*' as in *budō*), that is '*heihō no michi*' (the way of the art of war). This "way" is traversed in order to forge and heighten oneself throughout life. This is the way of thinking of the 'Way of the Art of War'.

Nowadays this is called *budō* (way of the martial). In *budō*, it is not merely a problem of technique, but rather about the mentality of the human being. This is what needs to be done to move from '*jutsu*' (technique) to '*dō*' (way). In general, these persons were the main representatives of this way of thinking in the first half of the 17th century, as they expressed it very clearly. This is the age when the foundations, the basis of *budō* were shaped.

This took place on the first half of the 17th century. In the second half of the 17th century no battles took place. This state continued to the 18th century and until late in the first half of the 19th century and it was a long period of peace. During this time, it was part of the duties of the *bushi* to learn their *ryūha* (school) of *kenjutsu* or *bujutsu*. However, the actual combat experience was gone. There was this problem that it was learned in practice in a school, but not really applied to real combat situations.

In Musashi's and Munenori's time it was a given to use a *katana*, but since practice could not be done with a live blade, a *bokutō* (lit. wood sabre; also '*bokken*', wood sword) was used. Each *ryūha* had its own particular way of striking and of teaching techniques and this was made into *kata*. For example, the determined way of pressuring for an attack was taught through *kata*.

The *bushi* of Japan emerged around the 10th century. Of course, before that the state army was based on the '*ritsuryō* system' (lit. criminal code and administrative code; legal system strongly based on Confucianism), which imitated China. This system was used to keep public order and subdue trouble in local territories and it is how *bushi* first appeared. Around the 10th century, the Japanese *katana* already had its main elements and shape such as the *sori* (depth of curvature), *shinogi* (straight ridge line on the side of the blade), fittings and so on, in other words, the Japanese style *katana* was conceived around the 10th century. In the case of China, there is a difference between '*ken*' and '*katana*'- the Japanese *katana*. In China the '*ken*' is used for stabbing and is double-edged. On the other hand, the '*tō*' (this is the Chinese reading of the same character as for *katana*) is single-edged and was used to mow down. In particular, the 'Japanese *katana*' is a midpoint between these two swords, as it can be used to both stab and cut (note the distinction between '*katana*' and 'Japanese *katana*').

The largest difference with China is that in Japan there was basically no war between different ethnic groups. Battles inside the country were civil wars. For this reason, war was waged between peer *bushi*. In the case of Japan, the *samurai* government was organized in the latter half of the 12th century. From then on after the second half of the 12th century, there were a series of consecutive shogunates (military governments) one after the other. In those days, horseback riding with a bow, shooting while riding the horse, was the basic form of combat. Only a *bushi* rode a horse, not vassals or servants.

In those times, a *bushi* was one who used a bow and rode a horse. A *bushi* was referred to as "one who undertook the life-habit of the bow and arrow". It was a particular way of living called '*yumiya no narai*' (lit. life as habit of bow and arrow). From the 10th century to the end of the 12th century the shogunate system and the *bushi* held power of the state.

The *bujutsu* from this age and modern *budō* are clearly different. In those times, especially *kyūdō* (bowmanship) and the way of doing *kyūdō* changed. From 12th century to around the 14th century, the Kamakura Shogunate started in the late 12th century.

The Kamakura *bakufu* (lit. tent government; military government; shogunate) was established. It lasted 150 years before an uprising destroyed it. The next *bakufu* was the Ashikaga (Muromachi) *bakufu*. It was 14th century middle age-style rule. These were times of the Nanbokuchō (Northern and Southern Court) period of war between two courts. *Ogasawara-ryū*, which was connected to Japanese archery and was a part of the Genji clan, was the one to create rules of *sahō* (etiquette) for warriors during those times. It can be said that those were the times when *ryūha* (schools of martial arts) have been born. Probably around the second half of 14th century.

During times of Muromachi *bakufu*, in 15-16th century, *geidō* (lit. way of performing arts, theater) and *nōga ku* (lit. musical talent; *noh* theater) were created. In the beginning of 15th century the idea of a '*dō*' (way) of '*gei*' (performance) was born. This was the time when the term '*do*' appears, as well as the idea of *ryūha*. Appearance of schools of martial arts in the second half of 15th century has the idea of 'way' in its background. What is more, since the end of the 14th century the idea of '*mushin*' (no-mind), that comes from Zen Buddhism, was said to appear in everyday life as well. *Mushin* has been connected to everyday matters like *nōga ku or 'cha no yu*' (lit. hot water for tea; Japanese tea ceremony), which has *zen* considered in every teacup. *Sadō* (lit. way of tea; Japanese tea ceremony) appears at around the end of 16th century. This way of thinking existed parallel. The creation of schools of martial arts in late 16th century had a background that had a philosophy like this.

Schools of Japanese martial arts had become less practical in combat in these times. When those schools have developed in 16th century, the country was in a state of so called *Sengoku jidai* (Warring States Period). These were times when wars happened all over the country. During battles big armies clashed.

There were no firearms during those times yet. Battles were fought using those long spears. Of course they did fight with *katana* but basically they were used at the end to cut down and claim an enemy's head.

When it comes to *kenjutsu*, there was not much of it in those times. It was good for a warrior to train in *kenjutsu* but it wasn't considered practical. In the next period firearms appear and there are accounts of cavalry that made charges, where the other army countered them with 3,000 firearms, which I believe to be an exaggeration. Nevertheless some armies fought with more than 1,000 firearms. These are times in which swords or spears often became useless.

In the past there were scenes in which one-on-one fights took place. Firearms and massive armies appear. Kamiizumi Ise no Kami is the founder of *Shinkage-ryū kenjutsu* who came from Jōshū in Gunma prefecture. He made a presentation before a *shōgun* in Kyoto and started teaching *Shinkage-ryū* to him. In those times one can talk about not individual warriors but a group of warriors fighting each other. *Shinkage-ryū* was meant to show the individual pride each of those warriors had. In teachings from the end of 16th century we can read that he wanted to teach *kenjutsu* not only in order to make one win over another.

He says in advance that his teachings are not meant to be the teachings for winning as a warrior. He created a school which followed one principle. Because the school's base was *Kage-ryū* (lit. shadow/yin principle style), he added '*shin*' (new) thus naming it *Shinkage-ryū* (lit. new shadow style). He emphasized spirituality and used in his *kata* ideas of '*satsujintō*' (lit. person killing sabre; also pronounced '*setsunintō*') and '*katsujinken*' (lit. person resuscitating sword; also pronounced '*katsuninken*'). In the 17th century's first half, the person I mentioned before, Munenori Yagyū, used the idea of 'life-giving sword', saying that in times of peace one's sword must 'give life' to people. So it developed like this. In the times we speak of, *kenjutsu* schools appeared as a way of expressing a warrior's individualism because they could no longer be solitary warriors.

As I said before, Kamiizumi Ise no Kami had gone to Kyoto, to a *shōgun* in 1566, and he met Yagyū Tajima no Kami. The Yagyū clan originated from Nara prefecture, a place known as Yagyū manor, where a man called Muneyoshi was a military commander. His family lasted for generations from the Kamakura period. To the time when Oda Nobunaga appears, Muneyoshi acts as a military commander.

When Nobunaga steps out to accomplish the so called '*tenka tōitsu*' (lit. unification of all under heaven; supremacy over the whole nation), he had to hide in Yagyū manor. During 20 years he trained in *kenjutsu* which he learned from Kamiizumi Ise no Kami. He wrote down the ways of teaching it as well. Twenty years later his successor, Ieyasu Tokugawa, learned that a great warrior exists, called Munenori Yagyū. Ieyasu had been training in *kenjutsu* since he was young so he was confident in his skills, yet he could not defeat an unarmed Munenori, so he became a disciple of Yagyū. At the end of the 16th century he orders Yagyū to teach his descendants. These are times when Ieyasu was under the command of Hideyoshi Toyotomi. Six years later Hideyoshi passed away and Ieyasu takes hold of hegemony after the Battle of Sekigahara.

His son, Hidetada, the second Edo shōgun and his son, Ieyasu's grandchild Iemitsu, were taught in the martial arts by Sekishūsai Yagyū's 5th son - Munenori. This Munenori becomes the *kenjutsu* teacher of the Tokugawa family and as I said, *kenjutsu* was the center of attention in everyday life during this period. Munenori Yagyū was the one who developed the idea of *heihō* (lit. army principles; art of war) that aimed to prevent wars and rebellions. So this is a story that connects with the history that I have told you so far.

Until the first half of 17th century the idea of *budō* has been established. The second half was a time of peace and many new rice fields were cultivated. It was a time of prosperity. In those times retainers of *daimyō* (feudal lords) had to perform '*sankin kotai*' (lit. alternated attendance to an audience; a *daimyō's* obligation of alternating their residence yearly between their own feuds and their lord's in Edo). While visiting such a prosperous and big city, one becomes influenced with its flourishing culture. Although *bushi* had duties, they were not so many of them. In their free time they went for example to watch theater, and that's a reason why *kabuki* (lit. singing and dancing skill; traditional form of drama and music) became so popular. The end of 17th century or the beginning of the 18th century is when *ukiyoe* (lit. painting of the floating/transient world; artistic woodblock prints) would start to appear.

Bushi were influenced by city culture and they lost the opportunity to use their fighting skills. In the times when warriors lost the opportunity to fight, in Saga province a book called '*Hagakure*' (lit. Hidden by leaves), which encouraged '*bushi* spirit', was written. There is a famous phrase that appears in the book, which is "I've found that the meaning of *bushidō* lies in death". This book was written at the beginning of the 18th century by a *bushi* who had never fought in a battle. He was a person whose predecessors had become successful thanks to military exploits. He had in mind that if there is a battle, he would need to be prepared for it. Young people today are somewhat playing around too much because there are no battles, and the book tells us that while going to battle one must be mentally prepared to die.

As I said, in those times there were almost no reason to fight. *Bushi* had *katana* with them all the time but they could not draw it in front of people. The only reason for drawing it was when one wanted to cut down another person. So it meant that one had to be prepared to kill another person, and that's why one would never draw a sword in everyday life. That's why *bujutsu* practice was done – in order to train oneself because one would never know when would he need to draw a sword. That's why a cultural form developed in which those ideals were taught in the *dōjō* of castle towns.

A *dōjō* (lit. place of the way/path; abbreviation of "place of competition of the path to perfect enlightenment", from skt. *bodhimanda*) was a place where, obviously, one would learn *kenjutsu* and simultaneously spiritual attitude and etiquette, a way of behaving and expressing oneself as a *bushi*. *Bushi* learned to be resolute, as a *bushi*, in those individual schools. What is different in Japanese schools of martial art compared to Chinese is that each school specialized in one skill. *Kenjutsu* was done in only *kenjutsu* schools. *Kyūjutsu* (bowmanship) only in *kyūjutsu* schools. *Sōjutsu* (spearmanship) in *sōjutsu* schools. Horsemanship only in horsemanship schools. *Bushi* learned those skills independently and they learned the way of behaving and etiquette.

A *dōjō* that a certain bushi would go depended on his place in hierarchy. So even in one feudal domain there would be different *kenjutsu* schools. In those times there were still no *kenjutsu* school specific for that one domain. *bushi* went independently to learn from different masters. That's what was going on in middle Edo period. In late Edo period, say, second half of the 18th century, *bushi* were divided into classes: lower, middle and higher. Depending on a *bushi's* skills, he could rise to become a high class *bushi*.

The society itself has changed as well. Because of such background, *bujutsu* change as well. In those times *kenjutsu* was always practiced by doing *kata*, and then new problem arose. What if one needed to fight for real? *Kenjutsu* is basically trained with *bokutō* (wooden sabre), however in *Shinkage-ryū* they use a *fukuroshinai* (lit. bag bamboo sabre; style of *shinai* where 8 or 16 thin slats of bamboo are covered in a leather bag), by doing s set forms as *kata*. Although forms were defined, changes would occur. Because of that *waza* would become more varied and of course these were tried out. However striking for real could not be done.

In the beginning of the 18th century *bōgu* (protective equipment) like *men* (helmet), *dō* (breastplate) and *kote* (wrist protectors) were being developed because one could not hit a partner for real. In the middle of the 18th century those protectors become popular. And these protectors have developed into modern ones. The modern *shinai* is made by putting together 4 slats of bamboo.

Keiko (lit. consider antiquity; routine practice) before the invention of protectors, was done with a *bokutō* (wooden sabre). And a little different to this, is *Shinkage-ryū*, which is made of bamboo and even when hit by this, it's not dangerous. It is said that Kamiizumi Ise no Kami had invented these, by putting split bamboo inside of a leather bag, thus the name is *fukuroshinai* (bag bamboo saber). This was developed during the 16th and

17th century. There is a school today that continues practicing with these.

Different than those two, in the 18th century, the modern *shinai* is invented. With this *shinai*, it became possible to safely strike a person. A *katana* is 2 *shaku* (60 cm) 4 *sun* (12 cm; total 72 cm) in length. The length may have gone up to 3 *shaku* (90 cm). This piece that is a grip has about 1 *shaku*, so in total 120 cm. Those are normal forms of *katana*, but in case of *shinai* it is a bit longer. It is 3 *shaku* 8 sun (78 cm).

In the second half of the 18th century a form of *kendō* that we know today had been developed and continues even today. Although *shinai* is not a *katana*, it is used as if it was one. Places one can hit the opponent are restricted by a placement of protectors. Before the Second World War one could aim for the legs that weren't protected and he could even knock a person down and take his *men* (protective gear) away. Such things were allowed before the War. So as I said these things had been developing since the second half of the 18th century. Especially among the lower class *bushi* who devoted themselves to this practice.

There were cases in which a lower class *bushi* would advance to higher ranks thanks to his skills in *kenjutsu*. In case of Japan there were cases where one could buy himself a rank of *bushi*. There were also cases that one married a *bushi* daughter and became adopted to her family. So those kind of people become a *bushi*, right? Because of that they can wear a *katana* which is a status symbol of a samurai. Only *bushi* could wear a *katana* since beginnings of 17th century. Thus such person needed to learn the way of wearing and using a sword by training in *kenjutsu*. They learned etiquette as well. *Kenjutsu* is a martial art that has the most number of schools. One theory says that there were about 500 schools.

In the Edo period system there were various *han* (feudal domains) and in each of it a *kenjutsu* school would develop. There were cases that the same school would be named differently in other domain or by adding one's ideas one would make it a new school. In the second half of the 18th century both the *bakufu* (centralized military government) and *han* (feudal local governments) political systems have become loose because of monetary economical development. *Kenjutsu* was a means of re-educating *bushi* in their spiritual attitude.

Different from the *kata* practice that had been done before, *gekken* (lit. attacking swords; fencing, also '*gekiken*') *ryūha*, in which practitioners hit each other, became adopted. In the second half of the 18th century *hankō* (lit. domain schools) are established, where *bushi* are educated.

That was a way of restoring a domain. These were built to educate *bushi* in their spiritual attitude. There were two main pivots of curriculum in those 'domain schools'.

Firstly, Confucianism was taught. Secondly, *bujutsu* and *kenjutsu*, which was emphasized, were taught. Of course spears, firearms and archery were taught as well, and these had individual schools. So these things were taught in places called 'domain schools' since the second half of the 18th century. In the 18th century domain schools of *kenjutsu*, in which people were hitting each other for real, appear. By doing so one can clearly see a person's real skills. People who showed great skill in a *ryūha* can build big *machidōjō* (lit. town *dōjō*; Municipal dōjō) in Edo. There were four big schools of swordsmanship. When a school becomes famous, many people from different domains start to practice there. At first information exchange was done between domains but then the exchange inside one school occurred as well. Such municipal *dōjō* start to appear in the middle of the 19th century.

When one wears *bōgu* (protective gear), he can train safely. The truth is that *bakufu* had abolished inter-school matches in 17th century. In those times there were no protectors so if there was a match, people got wounded. There was also a concern that the one who lost would take a bloody revenge on the winner. Although in the 17th century inter-school matches were abolished, in the middle of 19th century training martial arts became popular because of safety of training thanks to protectors. Those were feudal times thus no one could freely move between domains but when the person would have said that he's going for a martial arts practice, he could quite often go when he wanted. There were some big schools in Edo and in those places people from other domains were given a chance to practice. *Kenjutsu* training had a great meaning for low class *bushi* because it taught them a *bushi* ethos and it could grant them social advancement.

As I said, from the middle of the 19th century to its end, *kenjutsu* developed very rapidly. Captain Perry's 'Arrival of the black ships' had taken place in 19th century but before that information about Opium War in China had already reached Japan. Japanese authorities strongly felt that the West (Europe) and its military revolution possessed a great threat to them. Japan isolated itself from abroad since late 17th century but there were two exceptions: Netherlands and China. Japan was trading with these two countries. What needs to be emphasized is that Netherland had a duty to give reports about European affairs to the *bakufu*.

In fact, Japanese authorities had quite good knowledge of European affairs. They even knew about Napoleon's appearance. When 'The Black Fleet' came, they had already known about those kind of things. They even had known beforehand that the Chinese had lost against the British Empire's army. They were seriously concerned about European armies. So this is the background when Perry came with his military ships, and because of that, the policy of *sakoku* (lit. chained country; national isolation enacted by the Tokugawa shogunate) became lifted. The *bakufu* military government knew that it had to reform it's Japanese army. *Gunkan sōrenjo* (warship special training institutes) were established and manned by Netherlanders as a way of reforming the Japanese navy.

In Edo, a school called *Kōbusho* (lit. place for military lecturing) was built. That was a place for training in gunnery and artillery. The things taught there were not traditional Japanese gunnery skills but the western ones. At the place people were trained in bujutsu as well. This was an institution under *bakufu's* jurisdiction and people from domains learned there. At first, *jūjutsu, kenjutsu, sōjutsu* and *kyūjutsu* were taught as well but in the end the curriculum shrunk to *hōjutsu* (lit. artillery techniques; gunnery) and *kenjutsu*. *Kenjutsu* was left because it teaches a *bushi's* fighting spirit, which made it important. Because it was an institution established by central authorities of the *bakufu*, all the skillful masters were gathered from around the country.

Although each *ryūha* has its own set of *kata* (defined forms) all of them could be practiced together if protectors were worn. This was a place where *gekken*, fencing training with *shinai* and striking for real was done. Those were the times when modern length of *shinai* was decided. The *Kōbusho* was established in 1856 and it's a place where *kenjutsu* that transcended all the schools was born. And again, people from domains came to that place and started to learn new *kenjutsu*.

In 1868 an event called the Meiji Restoration (or Restoration of Meiji period) took place. This is the time when the *bakufu* has returned all authority to the emperor's court. Later there were struggles over this authority inside the court and Satsuma and Choshu domains create the Meiji government. At the end of its rule, the *bakufu* created a military advisor group manned by the French which aimed to reform the military system. Simultaneously the *bakufu* has established a school in which such arts like *kenjutsu* were taught.

Until this time a *shōgun's* family was the top of Japan's authority but since 1868 it was an emperor who was the most important and a government, that lay underneath him, was established. Originally an emperor had been living in Kyoto but in the second year of Meiji period (1870) he has moved to Edo. The *bakufu* handed over Edo Castle without bloodshed and the emperor moved in. This is today's Imperial Palace. Edo was renamed 'Eastern Capital,' which is the meaning of Tokyo and a new era named Meiji was born. This was the time when the new government, which was different from the *bushi* one and a new political system was created, and the country was integrated as a modern nation. Japan was divided into domains but it became united under centralized government. The land and people were returned to the Emperor. At the same time central government created prefectures administered by a governor in place of domains.

At first a position of a governor was given to a domain's lord but later they were replaced by an central government official. *Bushi* had been given *roku* (lit. stipend; salary) but in the new period that system was canceled. *Samurai* were given a payment as a conscript. Different than in the past they were no more given 'bonuses' – from now they were given a lump sum payment. At the same time the right of ownership, law in general and capitalistic economy were being established – in other words it was a rapid modernization. Because Meiji government knew of China's defeat to the West and for example Hong Kong's disadvantageous taking, it was obvious that Japan's independence was threatened.

That's why the establishment of central government and rapid modernization had to be done. To do that many western teachers were invited to Japan and hired for an exceptional salary at the best university, which was Tokyo University. Many technicians were invited as well. These were the methods to rapidly modernize the country. Japanese had been learning things from foreigners since long past, especially *bushi* from the Satsuma domain in Kyūshū and the Chōshū domain in Yamaguchi prefecture that had taken hold of authority in Meiji government.

In those times many Asian countries like India (Indian empire) had already been colonized and China had been forced to sign a disadvantageous treaty. So Japan's national independence was threatened. Because there was a need for rapid modernization, there was a need to establish a modern political system as well. Edo period was feudal so everything like this needed to be cut away. As you know *bushi* had been wearing *katana* but in the 9th year of Meiji period the '*Haitō rei*' (lit. sabre abolishment order; Sword Abolishment Edict) was introduced. *Bushi* were wearing special top-knot hairstyle – *chonmage,* and that was prohibited as well. The first 10 years of the Meiji period were a time when the government was not strongly established. A plan, in which the government wanted to accomplish a rapid modernization, included learning from and imitating the West. This plan developed fast in the first ten years. So in those times of westernization things like *kenjutsu* was considered 'antique'. Because the class of *bushi* ceased to exist, *bujutsu* practitioners ceased to exist as a profession. People who wanted to learn *bujutsu* were considered out of fashion as well, and thus their numbers began to decrease over time.

If you think of the Meiji Restoration as a middle point in a thirty-year period, many *ryūha* (schools) vanished in this time. That's because the Japanese Meiji nation had taken a big step towards modernization. On the other hand there were a lot of people who still developed *bujutsu*, believing in its educational value. A major example is Jigorō Kanō and his Kodokan school of *jūdō*. Jigorō Kanō was the son of a wealthy sake brewing family. In his childhood he had learned Chinese classics and English. His father was a person in Meiji government who had contributed in military matters. He was a second generation student of Tokyo University.

While Jigorō Kanō came from a wealthy family and was intelligent, he had a small body, for which he was made fun of and gave him a complex. One day he learned of *jūjutsu* – a *bujutsu* that allowed small people to throw bigger ones. He wanted to learn it badly, but could not get more information on it. At the age of eighteen years he entered university and finally found a master of *jūjutsu*, who was teaching at a *Kōbusho* established by the *bakufu*.

Sadly the master died after a year and a half. Then Kanō changed his *sensei* and also the school. The first school, *Tenjin Shin'yō-ryū* (lit. style of the heavenly true willow tree) was similar to today's *aikidō*. The second one was called *Kitō-ryū* (lit. style of 'origination and reversal', also 'rise and fall') and specialized in throwing. Because of this he wondered how these two schools being both *jūjutsu* were so different?

He was a modern person who was well educated and he thought that *jūjutsu* can be taught more logically. The second *sensei* kept on telling him to learn with his body. In response to that Kanō created a *jūdō* figurine that could show the posture when a move was done. So he was thinking and analyzing in terms of bio-mechanics. So that's how he learned. After he graduated the university and even though he did not have a certificate in *jūjutsu*, he created a private school named *Kōdōkan*. He also employed some people to do household chores and invite skilled practitioners of other *bujutsu* in order to research *jūjutsu*. By this he was creating a new form of *jūjutsu* with those early *Kōdōkan* members.

Kōdōkan was built in the 15th year of Meiji period and until the 22nd year – for 7 years - Kanō had been teaching in Gakushūin University as a professor, but at nights he would train with his pupils and practitioners of other schools in order to create a new *jūjutsu*. During this time he employed the rules that existed in western sports.

Jigorō Kanō understood western baseball and he knew its rules well. He wanted to create rules that allowed students to throw each other safely, and therefore he made *randori* (free practice) a centerpiece of his school. Dangerous techniques could only be done in the form of *kata*. This is how *Kōdōkan* school of *jūdō* was created during those seven years. Many of the regular *jūjutsu* schools had a secret move like *kuchikidaoshi* (lit. decayed tree throw) that were named figuratively. In place of those he created moves that depended on a part of the body – *ashiwaza* (leg techniques), *koshiwaza* (hip techniques), *seoiwaza* (back-carrying techniques), and so on. So one could throw and when one attempts throwing, there is *kuzushi* (to throw off balance), *tsukuri* (building, preparation), and *kake* (execution). This early *jūdō* form was made in 22 year of Meiji (1889).

At the same time, in *kenjutsu*, there was a person who was teaching 'shinai kenjutsu'. His name is Tesshū Yamaoka. He was a retainer in the *bakufu* and an enthusiastic *kenjutsu* practitioner. He was the person who played an active part in handing over Edo castle. Because of this he was even appointed the emperor's teacher and chamberlain. In his *kenjutsu* practice he had once met a person to whom he lost completely. It is said that the person's *tachi* (lit. long single-edged sword; way of fighting) was always on his mind, thus making him wonder what could he do to become stronger. Then came *Zen* Buddhism and he started practicing at a *dōjō* connected to *zen*.

In the background of his technique was the idea of 'kenzen icchi' (lit. sword and zen as one), that had appeared in the first half of 7th century and this even reached Tesshū Yamaoka that lived in the second half of the 19th century. Although he was practicing *gekken* (lit. attacking swords; fencing, also 'gekiken'), simultaneously he was practicing *zen* and even attained enlightenment. Because of this, his memory of an opponent to whom he had lost a fight had completely vanished. So he asked the person to fight him once more but this time Tesshū was in a state of *mushin* – very calm. Even the opponent admitted that he had reached an impressive level and recognized his skill. He was the person who built a *dōjō* named *Shunpukan* (lit. Hall of the Spring Wind) in 15th year of the Meiji period (1882) – in the same time as Jigorō Kanō built *Kōdōkan*.

In those modern times *shinai kenjutsu* and the spirit of *zen* were connected as an effective method. Tesshū also did *arageiko* (lit. rough *keiko* daily practice), because in order to attain *mushin* he believed one had to do very hard practice. He did a form called *tachikiri* in which one would hit an opponent one after another. This kind of person became a mediator between the modern world and *zen*. In the first 15-20 years of the Meiji period all the things from feudal Edo period were considered bad, and all the western things were desirable. In the 22nd year of Meiji period a Meiji constitution (Constitution of the Empire of Japan) was created and the national system became stable. After that a tendency to look at traditional things appeared. So this is the background to why, in the 20th year of Meiji, *kenjutsu* became popular again. Let me also mention that in the 10th year of Meiji (1877), when Meiji national system was becoming more stable, the Satsuma Rebellion took place. Takamori Saigō, a commander of Meiji government's anti-*bakufu* army, who was from Kagoshima, was an important person in the Meiji government.

Because of ideological disagreement (strong westernization) Takamori Saigō returned to Kagoshima. Because he had doubts about the government's policy and the overdoing of westernization, he started a rebellion. This is called the Satsuma Rebellion. An army of *bushi* becomes sup- pressed by a conscription army wielding firearms. This was the time when the *Keishichō battōtai* (lit. Drawn-sword Regiment of the Metropolitan Police Department) was created and was active.

It was the 10th year of Meiji, and from that time the Police Department has discovered new merits of *kenjutsu*. Of course police had to arrest thugs so *jūjutsu* was highly regarded. Educating policemen in *kenjutsu* and *jūjutsu* has begun around that time, say the 10th or 15th year of Meiji. One thing is that the Police had found new merits in *bujutsu*. There were also many people stating that because *bujutsu* was a part of education of *bushi*, it should be introduced into the educational programs. The Ministry of Education deliberated the effects of introducing *gekken* and *jūjutsu* to educational program.

In response to this, the Physical Training Institute was established and physical education in Japan was introduced. The main instructor was a foreigner, a North American physician called Leland. When he saw *kenjutsu* he thought of it a dangerous and not a good activity because of the striking without protection, so he removed *kenjutsu* completely. In the year Meiji 16 (1883) he considered it would not do as physical education. Until about the end of the Meiji era, *kenjutsu* was not considered acceptable as a means of development.

At the same time, the previously mentioned Jigorō Kanō was actively involved in the Ministry of Education. He was also appointed principal of the First High Secondary School, as well as the principal of the Tokyo Higher Normal School. This Tokyo Higher Normal School is what today is known as Tsukuba University. It is here, that all the country's high school teachers were trained. It was of course a very important place for education. He acted as the principal of such a place for 26 years.

Kanō was a person who was very active in the development of education. From the beginning when he practiced *jūdō*, he noticed that the body gained strength and that self-confidence increased. As he studied this, he realized also that more rational things could also be made through this. Until that point, he had been doing his practice as *jūjutsu*, but from then on he did it as *jūdō*. *Jūjutsu's* focus was on winning, as it had been since the Edo period. On the other hand, *jūdō* had a more pedagogical focus. First of all, it is physical education. Secondly, it is a method or a way of winning. How to win against an opponent. Thirdly, it is a moral and ethical method, in order to train the mind and heart. It contains these three aspects and by combining them, *jūdō* was developed from *jūjutsu*. In those times he was principal of the Fifth Higher Normal School in Kumamoto, where he was now teaching *jūdō*. There, a man named Lafcadio Hearn saw *jūdō*. This Lafcadio Hearn who was in Kumamoto was actually the first one to introduce Kanō's *jūdō* to the outside World. Hearn announced it to the World and Kanō, who was very proficient in English, kept a diary written in English which helped Hearn. Kanō used every trip to Europe as an opportunity to spread the system that he created, which is *jūdō*.

At this time *jūdō's* background and surrounding conditions were those of an educational tool, and as such it was to be included in the educational curriculum, but as an extracurricular activity. Students were to do it while having fun. It is in this shape that it started to spread.

On par with *jūdō*, the *kendō* people were observing this taking place. It had now been some time since *kenjutsu* had been called *kendō*, but the practitioners were also interested in introducing it into the educational system as *kendō*. This campaign then took place. Another important thing regarding *budō* is that in the time when the first external war took place since the beginning of the Meiji period from 1894 to 1895, the years Meiji 27 to 28, the Sino-Japanese War took place between China and Japan.

Until now, Japan had learned a lot from China, but at this time the recently created modern army seized victory over China. Due to this conflict, the traditional Japanese culture was widely promoted. In fact, in the year when the Sino-Japanese War ended in 1895, 1,100 years had passed since Kyoto was changed as the capital. In order to mark this commemorative event, the Kyoto industrial Exhibition was organized in the old capital of Kyoto.

During this event, *budō* was demonstrated and promoted and it was also an opportunity to have the Emperor as a spectator for the martial arts exhibition. It was here that for the first time *budō* was institutionalized in the form of the *Dai Nippon Butokukai* (Greater Japan Martial Virtue Society). This was the first national *budō* organization. For the first time since the beginning of the modern era there was an institution which focused in *budō*, and *budō* was established as an organization. The *ryūha* which had remained at various locations made presentations at this event.

The practitioners of various *ryūha* of *jūdō* and *kendō* did demonstrations and organized competitions after this, the *Dai Nippon Butokukai* was established. The royal family, the imperial family, and also the Japanese police organizations who had been practicing *jūdō* and *kenjutsu* also joined and the organization started to grow.

In the time of the Sino-Japanese War in the year Meiji 28, after achieving victory, a treaty was established and the Liaodong Peninsula in China was attached to Japan. However, a diplomatic intervention initiated by Russia, Germany and France requested Japan return this land to China. In return, they would receive a monetary reimbursement. Russia was concerned for the taking of the Liaodong Peninsula and it was they who pushed the request. For that reason, Russia had an intention to gain control and that led to the beginning of hostilities. Russia intervened after the victory over China and it could be seen as inevitable for Japan to be at war with Russia next.

After winning the Sino-Japanese War, Japan expected to enter into a war against Russia in the next ten years, as part of its military expansion. Meanwhile, *budō* had been established as an organization, and there was intent to promulgate Japanese *bujutsu* which marked its revival. In 1904-5 the Russo-Japanese War occurred. After great strain, the Russo-Japanese War was won by Japan. This was very surprising for the entire world. That a large country such as Russia would be defeated by Japan who had entered the modern era merely thirty years before. From this point it was recognized that Japanese *budō* had begun its international diffusion.

Inazō Nitobe wrote the English text book "Bushido: The Soul Of Japan" in the year 1899, which is just before the Russo- Japanese War. *Bushidō* was stated to be a unique Japanese moral criteria in this book. However, it gained popularity only after the Russo-Japanese War when people wondered what made it possible for Japan to be so strong and achieve victory. The North American president Theodore Roosevelt was one of the people who read *"Bushido"* and popularized it. In fact, there was a person from Japan who went over to Roosevelt to teach *jūdō*. Therefore Japanese *budō* can really be considered to have become international around this time.

The book "Bushido" was then translated into Japanese and named *Bushido* (it was originally written in English). Meanwhile, Japan had won the Russo-Japanese War and it came into fashion to diffuse the traditional things such as *jūdō* and *kendō*, and it developed rapidly during this time.

Finally, the Ministry of Education at the end of Meiji period accepted the instruction of *jūdō* and *kendō* at schools. From then on it developed for didactic teaching in schools. For the purpose of school instruction it was necessary to create a unified form or *kata*. As for *jūdō*, the aforementioned *Dai Nippon Butokukai* created the *jūjutsu kata*, while *kendō* created the *kendō kata*.

However in the case of *kendō*, there are many *ryūha* so it could not be very well unified, so it was amended a second time and the *kata* that were defined on this second attempt for unification are the '*Nihon kendō kata*' which are still practiced today.

As for school level instruction, its development took place in the Taishō era according to the Japanese year. In Japan, the duration between Meiji and Taishō periods which marks the modernization spanned some 40 or 50 years. In the cities, the 'salaryman' stratum also developed. For schools and the education system it was a period where sports popularized among the student stratum. Around the end of the Taishō period, various sports nationwide united to do the Athletic Meeting in the 1920's.

During World War One, Japan participated with the Allies but it did not enter actively on the battlefield. The Japanese industry increased significantly during this time. Blue-collar workers also increased correspondingly. In this era the radio was developed. There was also the development of other media. These contributed to the development of the Championship of the Athletic Meeting during the 1920's.

In the discussions about including *budō* into the school curriculum, it became necessary to have instructors who could teach *bujutsu*, and other *budō*. In order to train these instructors to teach, the *Dai Nippon Butokukai*, which acted as a vocational school specializing in *budō*, taught how to instruct. One more thing is that in Tokyo there was the Tokyo Higher Normal School that was mentioned before, a place where school teachers were developing teaching methods. Also a textbook describing how *kenjutsu* could be taught in schools was prepared. That textbook is one of the methods of instructing *kendō*. In Tokyo, this Tokyo Higher Normal School was instrumental in helping the martial arts to develop.

In Kyoto, the *Dai Nippon Butokukai* was able to supply the instructors in *budō* that would teach in schools serving as a specialized *budō* vocational school. These two institutions produced instructors, and were responsible for the development of *budō* as an educational tool for schools.

Around the end of the Meiji period and through the Taishō period, what had up until this point been called *gekken* was now named *kendō*. Likewise, what had been called *kyūjutsu* was renamed *kyūdō*. This is with the background and the important influence of *jūjutsu* evolving into *jūdō* by Jigorō Kanō. Therefore, *budō* contains an intrinsic educational meaning. This educational meaning is transmitted not by '*jutsu*' (applied technique), but by '*dō*' and with this development came the naming of *kendō* and *kyūdō*, and before those, *jūdō*. Therefore, '*budō*'.

Coming back to what I was saying before, in the 1920's the student stratum at schools were very enthusiastic for sports and this caused a further development in *budō* as the athletic competitions also developed. When the nationwide Athletic Meetings developed, the *budō* groups initially refused to participate. The reason for this was that *budō* was an educational thing and the competitive aspect of fighting for fun like a sport was not included. For this reason they did not participate. However, two years later they participated, which included the educational aspect. It is here that the aspect of achieving victory or defeat through a sports-like competition became part of the *budō* point of view. However, the National Tournament Championships served as a very significant condition for the development and diffusion of *budō*. *Jūdō* was the first to join the All Japan Championships.

Afterwards, for *kendō* it became a little bit later, but in 1929 a demonstration competition called *tenranjiai* (lit. bout under heaven's perusal; a match or game held in the presence of the Emperor) took place as a commemorative event for the enthronement of the Shōwa Emperor, with the Emperor himself as a spectator, which was a huge honor. For that purpose, there was the desire to organize the highest-level competition. For this, the best players from all over the country were selected to participate in the *tenranjiai*. At this time, some people still opposed it, stating that *kenjutsu* is not something to make a competition about victory or defeat, since doing that would ruin the spirit of *kenjutsu*. However, with the opportunity to appear before the Emperor, the National Championship was organized for the first time. Even so, many of the participants feared the criticism that it would invoke and question who is the strongest?

However, from then on, this championship took place several times since the 1920's as a tournament. What had been the martial arts for the *bushi* became institutionalized with the coming of the modern age. Additionally, martial arts were introduced into the school education, and also they were developed as tournaments. This was around the period of the 1920's and 1930's.

In the year 1922, Okinawan *karate* was first presented officially in the mainland. In fact, what is called Okinawa refers to the Ryūkyū Kingdom which had, since the 14th century been an independent country with prosperous trade. The Ryūkyū Kingdom traded with China and Southeast Asia, including Japan, and so Okinawa had a very important position. It was a country prosperous with transit trade, and in the 17th century the Satsuma Domain from Kagoshima gained control over half of Okinawa. However, it remained as the Ryūkyū Kingdom, set apart from Japan or China.

However, in the Ryūkyū Kingdom there was a prohibition targeted toward the 'samurae' (jp. samurai) stratum. Keeping weapons was very restricted. Around the end of the 14th century and start of the 15th century, when weapons became restricted, the martial arts of *kenpō* or *kara-*

te-jutsu was introduced through China. The '*kara*' in *karate* meant China. This martial art developed in Okinawa as a weaponless technique, called '*ti*' (the Okinawan pronunciation of '*te*', fist). This happened especially in the 17th century when the Satsuma Domain gained partial control and weapons were restricted.

Among the population, fighting techniques without weapons were refined as *karate-jutsu*. Beginning in the Meiji era, the Ryūkyū Kingdom was put down and it now came under Japanese rule known as Okinawa Prefecture. Within Okinawa there were progressive instructors who thought of transforming *karate-jutsu* for the modern era. These people intended to use Okinawan *karate-jutsu* as a means of physical training. For this purpose, they began exchanging what was previously transmitted only in secret and implemented as didactic teaching. It was developed in that form by 1922, and the same year it was presented to the Japanese mainland.

Okinawan *karate* was presented in the *bujutsu* Tournament of the Ministry of Education, and later it was also presented at Jigorō Kanō's *Kōdōkan*. Jigorō Kanō, as I stated earlier, is the person who created *jūdō* but he also had a very deep interest in all *bujutsu* and practiced as such. He very much wanted to learn Okinawan *karate*, and therefore a *karate* workshop took place in the *Kōdōkan*. In 1922, a person called Gichin Funakoshi was the first to come to instruct *karate* to Japanese students. Students learned and diffused *karate* among the student stratum. The Ryūkyū *karate- jutsu* was roughly divided into three sorts of *ryūha*, and people who were from a different *ryūha* also wanted to present their style in the mainland.

Gichin Funakoshi was in Tokyo, but in those days, when coming by boat from Okinawa one would come through Kansai area, where Osaka is located. So the different *ryūha* concentrated in the Kansai area and it is here various people developed *karatejutsu*, like Chōjun Miyagi. Various different *ryūha* simultaneously came into development around the 1920's decade. When Okinawan *karate* was presented for the first time, it was in the *Kōdōkan*, and at that time there were no outfits or uniforms for *karate* so they wore the *jūdōgi* (uniform). This is the origin of the *karatedōgi* (karate uniform), which was created based on the *jūdōgi* which Kanō had created.

At the time of this *karate* introduction, they learned to copy the shape of the Japanese *budō* system and saw that the *dan* ranking system was used to raise motivation, such things as the black belts and so on, and thus the black belts were also introduced into *karate*. The full-scale introduction of Okinawan *karate* to Japan took place from 1922 to the thirties, and through four major styles. These are called the '*Yondai ryūha*' (Four Great *Ryūha*). These four ryūha were then organized so they could be registered in the aforementioned *Dai Nippon Butokukai*.

In order to register them, the Okinawan teachers were asked about their method of instruction, what they included in their respective curriculum, and the theory behind them, and so on. For this, they took Japanese *jūdō* as their model and created their own textbooks and registered their own methods of teaching. The schools were individually registered. At that time the name *karate* changed just like *jūjutsu* did into *jūdō*. *Karate* was registered as *Karatedo*. These were all registered individually and therefore they have continued that way until today.

About *karate*, initially the '*kara*' character, which is also read '*to*' in Japanese and means 'China', was changed around the year 1929, to the character used nowadays which reads '*kū*' and means 'empty'. This implies that in *karate* nothing is used, as in no weapons, because it is done 'empty handed'. The character '*kū*' also is a significant character in the Buddhist sphere as it represents a higher state of mind. This character has this implied meaning. As a background to this, there was the expectation of Japan entering into a war against China, so this change from the influence of China to something deeper spiritually by changing the character '*kū*' in *karate* was welcomed.

This change was made around the middle of the 1930's. The Four Great *Ryūha* were also organized around this time and *karatedō* was extensively transformed into a Japanese *budō*. It adopted the shape of the modern Japanese *budō*, and this was how *karatedō* came into being in Japan.

In 1931 the Mukden Incident took place and as a consequence a war started and the Manchukuo (Manchu State) was established. In fact it was a state made not by Manchu people – it was a Japanese puppet state. China sued Japan through the League of Nations, who investigated the case and stated that Manchu was under the influence of Japan and its independence could not be acknowledged. Because of that Japan got a warning from the League of Nations and that was the reason for Japan to withdraw from League Membership. So we can say that Japan was becoming more isolated. Anyway, that happened in 1931. Then in 1937 Japan and China started a major war.

If we count from 1931 to 1945 and from 1937 to 1945, it means that the war lasted eight years or fifteen years. From 1941 Japan is in a state of war with the United States. The war started in 1939 and Japan had formed the Tripartite Pact with Germany and Italy. Japan did not possess oil resources so it looked toward Vietnam and Indonesia. That was one of points of confrontation with USA, which abolished oil and iron exports to Japan. That was one of the reasons Japan started the war.

During the war, *kenjutsu* in Japan was practiced as *battōjutsu* (lit. sabre drawing technique), a very practical form. If one sees an American propaganda movie at this time, the Japanese are always depicted as a person who swings a sword at somebody. So *budō* was seen as something dangerous. In Japan, soldiers always carried a *guntō* (lit. military sabre; modern military *katana*) by their side. There were situations in China, in which a soldier would cut down a person who was accused of spying. These were times when the image of a Japanese soldier and the *katana* connected with each other.

In 1945 Japan was defeated in the Second World War. The war ended after a nationwide broadcast in which the Emperor accepted the Potsdam Declaration. However, the Japanese army maintained its form. So it was totally different than Germany's resistance which was to the very end. Politics in Japan were governed by the GHQ - General Headquarters, the Supreme Commander for the Allied Powers.

Modern Japanese *budō*, therefore, begins in 1945. The occupation forces considered *budō* as something dangerous that encouraged militarism, and so it was abolished. Both educational (school) *budō* and private *budō* were abolished. At this time there was *budō* teaching in schools as well as teaching for the public. The teaching of *budō* had been a profession, but when it was abolished in 1945, these people lost their profession.

Some *budō* like *jūdō* at the *Kōdōkan*, where people practice throws were not prohibited as strictly, so the *Kōdōkan* survived. At the *Nihon Butokukai* (Japan Society of Martial Virtue) in Kyoto the masters lost their profession. Most of these people decided to teach in Europe. For example, Haku Michigami, who taught Antonius Geesink, was a person from this *Butokukai*. Geesink was the first non-Japanese *jūdō* practitioner to win gold at the World Jūdō Championships.

So when we talk about these things, *budō* had been vigorously spreading in Europe since 1930. In fact, during *budō*'s prohibition in Japan, a Budō Alliance in Europe was established. What is more, the IJF

(International Judo Federation) was established abroad and yet Japan could not be a member. It was established without Japan. Even Jigorō Kanō has been thinking about making an international federation of *jūdō*. This was in 1936. But then the IJF was created in post-war Europe. Japan was still in a state of *budō* prohibition. However, *karatedō* was made legal quite early in this period. One of the reasons was the fact that it wasn't included in the school curriculum as an educational tool.

The internationalization of *karate* was formed by American troops stationed on the island of Okinawa and by Japanese school students who afterward had gone abroad. This was a chaotic time for martial arts in Japan. Post-war *budō* was prohibited and even the term '*budō*' could not be spoken. That's why the only way for it to survive was to talk of it as a sport.

A typical example of this was *kendō*. *Kendō* recalled images of the *samurai* and the cutting down of people, so it was considered dangerous. Because of that *kendō* was practiced not wearing the traditional *dōgi* (martial arts uniform) and *hakama*, but wearing white European style sportswear. Also, a point system was introduced and *kendō* was cast as a sport, a '*shinai kyōgi*' (*shinai* competition). *Kendō* was resurrected by changing it into a *shinai* competition. There were six years in which *kendō* had to be strongly stated as a sport or it would not be acknowledged and the effect of this still exists today.

In post-war Japan, *budō* was emphasized as a competitive sport and at the same time, the spiritual and educational parts of it were denied. So the characteristics of post-war *budō* were as a competitive game, being a sport and its internationalization. These are the pillars of post-war *budō*. *Karatedō, jūdō* and *kyūdō* became legal fairly early after the end of the war, but *kendō* was kept under close supervision.

The modern form of what we can call 'resurrected *kendō*', could only be established after Japan regained its independence, as stated in the treaty of San Francisco. Simultaneously with regaining independence in 1952, the All Japan Kendo Federation was established, and it incorporated the already stated European sportswear competitive style of *kendō*. The development of this *kendō* started in 1952. In total the prohibition period lasted six to seven years. I think that Japanese *budō* changed its appearance greatly during this period when we talk about spirituality and tradition being prohibited.

Because of air raids in the war, many Japanese cities and industries were destroyed, and because of food shortages these were not the times when one could enjoy sports. However in 1955 industry started to re-generate. From 1955 through to 1973, the Japanese economy was in a state of high growth. During this time, the growth exceeded 10% and Japan recovered from the war and developed quickly. In those times Japanese society began to have more economical flexibility. This culminated in the 1964 Tokyo Olympics.

While this was acknowledged thanks to the earlier efforts of Jigorō Kanō, there was also a feeling that Tokyo hosting the Olympics should be rejected because of the not so distant war. There was a big meaning to the 1964 Tokyo Olympics – that it was a sign to the world that Japan had developed into a peaceful country.

Because of the Olympics, Tokyo was modernized and highways and the *shinkansen* bullet train began to show up. Color television also spread in those times. Thanks to mass production and mass consumption, Japanese people could start to live a rich material life. One of the aims of the Tokyo Olympics was to show the world that Japan's economy was healthy.

Jūdō was introduced to the games as a *budo*. The *Nippon Budōkan* was also built then as a home for *budō* tournaments. Afterwards, the *Nippon Budōkan* became an organization that united Japanese *budō*. It was built in the Imperial Palace grounds, in the center of Tokyo, as a place for *jūdō* competitions and other *budō* such as *kendō* and *kyūdō* which were shown to the public as open presentations.

This was also an opportunity for establishing the International Kendo Federation. As for as the International Judo Federation, this was established earlier in 1948 in Europe, when Japan was still prohibited and so Japan joined the organization later.

In 1964 *jūdō* was accepted as an official event of the Tokyo Olympic games. There were 4 *jūdō* classes: light, medium, heavy and open-weight. A non-Japanese competitor called Geesink, from the Netherlands, beat the Japanese favorite at the Olympics in the latter class. Although Japan won all the remaining *jūdō* classes, it was a shock for the Japanese when they lost in the open-weight class. On the other hand, the win by Geesink was one of the reasons *jūdō* became so popular in the world.

So this was an event that carried a very big meaning for *jūdō*. However in the next Olympic Games in Mexico, *jūdō* was removed from the games. In order to restore it, Charles Palmer from Great Britain, who was elected president of the International Judo Federation, put in a lot of effort and *jūdō* returned to the Olympics and stayed, as part of the games

Takashi Uozumi

today. I must point out that while becoming one of the events of the Olympics helped *jūdō* to spread internationally, *jūdō* became popular in Europe after the Russo-Japanese War in the first decade of 19th century, so it really developed even before the Second World War.

The appearance in the Olympic games also helped spread *jūdō* to third world countries. As far as *jūdō* is concerned, it is Europe that holds authority in meetings of the IJF, and Japanese people cannot even speak much during these. It has become something different from the original traditions but many schools became established in order to make *jūdō* more dynamic and entertaining in the Olympics.

Because of that *jūdō* became more sports-like. That is how Europeans think of it. There were many occasions in which Japanese would oppose this tendency, but gradually, the International Judo Federation's authority became concentrated in Europe.

The first president of the IJF was Risei Kanō, the son of *Kōdōkan*'s founder, Jigorō Kanō. However, Risei could not maintain enough authority, and Palmer became the president. After this time, many non-Japanese looked upon themselves as caretakers of *jūdō*. However Shigeyoshi Matsumae from Japan, become the president of IJF in 1979, and remained in this position for ten years. He was the person who has brought women's *jūdō* into the Olympics.

During the 1988 Seoul Olympics in South Korea, women's *jūdō* became an open event and in 1992 in the Barcelona Olympics it became official. Bringing women's *jūdō* into the Olympics was a great achievement by Shigeyoshi Matsumae. He was connected with the International Budo University because there was a demand for *jūdō* leaders and he became the principal.

As for as *kendō*, in the 1970's there was a person named Torao Mori, who was active in the U.S. He was a renowned *kendō* master even in Japan. He moved to America and started fencing, and eventually became U.S. champion. He spread *kendō* in the United States. He was also the person who organized international competitions between Japan, USA and Taiwan, which eventually lead to establishing the International Kendo Federation (IKF). Although *kendō* spread in Japanese communities, the problems in acquiring equipment like *bōgu* (protective gear) and *shinai*, did not help it spread outside Japan, to the same extent as *jūdō*.

On the opposite side to *kendō*, *jūdō* and *karatedō* spread quite well. As far as *karatedō* is concerned, its schools were not unified even after the war. *Jūdō* was included in the school education curriculum and it was unified by the *Kōdōkan*, but as for *karate*, there are four different major schools on the Japanese mainland. In the Okinawan Island many other *karate* schools had developed. When the Japanese *karate* instructors go to America and Europe to teach, each of them teaches a different style. Post-war *karate* concentrated on the university student and here is where *karate* competitions were introduced. Up until this time *Karate* was in a form of *kenpō* (Japanese boxing) but *jiyū kumite* (free sparring) was introduced. This meant that if one punched for real, then the opponent would get seriously injured. Therefore, '*sundome*' (lit. short measure stop; stopping just before impact) was introduced in tournaments and people would also fight wearing protectors.

This has developed into the All Japan Karate Federation. Although some unification was achieved, each school of *karate* is independent. As I said before, one of the characteristics of post-war *budō* is competitiveness, organization and internationalization. In this situation, *jūdō* and *kendō* became an important part of male school education. However what was emphasized was that *jūdō* was not a *budō*, but rather a *kakutō-gi* (lit. ranking combat technique; competitive one-on-one combat). In 1958, the Ministry of Education introduced the Standards of Education, and the martial arts were called a 'combative sports' during the whole Shōwa period, until 1989). It was only renamed as "*budō*" in 1989.

After the war, *budō*, including its traditional and spiritual elements were considered dangerous. For example, in school education one could see *budō* was restrained. That is how *budō* was until 1989. This is how *budō* was 'sportified' and made into a competitive discipline, and I also think that internationalization is one of the characteristics of this process. In the 1980's, it was a time of economical growth and factory construction all over the world. At the same time, there was a movement that aimed to internationalize and unify *budō*. This university where we are now, the International Budo University, was established in these circumstances. Also, the '*Budō kenshō*' (Charter of Budō) was created. The group called '*gendai budō*' (lit. present day *budō*; modern *budō*) included *jūdō*, *kendō*, *kyūdō*, *karatedō*, *aikidō*, *Shōrinji kenpō*, *naginata*, *sumō* and *jūkendō*. The 'Budō Charter' was composed for this group of nine *budō*, and it declared what their spirit and way of teaching will be.

This 'Budō Charter' was enacted in 1987. This was a way of showing what Japanese *budō* was in comparison to western sports. *Budō* has been developing for a long historical period of time and it is a way of training one's character through improving one's physical and spiritual attributes, so it emphasizes the educational value of *budō*. This meant not only focusing on competitions. One should see the importance of *kihon* (basics) and the need to practice in order to attain a good physical state. At the same time, one should not become arrogant because of a victory, and should not become sad or angry because of a loss; the *dōjō* is a place of physical and mental practice and one should behave according with etiquette and good manners. Teaching martial arts should be a way of cultivating one's personality. Those are the things stated by the Charter of *Budō*.

However, in the background was another way of thinking about *budō*, where all that mattered was winning. The 'Budō Charter' was created in opposition to this way of thinking. Before this charter, there was the '*Kendō no rinen*' (Principles of *Kendō*), which stated that *kendō* is a "method of practice that leads to the shaping of a human being". This was made a principle. As a reply to this, *naginata* created the 'Principles of *Naginata*'.

These were a way of emphasizing the educational value of the disciplines. Nowadays, *budō* is international. I think that we can see here two current thoughts: one is of making *budō* competitive and spreading it internationally, with the All Japan Karate Federation being a typical example of this. The second part of this development is by making *budō* an Olympic event, in which it is part of an educational curriculum and sports science is adopted. Another current thought is the one which emphasizes the traditional and spiritual aspects of *budō*. I believe that *kyūdō* depicts this tendency very well. The book "Zen in the art of Archery" is well read in both Europe and the USA. It was a book written by a German philosopher, Eugen Herrigel, who came to Japan to study with a Japanese *kyūdō* master in the 1930's. *Kyūdō* was depicted as something mystical in this book.

Kenzō Awa, the *kyūdō* master featured in this book by Herrigel, stated that while shooting an arrow, one should get into a meditative state of mind – that of *mushin* - and this is the objective of *budō*. That is why in the book he stated '*kyūzen icchi*' (lit. bow and *zen* as one). In the beginning of the 17th century there was an idea of '*kenzen icchi*' (lit. sword and *zen* as one) and he was influenced by this. Kenzō Awa was a person who said things like this. Consequently in *kyūdō* it's spirituality is often emphasized. However, there are also people who oppose this way of non-competitive *kyūdō* practice done by some modern practitioners. I think the book, *Zen in the art of Archery* is a typical example of emphasizing the spiritual aspects of a *budō*.

Published by the International Budo University and written by Professor Takashi Uozumi and Alexander Bennett

In *kendō*, there are people who passed down oral traditions from the Edo period who talk about *zen*. Especially older people were like this. People who started *kendō* after the war are different. I believe that there are many people who practice *kendō* competitively. What is understood in our modern world is a world of competition – winning or losing. Some people support this way of thinking but at the same time there are people who emphasize spirituality in *kendō*. As I said before, it is divided into two ways of thinking. Currently *kendō* is not aiming to become an Olympic Event. If a *budō* becomes an Olympic event, it will become much more international and the focus will be toward the competitive side. Because *kendō* is believed to have an educational value as stated in the 'Principles of *Kendō*' charter, then accordingly, it should not be entering the Olympics. However when looking forward, how is *kendō* going to be shaped in the future? There are many opinions on this question and there are no unified answers.

In the long history of *budō*, the International Budo University's mission is focused in the scientific research of *budō*. As for as *budō*'s history, there are the different histories for each of them – *jūdō*, *kendō*, *kyūdō*, *karate* and so on. However, this university is a gathering of *budō* specialists and there is a summary of what *budō* is among our publications. For example we have published two English versions of our work *(shown above)* titled "*History and Spirit of Budo*" and "*Budo in the Global Era*". Please make use of them for your own study, thank you.

GLOSSARY OF MARTIAL ART TERMS

Age Uke	Rising/upper block	*Geri*	Kick
Aikidō	Way of harmony	*Gi*	Uniform (as in judogi)
Aiki	Spirit in harmony	*Go No Sen*	Counter attack
Ashi	The leg or foot	*Gorin no Sho*	Book of Five Rings
Ashi Barai	Foot sweep/throw	*Gyaku Tsuki*	Reverse punch
Atama	Head		
Atemi	Strike to vital point	*Hachidan*	8th degree black belt
		Hachiji Dachi	Natural stance
Bō	Wooden staff	*Haitō*	Ridge/edge hand
Bōgu	Armour/protector	*Hajime*	Begin/First step
Bokken	Wooden sword/sabre	*Hara/Tanden*	Lower abdomen
Budō	Martial way	*Hanshi*	High level master
Bujutsu	Martial technique	*Heiko Dachi*	Parallel stance
Bunkai	Application analysis	*Heisoku Dachi*	Formal stance
Bushi	Warrior class (samurai)	*Hidari*	Left (side/direction)
Bushidō	Way of the warrior	*Honbu*	Headquarters
Chudan	Middle section	*Iaidō*	Drawing the sword
Choku Tsuki	Straight punch	*Ippon*	One point score
		Ippon Kumite	One step sparring
Dachi	Stance or posture	*Irimi Nage*	Entering throw
Dan	Black belt rank		
Deshi	Disciple or student	*Jiyū Kumite*	Freestyle sparring
Dō	The way/path	*Jō*	Short staff
Dōjō	Place of practice (way)	*Jodan*	Upper section
Dōjō Kun	School creed/rules	*Jūdō*	Way of gentleness
		Jūdōka	Judo practitioner
Empi	Elbow	*Juji uke*	Cross block
Empi Uchi	Elbow strike	*Jūjutsu*	Unarmed soft style
		Jūkenjutsu	Bayonet technique
Fudō-dachi	Rooted stance		
Fudōshin	Immovable mind	*Kake Uke*	Wrist/hook block
Fumikomi	Stamping kick	*Kamae*	Posture (ready)
		Karate	Empty hand
Gatame	Hold or lock	*Karatedō*	Way of the empty hand
Gedan	Lower section	*Kata*	Form or exercise
Gedan Barai	Downward strike/block	*Katana*	Japanese long sword
Gendai	Modern/Present day	*Keage Geri*	Snap kick

GLOSSARY OF MARTIAL ART TERMS

Kendō	Way of the sword	*O' Sensei*	Enlightened teacher
Kenshusei	Instructor program	*Ogoshi*	Large hip throw
Ki	Energy or life force	*Oi tsuki*	Front lunge punch
Kiai	Spirited yell	*Osoto Gari*	Outer reaping throw
Kiba Dachi	Horse riding stance	*Ouchi Gari*	Inner reaping throw
Kihon	Basic technique		
Kime	Focus	*Randori*	Free practice
Kizami Tsuki	Jab or front punch	*Renshi*	4th or 5th dan level
Kobudō	Traditional weapons	*Rōnin*	Master-less samurai
Kōdōkan	Judo headquarters	*Ryūha*	School of martial art
Kōhai	Junior student		
Kokutsu Dachi	Back stance	*Satori*	Enlightenment
Kokyū	Breathing/breath power	*Seiken*	Two knuckles (hand)
Koryū	Classical/traditional	*Seiza*	Sitting/kneeling
Kosa Dachi	Cross leg stance	*Senpai*	Senior student
Kote	Forearm at wrist	*Sensei*	Instructor or teacher
Kumite	Sparring or fighting	*Shiai*	Competition
Kuzushi	Breaking the balance	*Shihan*	Grandmaster (teacher)
Kyōshi	6th or 7th dan level	*Shihō Nage*	Four direction throw
Kyūdō	Way of Japanese archery	*Shin*	The mind or will
Kyūsho	Vital pressure points	*Shinken*	Real sword/live blade
Kyū	Rank below black belt	*Shōrinji Kenpō*	Shaolin Temple boxing
Maai	Distance/space in combat	*Tai Sabaki*	Body movement
Makiwara	Practice target	*Tsuki Waza*	Punching technique
Mawashi Geri	Roundhouse kick		
Men	Face/head	*Uchi Waza*	Striking technique
Migi	Right (side/direction)	*Uke Waza*	Blocking technique
Morote	Two/double technique		
Morote Tsuki	Double punch	*Waza*	Technique
Mushin	Empty mind/no mind		
		Yame	To stop
Nage Waza	Throwing technique	*Yoi*	Ready stance
Naginata	Japanese glaive (blade)	*Yoko Geri*	Side kick
Ne-waza	Ground fighting		
Nukite	Spear hand (empty)	*Zanshin*	State of awareness
Obi	Belt	*Zenkutsu Dachi*	Front (leg) stance

MORE BOOKS IN THIS SERIES

Masters of Tai Chi Chuan
Masters of Kung fu
Masters of the Japanese Sword
Masters of Kyudo

Find our books online at
emptymindbooks.com and emptymindfilms.com/books.
Also at major booksellers including Apple and Amazon.
For inquiries email: info@emptymindbooks.com